Independence without Freedom

Studies in International and Comparative Politics
PETER H. MERKL, SERIES EDITOR

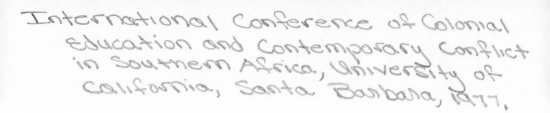

Independence without Freedom

The Political Economy of Colonial Education in Southern Africa

Edited and with an Introduction

by

AGRIPPAH T. MUGOMBA

and

MOUGO NYAGGAH

ABC-Clio

Santa Barbara, California   Oxford, England

Library of Congress Cataloging in Publication Data

International Conference of Colonial Education
   and Contemporary Conflict in Southern Africa,
   University of California, Santa Barbara, 1977.
   Independence without freedom.

   (Studies in international and comparative
politics; 13)
   Bibliography: p.
   Includes index.
1. Education—Africa, Southern—History—
Congresses. 2. Africa, Southern—History—
Congresses. 3. Education, Colonial—Congresses.
I. Mugomba, Agrippah T. II. Nyaggah, Mougo.
III. Title. IV. Series.
LA1501.1568   1977   370'.968   80-154
ISBN 0-87436-293-8

ABC-Clio, Inc.
Riviera Campus
2040 Alameda Padre Serra, Box 4397
Santa Barbara, California 93103

Clio Press, Ltd.
Woodside House, Hinksey Hill
Oxford OX1 5BE, England

Manufactured in the United States of America

For Barbara, Lynette, and Maria,
whose love, patience, and commitment exceeded the call of duty
and make them very dear to us.

Contents

Acknowledgments

Most of the chapters in this book were first presented at an International Conference on Colonial Education and Contemporary Conflict in Southern Africa held at the Santa Barbara campus of the University of California in November 1977. This was a follow-up to another conference, African Responses to European Colonialism in Southern Africa, from 1652 onwards, held in January 1976 at California State University, Northridge. The Santa Barbara conference, which was attended by participants from institutions throughout the United States, was sponsored by the Center for Black Studies, the Department of Black Studies, and the African Area Studies Program, all at the University of California, Santa Barbara; the African Studies Committee at California State University, Northridge; and the African Studies Center at the University of California, Los Angeles. We are grateful for financial assistance and other forms of support provided by these institutions. California State University, Fullerton, contributed funds to enable one of the editors to attend the conference; further supporting services were made available, which enabled us to coordinate our editorial work.

Without the assistance of numerous people, this book would never have seen light. In particular, Professor Chanaiwa was instrumental in organizing the conference from which this volume emerged. Throughout our editing, he served as an indefatigable consultant and ungrudgingly shared his vast knowledge of the subject with us, thus making our task both tolerable and immensely rewarding. We are especially grateful for his acceptance of the challenge to write the conclusion and tie the individual contributions together. Special appreciation should also go to our contributors; undoubtedly, without their active cooperation and their diligence in getting revised manuscripts to us on time, we would not have been able to meet the deadline.

We are also grateful to the following people, whose support or cooperation in many ways made it possible to convene the conference in the first place: Chancellor Robert A. Huttenback, Dean Robert O. Collins, and Professor Gerard G. Pigeon of the University of California, Santa Barbara, and Professor Boniface I. Obichere of the University of California, Los Angeles. During the editing, we benefited tremendously from the services generously provided by Mark Gilles and Joseph Dorsey, who compiled the bibliography. Alyce Whitted did splendid secretarial work for both the conference and the subsequent preparation of the manuscript. Without her invaluable assistance, the book would never have made it to the press. A special word of thanks must be reserved for Barbara Chanaiwa, who graciously welcomed us into her home and never complained about the imposition on her family when on numerous occasions we had to meet in their home midway between Santa Barbara and Fullerton for editorial consultations.

Other people we wish to thank are Professor Peter H. Merkl, editor of the ABC-Clio series on comparative and international politics, who took a rather unusual interest in the influences of colonial education in contemporary African politics, and Lloyd W. Garrison, Executive Vice-President and Publisher of ABC-Clio, who recognized the importance of the issue of colonial education in Africa as a whole and provided much needed encouragement while the book was in preparation. His editorial staff also assisted by compiling the index.

Above all, we take special pleasure in extending our appreciation to our wives, Maria Mugomba and Lynette Nyaggah, for their moral support and intellectual stimulation. They willingly sacrificed valuable time from their own academic interests in order to accommodate our demands and the accompanying inconveniences. In doing so, they contributed decisively to the realization of this collective enterprise.

While we have taken care not to overlook the insightful comments, remarks, and suggestions made by the conference participants, many of which have greatly improved the quality of the chapters contained in the book, we must accept, as editors, full responsibility for whatever shortcomings may be present in the final product.

Introduction

In Africa, as in other parts of the Third World, access to education remains a privilege—not a right—available to only a small minority. And just as the schools and universities are open to only a small sector in Third World societies, so too, they reflect the social values of the minority they serve. This is but one of the many legacies of a colonial past.

One of the most damaging legacies of imperialist and colonialist presences in Africa is the separation of education from the overall political, economic, social, and cultural development of peoples and nation-states. And yet, neither educational institutions nor the policies which govern them can be neutral because of their link to the economy and the dominant social values of the society of which they are a part. The essays in this volume are oriented towards the perspective of schools and universities reinforcing rather than challenging the existing patterns of dependence and inequality which impede relevant development in Third World nations.

HISTORICAL PERSPECTIVE

Indigenous African education was relevant and closely linked to the spiritual and material aspects of social life before colonization by European imperial powers. There was little separation of learning and productive labor nor any consequent division between physical and intellectual labor. This educational process reflected the realities of African society and produced people with an education which equipped them to meet the material, spiritual, and social needs of the society.[1]

The arrival of the European missionaries and "explorers" (who worked hand in glove with each other in promoting formal colonization) brought a new system of education which, like the colonial model of the political system, both subordinated and relegated to a peripheral role the African educational systems and the existing political, economic, and social orders. The newcomers introduced alternative theories of education and imposed a new set of educational institutions which in some cases partly supplemented and in most others replaced previous forms of learning. The colonial schools required students of a

1

specific age range to attend on a full-time basis rather than allowing them to be taught in the intervals between productive work, and on a lifelong basis. Rather than drawing the study content from the needs of students, school education was teacher-centered and focused on the culture of the colonial power. The experiences of students in British colonial schools in Africa, Asia, and the Caribbean revolved around efforts to instill deference to the foreign authority, unquestioned acceptance of hierarchy, the full embracement of Christianity (which was a requisite condition for school enrollment), and acceptance of the cultural superiority of the metropolitan country.

The colonizer's culture, history, religion, and way of life were thus promoted in the curriculum as well as in the discipline itself. The experiences of the colonized people were ignored in favor of such topics as the Peloponesian Wars, the Wars of the Roses, the Crusades, and Greek and Roman mythology. Students memorized European royal lineages, while the historic achievements of great African monarchs such as Shaka and Mwene Mutapa were either ignored entirely or buried in footnotes to the history of the military conquest and colonial occupation of Africa by the European powers. And because such schools were designed for the urban population in industrialized countries, they tended to devalue the peasant way of life, to edge peasants to the margins of colonial society. Indeed, the pertinent observation has been made that

> to most colonial educators, cultural development meant the expansion
> of a replicative school system that measured cultural and scientific
> advance by the number of students who could clearly demonstrate (by
> examination) that they had been pumped full of a foreign heritage.[2]

Thus, the colonial school was primarily a channel of social upward mobility for a tiny minority rather than a means of educating the entire population. As Walter Rodney has observed, it was never thought necessary to educate the masses "because only a minority of the [African] population entered the colonial economy in such a way that their performance could be enhanced by education."[3] This orientation was fully in keeping with the overall objective of colonial education, to produce an indigenous elite to ensure that the colonial settlers and various public services of the colonies could meet the personal requirements of the settlers themselves.[4]

EDUCATION AND UNDERDEVELOPMENT

With the recovery of formal independence, the former colonies found themselves saddled with an educational system unsuited to their requirements. They needed people trained for responsibilities previously reserved for the colonial administrators. They also needed to foster a whole new spirit of self-reliance and experimentation.

Substantial progress has been made throughout the ex-colonial world to reform colonial educational institutions and to introduce new philosophies and teaching methods. Demands for large-scale efforts in mass literacy and adult education have been heeded; the main response of political elites has been to expand existing schools and construct new ones to meet such demands. Nevertheless, the problems and contradictions of colonial education continue to be felt today throughout the Third World. In Africa, students must still read William Shakespeare, Charles Dickens, and other European literary giants before Chinua Achebe, Wole Soyinka, Aime Cesaire, David Diop, and Ngugi was Thiongo. They continue to learn about Victorian stagecoaches, fireplaces and top hats, none of which has any real meaning in their everyday lives. In many parts of the continent, students have their examination papers marked by European "specialists" before they graduate from high school or university. And, throughout the Third World, the colonial political economies which these schools were set up to serve continue to impede development. More important, postcolonial education in the Third World remains inextricably linked to the colonial period:

> Educational systems in the ex-colonies remain largely intact (long) after independence. Curriculum, language (of instruction), and, in some cases, even the nationality of the teachers, are carried over from the colonial period.[5]

The growth of the educational systems of many Third World nations has produced large numbers of graduates, at both the secondary school and university levels, but severe financial constraints and political pressures have prevented the economies from diversifying and providing the necessary numbers of appropriate jobs. The factors which have kept the economies from expanding through diversification have greatly reduced the numbers of jobs available, relative to the numbers of school-educated people qualified to fill them. The result has been a massive brain drain from the Third World to the industrialized nations, which has exacerbated the inherited problems of inequality, dependence, and underdevelopment. In a broader context, education tied to a colonial heritage has contributed immeasurably to the magnification and dramatization of the social distances between the educated and the uneducated.

It seems clear enough to leaders of Third World nations that they cannot afford to conceive of education as schooling in expensive institutions, even with huge investments, supplemented by educational assistance from capitalist and socialist industrialized nations. This catch-up or diffusionist approach to education is grounded in the cultural dependency of Third World nations. But just as the widening economic gap cannot be narrowed by importing solutions, the problem

of basic education for the majority of Third World people cannot be
solved by importing Western models (or even Eastern ones for that
matter).

EDUCATION AND NEOCOLONIALISM

In order to appreciate the influence of the postindependence
phenomenon of neocolonialism in Africa, it is vitally important to
realize the fundamental goals of colonial education practiced there by
churches and successive colonial administrations. Quite apart from the
fact that education (particularly the type taught in mission schools)
during the colonial era stressed the supposedly virtuous qualities of
humility, docility, and faithful acceptance without questioning, it also
taught the importance of individual achievement and personal gain
outside the context of a wider collective. Thus, the individualistic and
materialist ethic reinforced the spirit of capitalism, both essential ingredients of neocolonial dependence and underdevelopment.[6] Viewed
from a broader perspective, then, the theory and practice of colonial
education was

> to train Africans to help man the local administration at the lowest
> ranks and to staff the private capitalist firms owned by Europeans. In
> effect, that meant selecting a few Africans to participate in the
> domination and exploitation of the continent as a whole. It was not an
> educational system that grew out of the African environment or one
> that was designed to promote the most rational use of material and
> social resources. It was not an educational system designed to give
> young people confidence and pride as members of African societies,
> but one which sought to instill a sense of deference to all that was
> European and capitalist. Education in Europe was dominated by the
> capitalist class. The same bias was automatically transferred to Africa;
> and to make matters worse the racism and cultural boastfulness
> harboured by capitalism were also included in the package of colonial
> education. *Colonial schooling was education for subordination, exploitation,
> the creation of mental confusion, and the development of underdevelopment*
> [emphasis added].[7]

Any serious analysis of the political economy of colonial education
in Africa during the colonial period itself and in the postindependence
era would be meaningless if it divorced such education from the
ideological milieu which emphasized metropolitan cultural and racial
superiority and considered education to be one of the primary instruments to be used in cultivating European political and economic
hegemony over Africans. Whether one is looking at the ideals of
colonial education articulated by the French, Belgians, Portuguese,
British, or Boers, the similarities are striking although, of course, there
are variations in the degree of dedication which accompanied their
implementation.[8]

Colonial education had a special function: to provide necessary support personnel for the church, state, or colonial economy.[9] If the Africans receiving this education yearned for more knowledge or through their ingenuity read prohibited books or "misinterpreted" their sources, such as the Bible, and exposed the prevailing contradictions to the colonialists, they were considered dangerous to the existing colonial infrastructure and were often incarcerated in colonial jails because of their beliefs. During colonial times, the education provided produced both the "docile" or cooperative Africans and others who were able to penetrate the colonizers' minds and expose the colonizing myth for what it was in reality: the deliberate exploitation of the uneducated masses with the active collaboration of the new educated elite.[10]

Continuity in the role of education during the colonial period and in the postindependence era is provided by the neocolonial dependence arrangements which most African states accepted as the package deal for regaining their independence. Under these arrangements the metropolitan powers continue to provide school teachers and university personnel. They define the "right kind" of education either subtly or bluntly, depending on the degree to which their African clients are willing to play the neocolonial game from which derives the necessary external support for maintaining power and privilege, and they provide funding assistance for developing educational curricula and institutions. This continuity is an important factor to consider when we analyze education because it helps us understand what might happen in a region such as southern Africa when it regains complete independence under African majority rule. Familiarity with this concept of continuity helps us see the revolutionary impact of the educational models now being tested in Mozambique and Angola (and to a lesser extent in Tanzania). In these nations, we see genuine manifestations of the desire to completely restructure the inherited educational systems to make them serve the needs of relevant development and modernization. By contrast, the neocolonial systems which have proliferated elsewhere in the continent seem less effective.

STRUCTURE AND APPROACH

Since the region covered by this book has followed largely similar colonial educational policies, we found it worthwhile to adopt an interdisciplinary and a comparative approach, bringing together original studies by historians and political scientists. The book has been organized into four parts, allowing a logical thesis to develop and link directly the past and the present.

Part I contains two chapters. The first provides a general background and a regional perspective which focus on the role of humanist education. This chapter shows how a humanist education molded the minds of African intellectuals and produced among them the paradox of alienation from and admiration for their own tradition and culture, while they accepted at the same time alleged British cultural superiority. This kind of education was used to legitimize the "civilizing mission" of churches and colonial settlers and administrators. The second chapter shows the link between the neocolonial economic structures and political institutions which "departing" colonial powers bequeathed to the succeeding African elites and the type of education or miseducation the Africans got during the colonial era.

The second part, with three chapters, deals with the philosophical foundations of colonial education. The first chapter, on apartheid education, establishes the functional use of the educational system to advance missionary goals and to ease economic exploitation by rigid legislation providing constraints against equal education. The other two chapters deal with the attempts of white educators in South Africa to import a nonacademic educational model used in certain black institutions in the United States and apply it to African education in South Africa. Education similar to that provided at South Carolina's Penn School or the Tuskegee Institute in Alabama was believed to be an appropriate model for maintaining and supplementing the existing socioeconomic differentiation and racial stratification in South Africa.

The third part of the book provides comparative perspectives in the form of case studies which analyze the nature, function, and goals of colonial education in Malawi, Namibia, Botswana, and Mozambique. Of the two chapters on Mozambique, one goes beyond the colonial era and delves into the attempts of the postindependence leadership to decolonize the inherited educational system through Marxist revolutionary ideas. Lack of case studies for Zimbabwe and Zambia, two former British High Commission territories (Swaziland and Lesotho), and Angola does not present a serious drawback to the book since there are representative chapters that shed light on educational policy for former British Central Africa (Pachai), the High Commission territories (Bermingham), and the Portuguese-speaking areas (Azevedo and Mugomba). And as the bibliography amply demonstrates, many studies have already appeared covering these countries, particularly Zimbabwe and Zambia.

The final part presents a comprehensive historical evaluation of the political economy of colonial education in southern Africa and integrates the individual presentations.

The contributors to this volume fully recognize, individually as well as collectively, the continuity between the past, the present, and the future with respect to the neocolonial influences of colonial education in contemporary African political and socioeconomic development. Throughout the African continent, the retarding effects of societal disorientation brought about by colonization and dysfunctional education (or miseducation) continue to exercise an overbearing influence on the processes of modernization. The intellectual classes, the political, economic, and military elites, and the masses composed of workers and peasants, are now more separated from each other than they were during the precolonial period. Neocolonial values, institutions, and structures cannot possibly reduce this gaping distance. Above all, there is a clear recognition that colonial miseducation has had a profound impact on African society and that it has contributed immensely to the development of underdevelopment, dependence, and inequality, in both material and psychological terms. This may well be the major intellectual contribution of this book.

Notes

1. See Julius K. Nyerere, "Education for Self-Reliance," in his *Freedom and Socialism* (Dar es Salaam: Oxford University Press, 1968), p. 268; Henry F. Makulu, *Education, Development and Nation-Building in Independent Africa* (London: SCM Press, 1971), pp. 1–3; and Walter Rodney, *How Europe Underdeveloped Africa* (Washington, D.C.: Howard University Press, 1974), p. 239.

2. *Education and Underdevelopment* (Halifax, N.S.: Development Education Center and Development and Peace-Canada, 1976), p. 2. See also John Hanson and Cole Brembeck, eds., *Education and the Development of Nations* (New York: Holt, Rinehart and Winston, 1966).

3. Rodney, *How Europe Underdeveloped Africa*, p. 257.

4. Ibid. See also Nyerere, *Freedom and Socialism*, p. 269.

5. *Education and Underdevelopment*, p. 2. See also Martin Carnoy, *Education as Cultural Imperialism* (New York: David McKay, 1974).

6. Rodney aptly notes that "the model of personal achievement under colonialism was really a model for the falling apart and the underdevelopment of African society as a whole" (*How Europe Underdeveloped Africa*, p. 255).

7. Ibid., p. 241. Elsewhere, Rodney notes that "the colonial school system educated far too many fools and clowns, fascinated by the ideas and way of life of the European capitalist class. Some reached a point of total estrangement from African conditions and the African way of life. . . ." He further cites a critical observation made by an African educationalist that "colonial education corrupted the thinking and sensibilities of the African and filled him with abnormal complexes." See ibid., pp. 248–49.

8. For cogent analyses of these policies, see for example Makulu, *Education, Development, and Nation-Building*, pp. 17–19; Rodney, *How Europe Underdeveloped Africa*, p. 247; and L. J. Lewis, *Education and Political Independence in Africa* (Edinburgh: Thomas Nelson and Sons, 1962), pp. 1–2. The terms employed by the French, Belgians, the Portuguese to refer to natives who, through formal colonial education, has been assimilated or incorporated into the superior metropolitical culture and political ethos were, respectively, *assimilée*, *évolués* and *assimilado* (sometimes called *civilisado*). The British, and to a lesser extent even the Boers, spoke of the "white man's burden" to refer to the same process of culturally transforming Africans into "Afro-saxons."

9. This point is brought out forcefully in Rodney's brilliant analysis of the consequences and implications of colonial education, in *How Europe Underdeveloped Africa*, pp. 238–81.

10. Ibid., pp. 249, 253.

PART I

Regional Perspectives

CHAPTER 1

African Humanism in Southern Africa: The Utopian, Traditionalist, and Colonialist Worlds of Mission-Educated Elites

DAVID CHANAIWA

The theme of this chapter is African humanism in southern Africa before World War II, comprising the beliefs, values, actions, and life-styles of the mission-educated African elites. The chapter deals with the causes, history, and effects of African humanism. The major argument is that because of this humanism, the mission-educated elites imagined a utopian world of universalism, nonracialism, and moralism that was antithetical to the racist world of settler colonialism. But utopianism was unrealistic and self-defeating. The conclusion is that the mission-educated elites achieved minimal practical gains before World War II, although they did establish the foundation for nonethnic ideology and organization that was employed by the nationalist leaders of the post–World War II liberation struggle in southern Africa.

This is an analysis of the origins, dimensions, and effects of African humanism—here defined as the ideological commitment to individualism, nonracialism, nonviolence, and universalism—in the racioeconomic settler environment of southern Africa from 1850 to 1920. The focus is on the attitudes, goals, and actions of the mission-educated African preachers, teachers, lawyers, doctors, engineers, businessmen, and clerks in relation to (1) the utopian world of missionaries, humanitarians, and Cape white liberals, (2) the traditionalist world of the African masses among whom they lived and worked, and (3) the colonialist world of racism, exploitation, and oppression which determined their real personal and collective statuses.[1] Since we are dealing with the biographical and psychological aspects of the individuals (e.g., family background, education, habits, hobbies, and friendships), as well as the cultural-historical environment of southern Africa, one should expect a drama of personalities, motives, expectations, and actions. Additionally, there is a discussion of an African search for both personal and corporate identities in a colonial society.[2]

The humanists we are discussing either observed or participated in the settler conquest and occupation of their African societies, in the Anglo-Boer War, the Zulu rebellion (1906) and World War I. More important, they were among the first Africans to bear the heaviest burden of settler colonialism, under the notorious Natives' Land Act (1913), pass laws, Urban Areas Act (1918), and racial segregation. They were witnesses of fellow Africans who, as described by Davidson Don Tengo (D. D. T.) Jabavu in *The Black Problem*, were "landless, voteless, helots, pariahs, social otucasts in their fatherland with no future in any path of life."[3] Furthermore, traditional African societies, groups, and cultures had then been incorporated under alien national boundaries, culture, institutions, and values. The Africans—whether traditionalist or Christian, rural or urban—were thus placed in a culturally and psychologically disturbing and oppressive environment. They also were being taught that they had no civilization and history and that their future depended on their ability to imitate the very settlers who had enslaved them. In reaction to such condescending rhetoric and to the problems of African dignity, unity, and adaption, the educated elites began to respond with a humanist ideology.

Fortunately, little is obscure about both the private and public lives of the elites due to their penchant for intellectualism, scholarship, and publication. Through their letters, petitions, editorials, sermons, autobiographies, constitutions, speeches, and testimonies on diverse topics, they adequately spoke for themselves, and about the inner workings and effects of settler colonialism.[4]

THE UTOPIAN WORLD

The most important point to remember is that the African elites we are discussing were first and foremost exemplary Protestant preachers, teachers, and intellectuals.[5] For example, John Tengo Jabavu (1859–1921), the famous founder-editor of *Imvo Zabantsundu,* was a devout Methodist; Walter B. Rubusana (1858–1916), the only African ever elected to the Cape Provincial Council, was a Congregationalist minister; and John Langalibalele Dube, the first president of the South African National Congress, was a Methodist minister. Tiyo Soga (1829–1871) was the first African missionary to be ordained (United Presbyterian) in Britain. He founded the Mgwali Mission, where he preached to both Africans and Europeans. His famous Xhosa translation of John Bunyan's *Pilgrim's Progress* [*U-Hambo Lom-Hambi*] was the first African book published by the Lovedale Press (1867).

As true believers these elites internalized the nineteenth-century European missionaries' cultural chauvinism, pseudoscientific racism, and belief in the redemption and perfectibility of the "noble savage." They joined the missionary in condemning traditional African societies as heathen, superstitious, warlike, tribalistic, backward, and inferior.

The Christian doctrine was then reinforced by a culturally isolationist and elitist education at mission schools. According to Peter Walshe, there were 9,000 African students in 1850, 100,000 in 1900, and 170,000 in 1909 receiving education in South Africa.[6] The most famous mission school was the interdenominational, interracial Lovedale Free Church Missionary Institution, established by the Glasgow Missionary Society in Cape Colony in 1841. The institution also had a seminary, a girls' boarding school added in 1868, and it had 813 students by 1897.[7] Lovedale had an interracial student body and staff. There, blacks and whites sat in the same classes, same literary societies, and same dining room. They, however, slept in separate dormitories. As stated by Andrew Smith, one of the teachers, there was at Lovedale a practical recognition that the Africans were fellowmen, that they were a permanent fixture, that whites had to accept them as fellow citizens, that they had all the rights of British subjects and had to be treated according to the laws of the British Empire.[8] The educational process was also very elitist because the first principal, Rev. William Govan, believed in advancing Africans by "the higher education of a few rather than the elementary education of the many."[9] Several other African youths were being Christianized and educated in mission schools throughout South Africa, especially in the Ciskei and Transkei.

As exemplified by Lovedale, mission schools were mainly indoctrination centers for an alien culture, where impressionable African youths were introduced to the capitalist-Protestant ethics of piety, thrift, industriousness, sobriety, and respectability. They lived in an experiential educational environment of spiritualism, strict discipline, as well as nonethnicity, nonracialism, and universalism—all of which provided them their principles and values for private and public life. Thus, their education was not just a process of acquiring knowledge; it also was a way of living and feeling.

Beside the mission church and boarding school, the mission press also exercised considerable influence on the African elites.[10] The most famous and exemplary mission press was at the Lovedale Missionary Institution. As stated by Robert H. W. Shepherd, one of the principals, the Lovedale Press was founded to publish works of "spiritual and devotional character" and textbooks for African schools "for the prosecution of the evangelistic and educational tasks."[11] The press was essentially another instrument of missionary indoctrination, for it (1) assumed "all the costs of publication and paying a royalty on sales" to African authors and composers, (2) confined its publications to Bantu traditions, literature, colonial conditions, and missionary activities, (3) recruited and assisted African authors, (4) organized literary workshops, and (5) insisted on the publications being printed and bound by African workers.[12] Rev. D. Fred Ellenberger, author of books such as *History of the Basuto: Ancient and Modern* (1912), and Prof. C. M. Doke, coeditor of *Bantu Studies*, were among the permanent referees of African manuscripts.

Consequently, the topics, sources, and scholarship of missionaries and African elites were similar. African authors had missionaries or white liberals as father figures and intellectual mentors, similar to Booker T. Washington's Samuel Armstrong. Thus, Tiyo Soga had Rev. William Govan,[13] Dube had James Stewart,[14] John Tengo Jabavu had Davidson Don, and Jabavu's son, Davidson Don Tengo Jabavu, had Dr. C. T. Loram.[15] Likewise, Solomon Plaatje had Rev. G. E. Westphal[16] and Pixley Seme had Rev. S. Pixley of the American Board of Missions.[17] Like their missionary patrons and editors, first generation African authors (1820 –1900) were motivated by religiousness, intellectualism, and didacticism.[18] They were primarily concerned with the "triumph" and "forward march" of "Christian civilization" against the "heathenism" and "wretchedness" of the "dark continent." They acquired the derogatory terminology for Africans of the missionaries and settlers, such as "natives," "heathens," "primitives" and "Kafirs," and the same stereotypes about the African past and culture. They saw themselves as the African replicas of the European missionaries, as dauntless disciples of God, and as ordained leaders.

The first major African work published by the Lovedale Press, Tiyo Soga's Xhosa translation of *Pilgrim's Progress*, is full of spiritualism, symbolism, and drama.[19] Christian and his companions Faithful and Hopeful go through a series of trials and tribulations in their successful search for God and salvation. The villains are Messrs. Fearing, Ready-to-Halt, Much-Afraid, and Feeble-Mind. Every episode in the book assumes a spiritual and moral lesson.

Soga began his "translation labors" when he was a student and completed *U-Hambo Lom-Hambi* on November 21, 1866. He dedicated it to "the Rev. Govan, _____, one of the long-tried, unwearying, constant friends and benefactors of the native races of South Africa, by his friend and pupil, Tiyo Soga."[20] There was also a Sotho adaptation of *Pilgrim's Progress* by Thomas Mofolo, *Moeti oa Bochabela* [East-bound traveller].[21] The hero, Fekisi, starts as a civic-minded philanthropist in a traditional Sotho society that was "clothed in great darkness, a fearful darkness, in which all the things of darkness were done" (drunkenness, adultery, murder, violence, etc.). After an unsuccessful attempt to reform the society, Fekisi, like Christian, leaves his familiar homeland and people on a pilgrimage to find the Christian God and salvation. After some "miraculous hair-breadth escapes" from a lion, crocodile, snake, starvation, and thirst, Fekisi reaches the sea, where he sees three men "white in color, with hair like a horse's mane, with blue eyes," who speak a strange language. After informing them that he has abandoned his village because of its heathenism and is seeking salvation, the three White men lead him to God, Christ, and the Holy Spirit.[22]

There were several didactic lessons in both *U-Hambo Lom-Hambi* and *Mocti oa Bochabela* for the emerging African elites. Both authors were crusading for a "pilgrim's progress" from "heathenism" to salvation and "civilization." To escape from the "pitch black darkness" of heathenism, communalism, nakedness, and ignorance, and from the anonymity of the "communal herd" where everyone behaved alike, one had to be capable of making difficult decisions, accepting suffering, conflicts, and loneliness, and succeeding through the Christian virtues of faith, hope, and courage. As stated by Daniel Kunene, "Fekisi thus takes a symbolic journey, a journey across cultural boundaries occasioned by his total rejection of his own cultural values and his yearning for the values brought by the white missionary."[23] In both books we can see the expression of the individualism, idealism, elitism, and self-determination of the new elites. The books portray Christian life as an expression of a dynamic will and activity but also strewn with obstacles, and the heroes as distinct, sainted individuals. We can also perceive what Frantz Fanon, Aime Cesaire, and Albert Memmi have called the intellectual and psychological alienation of the African elites since their God, Christ, angels, saints, and idols are always white.[24]

In addition to translating religious-oriented English literature into African dialects, the new elites also wrote poems derived from European themes, as well as African history, customs, and proverbs (e.g., Tiyo Soga's *U-Tywala* [Beer]. They composed a lot of music, mostly hymns, such as John Knox Bokwe's *Amaculo ase Lovedale* [Lovedale hymns], the most common being "Give a Thought to Africa," Tiyo Soga's "Lizalise Dinga Dingalako Tixo We Nyaniso" [Fulfil thy promise God of Truth], Enoch Sontoga's classic "Nkosi Sikeleli I-Africa" [God bless Africa], and Ntsikana's classic "Ulo Thixo Omkhulu, Ngose Zul-wini" [He, the Great God, high in Heaven]. There also was a prolifera-tion of African newspapers, e.g., John Tengo Jabavu's *Imvo Zabantsundu,* William Wellington Gqoba's *Isigidimi,* and Nathaniel C. Mhala's *Izwila Bantu.* Newspapers were the most successful business enterprise operated by Africans for expressing the opinions of the emerging intellectuals.

These Africans were writing religious and didactic literature "to meet a want being gradually felt amongst the Christian natives for a Christian literature in their homes, and also as a guide to evangelists in their preparation for addressing their countrymen at the services in various villages."[25] The audience consisted of what Tiyo Soga referred to as "our Kafir-reading native population,"[26] missionaries, and white liberals. Thus, the authors primarily wrote sermons in the guise of poems, novels, music, and biographies. For example, Thomas Mofolo's *Shaka*[27] is essentially a moralist indictment of the Zulu society for its ignorance, superstition, and witch doctors *(Isanusi)*, and of Shaka for his tyranny and bloodthirstiness; so is Dube's *Insila ka Shaka.*[28] Like the missionaries, the elites did not see God or greatness in the African past.

The same correlation existed between missionary and African writings of the second generation (1900–1950) mission-educated elites. By then missionaries were proselytizing conquered and dominated Africans, whose gods and spirits had been proved vincible and power-less, and whose culture had been disturbed. There was security for them and their converts, while African customs considered un-Christian were prohibited by colonial decrees. Furthermore, there was an abundance of European manufactures to overhaul African societies. In this favorable atmosphere, the missionaries not only shed some of their aggressive messianic traits, but also undertook a well-meaning but haphazard study of the African past.

The missionaries primarily were motivated by the nineteenth-century belief (shared by the African elites, by white liberals who then controlled the legislative council of Cape Colony, and by philan-thropists) in the positive response of any electorate and leadership when alerted to existing evils, problems, and racism, through educa-tion, publicity, demonstrations, and public debates. Some missionaries wanted "to prevent making the most dangerous mistakes from mere ignorance of the true nature of (African) rites or superstitions."[29] Some intended to effect some corrective censure of European prejudices, racism, and exploitation, especially after the unification of South Africa, the erosion of Cape liberalism, and the increasing victories of the Nationalist party. They hoped to influence district commissioners, settlers, fellow missionaries, and educated Africans. Henri A. Junod's *Life of a South African Tribe* is "addressed to those who can influence the development of the African, to the authorities dealing with the so-called native problem, and to educated Africans. . . ."[30] Others actually hoped to initiate an historiography of the African past.

> The importance of this work may not be fully realized at the present moment; but its lasting value will be better appreciated a hundred years hence, when native-born historians, then beginning to emerge, will be highly thankful for our having herein put on permanent record this account of the simple civilization of their forefathers.[31]

These first Africanists, Bantuists, or antiquarianists (as they called themselves) began the "investigation" of African history and observation of the African's physical, mental, social, and moral life, which led to a prodigious output of books.

Similarly, African intellectualism and politics centered on exposing and (hopefully) reforming the racism, brutality, and repression of settler colonialism. The founders of the South African Native National Congress (1912) stipulated some of their major objectives:

> To be the medium of expression of representative opinion and to formulate a standard policy on Native Affairs for the benefit and guidance of the Union Government and Parliament (article 12, section 3); to educate Parliament and Provincial Councils, Municipalities, other bodies and the public generally regarding the requirements and aspirations of the Native people (section 4); and to educate Bantu people on their rights, duties, and obligations to the state and to themselves individually and collectively (section 5).[32]

Perhaps the most typical of these reform-oriented intellectuals was Solomon Tshekisho Plaatje, whose *Native Life in South Africa, before and since the European War and the Boer Rebellion* (1916) deals with the history of the Land Act and of segregation in South Africa. His objective was to present

> a sincere narrative of a melancholy situation, in which, with all its shortcomings, I have endeavored to describe the difficulties of the South African Natives under a very strange law, so as most readily to be understood by the sympathetic reader.[33]

He was appealing to the British government and public "on behalf of five million loyal British subjects (Africans) who shoulder the 'black man's burden' every day, doing so without looking forward to any decoration or thanks."[34] He collected most of the material on personal tours throughout the Transvaal, Orange Free State, which he referred to as the 'Only Slave State,' and the Cape Colony.

Another great and even more historically oriented intellectual was S. M. Molema, who wrote *The Bantu Past and Present: An Ethnographical and Historical Study of the Native Races of South Africa* (1920) to present "to the public some facts about my people, the Bantu . . . and that it might increase the public interest in them."[35] The book was based on Molema's "personal observation and experiences, and more correctly interpreting the psychological touches which must be unfathomable to a foreigner."[36] But the most prolific intellectual was D. D. T. Jabavu, who wrote *The Black Problem* (1920), *Native Disabilities in South Africa* (1932), *Criticisms of the Native Bills* (1935), *The Findings of the All-African Convention* (1935), *Native Views on the Native Bills* (1935), and *Bantu Literature: Classification and Reviews* (1921), all published by the Lovedale Press. Jabavu's avowed aim was to present "an all-round practical exposition of the Native problem by a Native . . . providing both negative and constructive criticism." Other intellectuals wrote novels, biographies, and poems, translated English works, composed music, and edited newspapers as was done in the first period.

Complementing the religious world of the missionaries was the secular world of Cape liberalism.[37] African elites wholeheartedly accepted the famous maxim: Equal Rights for All Civilized Men South of the Zambesi. Plaatje described the Cape franchise as "the most liberal, logical, just, and humane" voting system because it had

> . . . recognized that, socially and politically, the Bantu people are in their teens. It made a point to shape and help on their development by all possible means—education in arts and crafts, instruction in the use of political privileges, exercise of power, and self-government after the British representative system.[38]

He denounced the Natal "Native Policy" as being "at once illiberal and illogical, unjust and inhumane, a policy entirely subversive of the British traditions and sense of fairplay, such as we see were more or less adhered to in the Cape Province," because it had devised "obnoxious legal distinctions" between blacks and whites.[39] To the African elites, the theory and, to some extent, the practice of Cape liberalism represented nonracialism, justice, democracy, and common citizenship. Through it, mission-educated Africans wielded a limited but real influence in Cape elections. Overall, the African vote was less than 10 percent of the electorate, but in some eastern Cape constituencies it was as high as 47 percent.[40]

The most important convert to Cape liberalism was John Tengo Jabavu.[41] He was educated at Lovedale and became the editor of *Isigidimi Sama Xhosa* [The Xhosa messenger] and president of the Native Election Association of the eastern Cape. He maintained influential contacts with white liberals in the Cape and England, such as James Rose-Innes and John Sauer. Rose-Innes and his friends launched Jabavu as the founder-editor of *Imvo* (1884) "to open the eyes of the Natives to their rights," through which he became the most influential African in nineteenth-century Cape politics.[42] He preferred Cape liberalism and imperial trusteeship to the "cruel and unreasoning majority of the Dutch Boers, the eternal enemies of Native political rights."[43] He and his followers organized themselves and worked with sympathetic whites to promote the so-called color-blind Cape franchise, under which an African who earned a minimum of £ 50 a year or who owned immovable property worth £ 75 and had passed a literacy test could vote and be voted to the Cape legislative council. Jabavu also sought to promote African interests through political journalism and lobbying.

Jabavu and his followers refused to join the South African National Congress in 1912 because it advocated the election to Parliament and other public offices of Africans, who would be "under the control and for the purposes" of the congress. Instead they formed the nonracial South African Race Congress to promote the objective of living "in absolute peace and harmony with every race in this country, be it black, or be it white, green or yellow." They were "perfectly convinced that race and color hatred are the curse and blight of any country," and were determined "to fight them to the utmost."[44] Jabavu ran against Rubusana, the National Congress candidate, in 1914 and, by splitting the African vote, caused the victory of a white candidate. Thenceforth, he became unpopular among Africans.

Despite its subsequent erosion due to Afrikaner nationalism and apartheid under the Union of South Africa, Cape liberalism had a definite influence on African humanism in South Africa. The elites already had been committed to parliamentary democracy and constitutionalism. Their friendships with white liberals who advised and encouraged them, and their electoral leverage led to undue optimism, naiveté, and imitation. Consequently, they misconceived European motives as being basically noble, and settler colonialism as a curable disease. Due to their false sense of common identity of interests with white liberals, they failed to develop their own racial or class consciousness and, thus, caused their political alienation from the African masses.

African trust of local missionaries and Cape liberals was further reinforced by international forces of the nineteenth-century humanitarian movements, especially the Aborigines Protection Society (APS) and the Brotherhood Movement in England. The APS was born (1837) out of the Boer-Khoisan and the Anglo-Xhosa frontier wars, of the Great Trek, and the Boer-Zulu wars.[45] Initially, it was Rev. John Philip who lobbied among members of the House of Commons, such as Thomas Foxwell Buxton, William Wilberforce and Dr. Stephen

Lushington, on behalf of the Khoi Khoi. He visited them in 1822 and 1826 and also published *Researches in South Africa.*[46] Consequently, the House of Commons established the Parliamentary Select Committee on Aboriginal Tribes (1828–1836). An immediate result of the committee was the Kat River Settlement of some five hundred Khoi, in which schools were established and named after Wilberforce and Buxton.

The committee condemned the commando system, the Anglo-Xhosa wars, and the Great Trek, and was very critical of the colonists. Buxton later exclaimed:

> Oh! We Englishmen are, by our own account, fine fellows at home!
> Who among us doubts that we surpass the world in religion, justice,
> knowledge, refinement, and practical honesty? But such a set of mis-
> creants and wolves as we prove when we escape from the range of the
> laws, the earth does not contain.[47]

When the committee was abolished, several members became leading figures of the Aborigines Protection Society. Buxton was its chairman.

The founding father of the APS was Dr. Thomas Hodgkin, a Quaker humanitarian, professor of anatomy at Guy's Hospital, and the APS secretary from 1837 to 1866. The APS' thirty-member Executive Committee included seven earls and viscounts, four bishops, five lords, and six members of Parliament. At first, the society mainly consisted of the most actively philanthropic and nonpartisan sector of the British public, but it gradually became part of the nonconformist conscience of Victorian England, and closely associated with the Liberal party.

The prime objective of the APS was "to watch over and protect the Aborigines of the British Empire" against the "unrestrained expansion," "unjustified wars," and "land-jobbing sophistry" of the colonists. Like the missionaries and African elites, the aboriginists were committed to the ideology of Christianity, nonracialism, universalism, parliamentary reforms, and laissez-faire. They were confirmed imperialists, monogenists, and assimilationists.

> The British empire has been signally blessed by Providence; and her
> eminence, her strength, her wealth, her prosperity, her intellectual, her
> moral and her religious advantages are so many reasons for peculiar
> obedience to the laws of Him who guides the destinies of nations.
> These were given for some higher purpose than commercial prosperity
> and military renown.[48]

Like the missionaries and Africans, the aboriginists believed in a universal "Empire of Man," in trusteeship, and in the progressive perfectibility of people. They conceived the Africans, Indians, Maoris, and aborigines as integral parts of a universal imperial community which was to be patterned along British culture, institutions, values, and socioeconomic classes. They admired the French "assimilationist impulse," and stated in the APS *Annual Report* of 1840: "This Society asserts the absolute necessity of admitting the Aborigines in our colonies and settlements, to the fullest participation in all the rights and privileges of British subjects."[49] Thus, their concept of the "white man's burden" was a British "Empire by justification" based on Christianity, education, assimilation, brotherhood, and equalitarianism.

The aboriginists were as committed to the "battle for the aborigines" as they were opposed to unrestrained, "unauthorized" settler colonialism. When their efforts to reconcile monogenist imperialism with settler colonialism failed, they, like the African humanists, increasingly became anticolonist. The settlers became "ministers of evil," whose oppression was "so grievious, and cruelty so atrocious," that they were "steeping England in deeper infamy by their inhuman conduct." The aboriginists denounced the Great Trek as "not only unauthorized but absolutely forbidden, and condemned." They urged the British government to "reduce the rebellious subjects to order," and opposed the Boer settlement in Natal as "a Texas in the heart of Africa."[50] They also declared the Anglo-Zulu and Anglo-Ndebele wars unjustified.

Like the missionaries and African elites, the aboriginists believed that ignorance was the "root of all evils. . . . It is from ignorance that much of the cruelty and unjustice which oppress our poor clients has flowed and continues to flow."[51] Thus, like the missionaries and Africans of Lovedale, they concentrated on collecting and diffusing "correct information concerning the character and condition of the aborigines," and appealing to the government, Parliament and the public to exert their "proper influence in advancing the cause of justice." The APS stated its purposes: "The Society seeks, by persuasion, by the exhibit of the evil, and by careful search after measures of a practical character, to obtain the application of the remedy.[52] They relied on the humanity and conscience of the British public for reformist action.

The aboriginists had so much influence on African elites that reading chapter 30, "A Charge to Keep," in Molema's *The Bantu Past and Present*, and chapter 16, "The Appeal for Imperial Protection" in Plaatje's *Native Life in South Africa* is like reading the APS' *Extracts, Aborigines' Friend* and annual reports on imperialism and trusteeship. According to Molema,

> The history of the relation of Britain to the Bantu is the history of the British government over the subject races all over the world, a history which, whatever its faults and blemishes, is characterized by justice and respect for human rights. These facts are even more forcibly borne out in South Africa, where they stand out in shining relief against the diametrically opposed Boer system.[53]

He claimed that the Boers had "won for themselves among blacks a notoriety for repression, inhumanity, and injustice, [while] the British people and government have drawn the sword, time and again, to assert Bantu rights [by saying] hands off to aggressive European colonists."[54] He characterized Britain as the "protector, friend and mother of the black races" and concluded that "in South Africa, as in India, and, in fact, as in all colonies, the good that Britain did for the natives far outbalances the evil."[55]

There also was a great deal of correspondence between individual African elites and aboriginists, as well as publications of African petitions and speeches in the *Aborigines' Friend*. Both sides made conscious efforts to coordinate their protests against settler colonialism and pleadings for imperial intervention, by exchanging ideas, information, and visits. For instance, when National Congress delegates Dube, Rubusana, Plaatje, Saul Masane, and T. M. Mapikela arrived in London in 1914 to seek imperial repeal of the notorious Natives' Land Act, they first visited and briefed the Anti-Slavery and Aborigines Protection Society.[56] In turn, Thomas Buxton and John H. Harris, secretaries of the Anti-Slavery Movement and APS, respectively, arranged for the delegates' meetings with the colonial secretary and sympathetic members of Parliament.

The meetings ended in complete failure, but the delegates were deeply impressed by the friendship and goodwill of the aboriginists, several members of Parliament, the English press, and the Brotherhood Movement. Several aboriginists and M.P.s entertained the delegates in their homes. Then on Sunday afternoon, March 14, the delegates took part in an "Imperial jubilee" in the Central Hall, sponsored by the Brotherhood Movement. According to Plaatje: "There was a great resemblance between Brotherhood and Empire. In it all kinds of religion were represented, yet all were united in one great principle."[57] To him the movement represented "practical Christianity which knows no distinction of colour or boundaries between nations," and whose members were "always ready to practice what they preach." The speakers supposedly were representing the integral parts of the British Empire: William Cross for England, T. Owens for Wales, S. S. A. Cambridge (black) for British Guiana, Ruth Buckwall for Australia, Lionel Boote for New Zealand, and Plaatje for South Africa, "the baby member of the British family."[58] The African delegates particularly were impressed by Cross's statement:

> The principle of freedom underlies Empire as it underlies Brotherhood also. There is no limit to Empire that is founded upon unity, toleration, justice and liberty; it surely has no end.[59]

While in England, the Africans spoke to about sixty brotherhoods, as well as to sisterhoods, adult schools, and numerous churches.

Like the aboriginists, the African elites strongly believed in the "potency of words" and ideas in the "war against the demon of ignorance, prejudice and error." They also were strongly anticolonist, especially the Afrikaners, whom Plaatje often described as "Backvelders" and "colour-phobic emotionalists." Plaatje, like the rest of his peers, preferred imperial trusteeship because "Imperial lines are benevolent while South African lines are cruel; consisting largely of repression and slavery."[60]

Thus, in their search for identity in the alien settler society, the African elites adopted the humanitarianism of Victorian England and, in turn, used it to guide and fortify their private and public lives. They acquired the pious optimism, utopianism, and universalism of missionaries, white liberals, and, especially, aboriginists. Considering the realities of racism, exploitation, and repression of their settler society, their humanism made them unduly naive, self-deceiving and even otherworldly. The spiritualism, universalism, nonracialism, and nonviolence inherent in their humanism became the predispositional factors which determined the elites' perception of and actions for or against the African and settler worlds.

ELITES AND THE TRADITIONAL AFRICAN WORLD

Due to the operative predispositional factors we have discussed, mission-educated elites perceived and portrayed the traditional African world primarily from the point of view of the missionaries, white liberals, and aboriginists. The "heathenism," "tribalism," ignorance, and technology of traditional Africa shamed and distressed them. For example, Molema's *The Bantu Past and Present* (1920) reads like Rev. A. T. Bryant's *The Zulu People as They Were before the White Man Came*, Rev. D. Fred Ellenberger's *History of the Basuto*, or George M. Theal's *Ethnography of South Africa*. To Molema, Africa was a "dark continent" in a "threefold sense": namely, being "terra incognita," being "peopled by dark-skinned races," and "perhaps most important of all, these dark-skinned Africans had no light; they were in darkness—the gross darkness of ignorance."[61] Southern Africa was even "more truly shrouded in the dense darkness of ignorance—a darkness almost palpable.[62] According to Molema, Egyptian civilization was not African but Asian because the Egyptians were "chiefly Hamitic people, with strains of Negro blood."

Concerning the Bantu, Molema stated:

They are said to have sprung from the mingling of Negro blood with that of the Hamites of North Africa and also Semites of North and East Africa—that is, in short, the Bantu are a hybrid race—Negroes modified by considerable infusions of Caucasian blood.[63]

He claimed, as did the missionary and colonialist historians of his time,

very little progress they have achieved," which would lead to "over-confidence and to national or individual arrogance."

The elites were especially worried about the incidences of alcoholism, promiscuity, venereal diseases, and materialism among the Christianized/urbanized Africans. They were also opposed to African racialism against whites, the Ethiopianism (religious separatism), Garveyism (Marcus Aurelius Garvey's Africa-for-Africans ideology), trade unionism, and especially to "Bolshevism and its nihilistic doctrines." D. D. T. Jabavu particularly was sensitive to those he characterized as "agitators" who were "rallying catch phrases and a copious socialistic vocabularly" with which they played "as easily as on a piano upon the hearts of the illiterate mine-labourers." According to Jabavu,

> The cure [to African unrest] here lies in our being able to produce well
> educated native leaders trained in a favourable atmosphere (e.g., Fort
> Hare), who will be endowed with commonsense, cool heads, with a
> sense of responsibility, endurance and correct perspective in all
> things.[80]

Thus, the elites actually were afraid of historical, racial, or nationalist consciousness among the African masses, to the extent of advocating gradualism and patience on the premise that Africans "must pass through the mill and serve their time as advanced races have done." According to Molema, to expect that "what has been brought about by centuries of steady application in one race—the European—can be effected by a few years' training in another race—the African—is, to say the least, rash."[81]

While the elites agreed on the ideology and goal of Westernism, they differed in emphasis on the means. John Tengo Jabavu emphasized political representation through an alliance with white liberals and through political journalism. His son emphasized Christianity, education, and economic self-determination along the Tuskegee model of Booker T. Washington.[82] Dube was the strongest advocate of economic self-determination, for which he established the Ohlange Institute and a business league, to make "Anglo-Saxons of Africa" who would "build farm houses, manage plows, make wagons, and raise sugar cane, tea, and coffee."[83] He was looking forward to the "great day" when a "schoolhouse and a church" would rest "on every hilltop" of the "dark continent" to develop "our peoples' minds, hands, and hearts by establishing industries and instruction in the various trades."[84] Dube and D. D. T. Jabavu both actually visited Washington and the Tuskegee Institute and were deeply impressed.

It should be noted that we are dealing with complicated personalities. So far, I have portrayed the image of alienated, elitist, and intellectual humanists and politicians who had forsaken their African heritage and peoples for Christianity and Westernism; who had learned to despise African history, customs, institutions, and values; and who were afraid of African resistance, racialism, nationalism, and independence because they considered them irrational, impractical, irresponsible, and, of course, un-Christian. They would not support a truly African liberation struggle because it would have created a different order, with no room for their Christian, utopian, and universalist humanism. Viewed from this angle, as Leo Kuper has done, the role of the elites was "not unlike that of the switches in the telephone exchange, passing the word—religious, educational, and administrative—from Whites to Africans."[85]

Even so, the elites derived their historical, racial, and cultural roots from the traditional African world. The classic example was Tiyo Soga. He was not only the first African missionary, and famous translator of *Pilgrim's Progress*, but he was also married to a white woman. Yet, Rev. Robert Johnston, one of his fellow missionaries who knew him best, described him: "He was a black man. He knew it; and, like Othello, never forgot that he was black."[86] To Johnston, "Tiyo Soga had an honest pride in his manhood as a *pure Kafir.* He was disposed to glory in his Kafirhood. He would not bow down before any one, because of his own black face." According to Johnston, Soga actually was "oversensitive" to racialist remarks about himself or any African. Johnston related a case in 1867, when Soga had been chosen to leave the Mgwali Mission to start the Kutura Mission among the Kreli. Soga asked the missionaries to inform officially Chief Sandili of the Mgwali area that he was leaving. The missionaries objected that since Sandili was a heathen chief and had nothing to do with the transfer, it was unnecessary to inform him officially. Soga was furious and "in a few pointed, burning sentences, exhibited to perfection the Kafir patriot and the Christian missionary."[87] He told the missionaries that Sandili and his people "although heathens, were still men, and could not be treated as if they had no claim to manhood," and he forced them to apologize and to inform the chief. Johnston concluded: "Few men possessed his degree of self-respect."[88]

Soga himself spoke out in a memo, "The Inheritance of My Children," in which he advised, *"take your place* in the world as *coloured,* not as *white* men; as *Kafirs,* not as Englishmen [and] never appear ashamed that your father was a Kafir, and that you inherit some African blood. It is every whit as good and as pure as that which flows in the veins of my fairer brethren."[89] Racism was to him "the height of ingratitude and impiety [and] equally the height of wickedness, a libel against God's creation." Africans, he said, may have "many unamiable points," but they stand "second to none as to nobility of nature," and they have "the elements out of which a noble race might be made." Africans' "natural capacity and intelligence" are equal to whites', "but education, civilization and the blessings of Christianity have made differences among men."[90]

Molema acknowledged many redeeming values of African traditions. He preferred the "raw, untouched, unsophisticated, purely uncivilized, but none the less observant, self-respecting, often virtuous, and always healthier and happier Bantu" to the "half-civilized" Bantu. He admired traditional midwives because "in spite of the entire ignorance of obstetrics prevailing among the Bantu people, labour was generally conducted very successfully," and polygamy because there were no harems, widows, orphans, illegitimates, and prostitution among the Bantu.[91] According to him, "the law of the Bantu people not only made no difference between males and females, but it also afforded greater protection to the latter, injuries to them being more seriously punished. In domestic affairs, the wife took the first place."[92] He was impressed by what he called "Bantu tribal communism," because "the unselfishness of the people was surprising." The Bantu society was, to him, a classless society which provided individual security and group harmony because "the moral and intellectual conduct of all members of the tribe was regulated by the prevailing moral and intellectual ideas of the time."[93] He argued that *lobola* (bride dowry) was not a commercial deal and the wife was not a "negotiable commodity," and traditional African dancing, "crude as the whole thing was, it was not totally devoid of beauty."[94]

In his essay, "The Regeneration of Africa," Pixley Seme emphasized, "I am an African and I set my pride in my race over against a hostile public opinion."[95] He was also an adviser to the Swazi royal family, a close confidant of the Swazi queen, Natotsbeni, and he married Dinizulu's daughter. He worked closely with African chiefs before and after the formation of the National Congress. "Although I had the honour to be the initiator of this Conference, Chiefs Maama, Sayso, Molembo, Sekukuni, and others were the men who really created Congress."[96] Seven chiefs were made honorary presidents of the National Congress, and while leadership of the Lower House of Congress mainly consisted of the educated elites, that of the Upper House of Nobles consisted of chiefs.

According to Dube, the Zulu had "well-formed bodies—straight, sinewy and well proportioned" and they "generally resemble the Aryan race but with higher foreheads and cheek-bones."[97] He also stated that they were "keen observers of men and things, intelligent and quick-witted"; "capable of great physical endurance"; and "sociable, polite and hospitable in times of peace." Jabavu was a relentless advocate of African unity, leadership, heritage, and historiography. He wanted "Native history written by black hands" because

> ... however sympathetic and good a European may be, he cannot
> undertake such a task with the minuted knowledge and enthusiasm that
> can belong only to the Native African, who must himself be the victim
> of the untoward circumstances and difficulties under discussion.[98]

He claimed that books on African history written by whites were
inadequate because they had been written "by white authors who
naturally must take care of their own interests first, and one cannot
blame them, for blood is thicker than water."[99] He advocated the
necessity for Africans to work out their own destiny by a selective
process of adapting, and amalgamating "all that is good in the white
man's civilization, eschewing the bad."

The relationship between the educated elites and the traditional
world of chiefs and masses was full of contradictions, ambiguities, and
surprises. The elites' commitment to the Christian pedantry which
equated Christianity with civilization and traditionalism with savagery
and, thus, engendered deep-seated inferiority complexes and imitation
is in contrast to their apparent racial consciousness and "pro-
tonationalism." And, while they were jealous of the chiefs, whose authority was vested in birth and traditionalism, they nevertheless gave the
latter honored positions in their National Congress. While they shared
the nonracialism of missionaries and white liberals, they questioned
and undermined the latter's legitimacy to be leaders of the African
masses.

Besides, the National Congress actually was in favor of either racial
equality or what Molema called "equitable separation." Dube, D. D. T.
Jabavu, Molema, and Plaatje accepted the land-division concept of the
Land Act with the proviso that "first and foremost, the separation must
be equitable." Molema wanted the Land Act to lead to "complete
national independence and absolute autonomy [for] each
community—black and white." He and his fellow elites were vehemently opposed to the racial segregation of the act, and were advocating land distribution to be determined "on a proper constitutional basis
by the co-operation of both parties—black and white, or through
arbitration."[100]

From this angle, the elites appear neither to be aping the white
man and his culture, nor to be advocating color-blind nonracialism and
universalism. Their inferiority complex becomes cultural and
psychological, but also temporary, and certainly not racial. Overall,
their predisposition (through Christianity, education, and friendships)
to the universalist, utopian world of missionaries, white liberals, and
aboriginists was so deeply rooted that it predominated and determined
their policies and actions against settler colonialism. Their apparent
admiration of selective elements of traditional African culture and

especially of the "noble savage" was predicated upon patronal self-righteousness and personal detachment. If successful, their religious, educational, and capitalistic programs would have wrecked the social system and, thus, the destiny of African societies; turned the elites themselves into merely assimilated conveyors of an alien culture; and also turned the African masses into lumpen proletariats. Their racial and cultural assertiveness, though genuine and sincere, largely was forced upon them by the racism and segregation of the settlers.

ELITES AND THE SETTLER WORLD

The elites' attitudes, policies, and actions towards settler colonialism were predicated upon their futile attempt to reconcile imperial and colonialist factors. In fact, they imagined a similar infinite antithesis between imperial trusteeship and settler colonialism as they did between Christianity and African tradition. On one hand, they saw the British Empire as "the epitome of Justice, Freedom, Equal Rights and the Natives' only bulwark"; on the other hand, they saw "the Union of White South Africa" as the epitome of racism, slavery, concentration camps, passbooks, and ignorance.

Historically, the elites of South Africa had the bitter experience of witnessing the increasing degeneration of their socioeconomic situation from the "colour-blind" Lovedale Institution and Cape Franchise, parliamentary representation, and exempt status to disenfranchisement, segregation, and harassment. This was particularly true of the first postwar decade of the Union of South Africa, characterized by the succession of notorious acts such as the Natives' Land Act (1913), which divided South Africa inequitably into 87 percent for the white minority and 13 percent for the African majority, and the Urban Areas Act (1918), which divided South African cities into African, Asian, colored, and European residential sections.

The elites had erroneously perceived the cause of the Anglo-Boer War (1898–1902) as "the avowed cause of Justice, Freedom and Equal Rights," to affirm their "full recognition as citizens of the Empire" and to extend Cape liberalism, franchise, and parliamentary representation to Natal, Orange Free State, and the Transvaal. But, to their amazement, the war ended with the infamous Article 8 of the Treaty of Vereeniging, which abolished imperial trusteeship, shirked the "Native Problem," promised responsible government to the Afrikaners, and thus assured a white-dominated Union of South Africa. Africans formed all sorts of organizations (e.g., the Natal Native Congress, the Transvaal Native Congress, the Orange River Congress, and a joint South African Native Congress) to plead for imperial trusteeship, but to no avail. On April 10, 1906, the South African Native Congress petitioned "His Most Excellent Majesty Edward the Seventh [that] . . . it would be preferable for the natives to be taken over by the Crown and be governed from Downing Street through a Department of Native Affairs in the Home Government."[101] Then, as their fears and forebodings were being vindicated by Union legislation, the elites reacted in a sorrowful sense of disbelief, disillusionment, and betrayal.

Plaatje particularly was amazed at the passage of the Land Act:

Personally we must say that if anyone had told us at the beginning of 1913 that a majority of the Union Parliament were capable of passing a law like the Natives' Land Act ... we would have regarded that person as a fit subject for the lunatic asylum.[102]

He had hoped that "a body of men like the ministerialists in Parliament would in the course of days attend the Holy Communion, remember the 11th Commandment, and do unto others as they would that men should do unto them."[103] He denounced the act as a "tyrannical enactment," and African reserves as "human incubators" for "breeding slaves for our masters" which were much cheaper than slaves had been in the United States where the masters provided shelter and clothes, because in South Africa "the pens" were "maintained entirely by the slaves, at their own cost, the farmer's only trouble being to come to the gate and whistle for labourers."

He lamented "the passing of Cape ideals" and "the fast degenerating land policy of Cape statesmen." He rhetorically asked,

Who ... could have thought that the *Cape Times* would in this manner have destroyed its great traditions, built up during the nineteenth century, by sanctioning a law under which Cape magistrates would be forced to render homeless the Natives of the Cape in their own Cape of Good Hope.[104]

To him, settler politics had made "strange bed-fellows" of Cape liberals and the Boers, leading Africans to sing "the funeral dirge of Cape ideals," while Boers sang "songs of gladness." He regretted the abandonment of "the suzerainty of Great Britain, which under the reign of Her late Majesty Victoria, of blessed memory, was the Natives' only bulwark," and the triumph of the Boers, who "like a lot of bloodhounds long held in the leash" had curtailed Cape liberalism and entrenched racism. Wondering if "the Victorian Englishman and the Twentieth Century Englishman are creatures of a different clay," he pleaded for imperial intervention "to assist South Africa in recovering her lost senses" and "avert the nemesis that would surely follow."

Molema was disillusioned especially with Cape liberalism, which was "an astounding platitude," but one full of "hollow, meaningless words and egregious tricks," and was "offering nothing to the Bantu of South Africa except such morbid creations and fancies as 'The Native Problem.' " Settler politics was, to him, predicated upon economic self-interest alone. On the basis of "historical grounds" and "the trend of British Rule in South Africa regarding the Bantu," he concluded,

> No intelligent observer can fail to realize that, whatever it might have
> been yesterday, Western Liberalism is today nothing more than
> verbiage—mere sound and fury—signifying nothing; that morality in
> politics, especially international politics, is apparently purely theoretical,
> that self-interest and self-interest alone is, and must perhaps always be
> the chief and dominating principle. . . . [105]

To him the South Africa act was "a death-knell" which replaced "British
ideas of Political morality" by "repressive Boer Republicanism," and the
Land Act was "the most cruel bill ever put before a Parliament."

Given their humanistic predisposition, the elites perceived a great
need for moral denunciation of racial discrimination and the exclu-
siveness of Afrikaner nationalism, and for the affirmation of God,
brotherhood, and goodwill. They not only presumed racism to be the
root cause of African suffering and of the elimination of trusteeship,
but they also began scapegoating the Afrikaner. According to Molema,
Afrikaner racism was not only "illegitimate, unethical, and unchris-
tian," but also of "unusual complexity." He distinguished between the
Boers (another name for the Afrikaners), who were more racist, ignorant, and "far behind their British kinsmen intellectually and socially,"
and the Anglo-Saxons, who were liberal, educated, and, together with
the French, "intellectual and social superiors of the Boers by a long
way." He claimed:

> All the prejudice that can possess an untutored mind, enhanced by
> some natural or unnatural tendency and torsion of the soul, inflamed
> by its earnest ascription to divine source, and quickened by aggression
> on the part of the object, is to be found in the average vee-Boer.[106]

He also distinguished between the Cape colonists who believed in
"Equal rights for all civilized men, irrespective of race and color" and
colonists of Natal who accomplished "what the Boers denied the Bantu
in concise, unequivocal terms, [by] unnecessary parry, circumventing
the exercise of franchise by the Bantu with well-nigh impossible conditions."

Plaatje was convinced that Afrikaner racism was caused by the
Dutch Reformed church, which to him was the "State Church of South
Africa."

> The Dutch almost worship their religious teachers; and they will
> continue these cruelties upon the natives as long as they believe that
> they have the approval of the church. Let the predikants [Afrikaans
> word for preachers] then tell their people that tyranny is tyrannical
> even though the victims are of a different race, and the South African
> Dutch will speedily abandon that course, for a course of political
> righteousness.[107]

He also believed racism was caused by ignorance and that it was unethical and un-Christian.

Retrospectively, we can see that the elites were often so carried away by their humanistic impulse towards the universal person, towards nonracialism, and towards brotherhood based on Christianity, reason, and goodwill that they consequently missed the real, specific, and immediate problem of predatory settler colonialism. They were what Albert Memmi has called "sentimental anti-racist" suffering from "the sociology of good intentions,"[108] who perceived settler colonialism in religioracialist terms instead of economic self-interests. They treated racism as a monstrous and immoral aberration of the sick, ignorant, and sinning Boers, instead of a symbol and function of colonial conquest, economic exploitation, and privileges. Elites attempted to distinguish between the liberal Anglo-Saxons and racist Boers, when, as Aime Cesaire says, " . . . no one colonizes innocently."[109]

They misjudged the parliamentary struggle between English and Afrikaner colonists, which was nothing more than family differences between groups of privileged white settlers over economic and social dividends and over some of the psychological qualms of colonial domination and exploitation, for a clash about humanistic fundamentals. Consequently, they overlooked the underlying ideological consensus and preoccupation with political power, economic self-interests, and raciocultural self-preservation, and, thus, erroneously presumed that while the Boer was *enfant terrible,* King George was their liberator.

> That the petitioners, in their capacity as representatives of the South African National Native Congress, which is again the representative body of natives of the Union of South Africa, most humbly approach Your Majesty as their King, their father and protector.[110]

The elites did not even see themselves as responsible for or capable of liberating the African masses; that was for an imperial trusteeship. Instead, they concentrated on educating the British government, Parliament, and the public, on reminding the British of their "Imperial charge," and on encouraging corrective measures by professions of loyalty, common sense, and gratitude.

The elites' "program of action" mainly consisted of successive meetings and conferences of the National Congress or its branches, which always ended with formalist and verbose petitions, mostly reading

> To His Most Excellent Majesty . . . by the Grace of God, of the United Kingdom of Great Britain and Ireland, and of the British Dominions beyond the Seas. King, Defender of the Faith, Emperor of India. . . . petitioners are Your Majesty's most loyal and humble subjects, who have always been loyal to Your Majesty's throne and person, and still desire to continue being loyal to Your Majesty's throne and person.[111]

The petitions largely pleaded for imperial intervention against "the selfish mismanagement of inter-racial affairs" by white settlers whose rule was "as harsh as its instigators were callous," before "the whole white community must deal with a situation overwhelmingly beyond their control."

Simultaneously, the elites sought to demonstrate their common sense approach by disassociating themselves and the National Congress from Ethiopianism, meaning African religious separatism from the missionary Christian churches, characterized by the boycotting of Western education, values, goods, and medicine, and by the practice of polygamy. The elites also disassociated themselves from the Africa-for-Africans and black-is-beautiful ideology of Marcus Aurelius Garvey, from communism and from trade unionism, especially that of the Industrial and Commercial Workers' Union. They emphatically stipulated in the constitution of the National Congress that "the work of the Association shall be effected and advanced by means of resolutions, protests and a constitutional and peaceful propaganda." Meeting in Johannesburg on July 25, 1913, to discuss the Land Act, right at the peak of a white labor strike, National Congress delegates addressed a resolution to "His Majesty's Government" (South African) disassociating themselves "entirely from the industrial struggles on the Witwatersrand and elsewhere," and promising "to seek redress for our grievances through constitutional rather than by violent means."[112] As reported by Plaatje, even the archracist Malan, then minister of native affairs, "confessed to a feeling of relief at the moderation of their tone."[113]

They always felt the urge to reaffirm their loyalty, especially in crises. For example, after its delegation had failed to obtain imperial repeal of the Land Act and had returned home, the National Congress convened a special meeting in Bloemfontein in August 1914 to express its disappointment at the cold reception given to the native deputation by the Imperial Government, [to] express its thanks to the British public for the kind reception given to the deputation, and to devise means for another deputation.[114] But when the delegates arrived, Britain had declared war on Germany and as reported by Plaatje, the secretary,

> ... the Native Congress, in view of the situation, resolving itself at once into a patriotic demonstration, decided to hang up native grievances against the South African Parliament till a better time and to tender the authorities every assistance.[115]

The executive went to Pretoria to offer Botha, the prime minister, their allegiance and "all possible services." Rubusana wrote Botha promising to raise "a native levy of 5,000 able-bodied men to proceed to German South-West Africa, provided the Government is prepared to fully equip this force for the front." Plaatje recommended that Botha

our Prime Minister, who is also Minister of Native Affairs, should now
postpone the constant pampering of the back-velders [Boers], hang
colour prejudice for a more peaceful time, call out the loyal
legions—British, Boer, and Black—and annex German South-West
Africa without delay! As a British General and Minister of Native
Affairs, he should himself lead the black contingents and leave the
whites to be led by their regular officers.[116]

But the governor-general, prime minister, and secretary of defense all
told the elites, "in true South African style, that it was a white man's
war" and that "the Government are anxious to avoid the employment
of its native citizens in warfare against whites." The rejection obviously
was due to "a repugnance to the idea of armed Natives shooting at a
white enemy," and fear of rebellion by trained African soldiers, using
European weapons. The elites, however, were furious at the "wretched
South African colour prejudice" exerting itself "even in critical times."

Needless to say, the elites' program of action and strategy were
supported fully by some missionaries, white liberals, and aboriginists
who continued to advise and encourage them. Several of the petitions
were published in *Aborigines' Friend,* and the aboriginists hosted African deputations (1914, 1919) and arranged their meetings with public
officials, as well as their speeches and interviews before churches,
brotherhoods, and press clubs. In South Africa, the elites participated
in multiracial joint councils led by liberal white professionals whose
intention was to "keep African leaders on peaceful and constitutional
lines, to educate and inform European public opinion, and to seek the
maximum possible concessions for African economic and political advance."[117] But, as Walshe has stated, these white liberals, like the elites,
lacked a political base, and they were then relying on "moral asserta-
tion, argument, research, the facts, and an awakening of European
concern for colour-blind justice."[118] In the end the African elites and
their missionary, liberal, and aboriginist "allies" lost the contest to
settler nationalism and apartheid.

Conclusion

We have chosen to call the elites humanists because of their apparently
overwhelming commitment to the ideology of individual dignity, nonracialism, and the brotherhood of mankind, which was not merely a
philosophy of life, but a moralist crusade against evil, ignorance, and
racism. The elites acquired this humanism from their Christian up-
bringing and education and from personal friendships and joint
crusading with missionaries, white liberals, and aboriginists.

They were not merely seeking acceptance in the white man's world
or aping white bourgeois values; they were more than just the *African*

Bourgeoisie of Leo Kuper. Their ideology of nonracialism and universalism actually transcended both the African and settler societies. Even
their notion of education was much broader than the mere production
of clerks, mechanics, farmers, and teachers for bread-and-butter occupations. To them, education had to include programs for elevating the
material, health, political, civil, and moral aspects of the whole community. Above all, it had to aim at providing the community with
well-trained, conscientious, and trustworthy leadership—capable of
transforming human life and the world into something higher, more
harmonious, and better. They created a utopian, universalist, and
moralist world of their own to which they attempted to lead both the
African and settler worlds. Thus, their main hubris was not that they
disowned their fellow Africans for the settler society which they despised, but that they transcended the nasty realities of settler colonialism into existentialist humanism.

It was a terrible mistake that the elites treated settler colonialism
mainly as a humanistic tragedy instead of a worldly, deliberately orches-
trated racioeconomic system. The apparent "shroud of ignorance
which surrounds the Native policy of the Union of South Africa," the
English-Boer, and the British-settler rivalries that Plaatje, Molema,
Jabavu, and their colleagues saw were family squabbles among fellow-
colonizers over "a piece of the pie." By 1900, the British colonial policy
was predicated upon the devolvement of self-government and, eventually, dominion status to white settler colonies, at the expense of the
indigenous populations if necessary. The elites' missionary, liberal, and
aboriginist allies by then were a powerless minority and a remnant of a
bygone nineteenth-century humanitarianism.

The elites also were not necessarily nationalists. They not only
condemned African history, customs, beliefs, and values, but also disassociated themselves from the mass-, nation-, and independence-
oriented Ethiopianism, trade unionism, and Garveyism. Ironically,
their condemnation of traditional Africa bolstered and upheld the
colonialist racioeconomic ideology. They psychologically weakened the
African's capacity to resist colonialist propaganda and hindered the
development of a truly African historical, racial, and liberationist consciousness. Given their cultural and psychological alienation from the
African masses, and the rejection by the settler society, the elites lost
their power base and legitimacy. Consequently, they became mere
expressions of themselves and, thus, a negligible group in the multifa-
ceted colonialist crisis of South Africa. They became loners and proph-
ets, filled with delusions, fantasies, ambiguities, and otherworldliness.
Nevertheless, a moderate version of their nonracialism and universalism has become a permanent feature of modern African nationalism. Through their examples and, especially, the National Congress,

they were also the first to undermine ethnicity and sectional collaboration by African chiefs, groups, and individuals.

Their real historical significance lies not so much in what they did as in what they said. Their prophecies of a doomsday of the British Empire in South Africa and of the inevitable violent confrontation between settler colonialists and African nationalists have come true in less than fifty years. Their familiarity with the English language, culture, and institutions, as well as their having been born, raised, educated, and discriminated against in the settler environment, enabled them to infuse into their writings the riches of their authentic experiences and the actual daily operations and machinery of settler colonialism.

Notes

1. Mission-educated elites have been discussed before in the context of African nationalism in southern Africa. See for example, Peter Walshe, *The Rise of African Nationalism in South Africa: The African National Congress, 1912–1952* (Berkeley and Los Angeles: University of California Press, 1971); Leo Kuper, *An African Bourgeoisie: Race, Class, and Politics in South Africa* (New Haven: Yale University Press, 1965); Manning Marable, "John Langalibalele Dube, Booker T. Washington and the Ideology of Conservative Black Nationalism" in *Profiles of Self-Determination: African Responses to European Colonialism in Southern Africa, 1962 to the Present,* edited by David Chanaiwa (Northridge: California State University Foundation, 1976), pp. 320–45; and J. Mutero Chirenje, "The Afro-American Factor in Southern African Ethiopianism, 1890–1906" in *Profiles of Self-Determination,* edited by Chanaiwa, pp. 250–80. This essay, however, treats the philosophy and behavior of the elites as humanism and not necessarily nationalism.

2. For detailed discussion of this search for identity and of the various African responses to colonialism in southern Africa, consult *Profiles of Self-Determination.*

3. Davidson Don Tengo Jabavu, *The Black Problem: Papers and Addresses on Various Native Problems* (Lovedale, S.A.: Lovedale Press, 1920), p. 16. Also Solomon Tshekisho Plaatje, *Native Life in South Africa before and since the European War and the Boer Rebellion* (London: P. S. King and Son, 1916); and S. M. Molema, *The Bantu Past and Present: An Ethnographical and Historical Study of the Native Races of South Africa* (Edinburgh: W. Green and Son, 1920); and J. Henderson Soga, *The South-Eastern Bantu* (Johannesburg: University of Witwatersrand Press, 1930); and *Ama Xosa: Life and Customs* (Lovedale, S.A.: Lovedale Press, 1931).

4. See for example Molema, *The Bantu*; Jabavu, *The Black Problem*; Plaatje, *Native Life*; and Thomas Karis and Gwendolen M. Carter, eds., *From Protest to Challenge: A Documentary History of African Politics in South Africa 1882–1964* (Stanford: Hoover Institution Press, 1972–), vol. 1, *Protest and Hope,* by Sheridan Johns III (1972).

5. For more details on Christian influences on the elites, consult John A. Chalmers, *Tiyo Soga: A Page of South African Missionary Work* (London: Hodder and Stoughton, 1877); H. T. Cousins, *From Kafir Kraal to Pulpit* (London: S. W. Partridge, 1899); Robert H. W. Shepherd, *Lovedale, South Africa: The Story of a Century, 1841–1941* (Lovedale, S.A.: Lovedale Press, 1940), and *Lovedale and Literature for the Bantu* (Lovedale, S.A.: Lovedale Press, 1945).

6. Walshe, *The Rise of African Nationalism,* p. 7.

7. Robert H. W. Shepherd, *Lovedale, South Africa, 1824–1955* (Lovedale, S.A.: Lovedale Press, 1971), p. 43.

8. Ibid., p. 14.

9. Ibid., p. 30.

10. For further discussion of African literature of this period, consult Daniel P. Kunene, *The Works of Thomas Mofolo: Summaries and Critiques,* occasional paper no. 2 (Los Angeles: African Studies Center, UCLA, 1967), and *The Beginning of South African Vernacular Literature: A Historical Study* (Los Angeles:

African Studies Center, UCLA, 1967); Davidson Don Tengo Jabavu, *Bantu Literature: Classification and Reviews* (Lovedale, S.A.: Lovedale Press, 1921); and Shepherd, *Lovedale and Literature for the Bantu.*

11. Shepherd, *Lovedale and Literature for the Bantu,* p. 10.

12. Ibid., pp. 16–17.

13. Chalmers, *Tiyo Soga,* p. 341.

14. Marable, "John Langalibalele Dube," p. 330.

15. Jabavu, *The Black Problem,* p. 14.

16. Plaatje, *Native Life,* dedication.

17. Walshe, *The Rise of African Nationalism,* p. 14.

18. David Chanaiwa, "The Historiographical Traditions of Southern Africa" (paper presented at the Internal Conference on the Historiography of Southern Africa, Gaberone, Botswana, March 7–11, 1977), pp. 3–11.

19. See John Bunyan, *The Pilgrim's Progress from This World to That which is to Come* (Cambridge, Eng.: Sever and Francis, 1864).

20. Chalmers, *Tiyo Soga,* p. 341.

21. Kunene, *The Works of Thomas Mofolo.*

22. Ibid., pp. 7–8.

23. Ibid., p. 8.

24. Aime Cesaire, *Discourse on Colonialism,* translated by Joan Pinkham (New York: Monthly Review Press, 1972); Albert Memmi, *Dominated Man: Notes towards a Portrait* (New York: Orion Press, 1968), and *The Colonizer and the Colonized* (New York: Orion Press, 1965); Frantz Fanon, *The Wretched of the Earth,* translated by Constance Farrington (New York: Grove Press, 1963).

25. Chalmers, *Tiyo Soga,* p. 359.

26. Ibid., p. 365.

27. Kunene, *The Works of Thomas Mofolo,* pp. 17–24.

28. John L. Dube, *Jege the Bodyservant of King Shaka* [Insila ka Shaka], translated by J. Boxwell (Lovedale, S.A.: Lovedale Press, 1951).

29. Henri A. Junod, *The Life of a South African Tribe* (London: Macmillan, 1927), p. 8.

30. Henri P. Junod, *Bantu Heritage* (Westport. Conn.: Negro Universities Press, 1970), preface.

31. A. T. Bryant, *The Zulu People as They Were before the White Man Came* (New York: Negro Universities Press, 1970), p. xi.

32. Constitution of the South African Native National Congress, September 1919, Doc. 23, in *From Protest to Challenge,* edited by Karis and Carter, vol. 1, p. 77.

33. Plaatje, *Native Life,* p. 11.

34. Ibid., p. 15.

35. Molema, *The Bantu,* p. vii.

36. Ibid., p. viii.

37. For Cape liberalism see, for example, R. F. Alfred Hoernle, *South African Native Policy and the Liberal Spirit* (Lovedale, S.A.: Lovedale Press, 1939); and Janet Robertson, *Liberalism in South Africa* (Oxford: Clarendon Press, 1971).

38. Plaatje, *Native Life,* p. 240.

39. Ibid., p. 241.

40. Walshe, *The Rise of African Nationalism*, p. 3.

41. Davidson Don Tengo Jabavu, *The Life of John Tengo Jabavu* (Lovedale, S.A.: Lovedale Press, 1922).

42. Walshe, *The Rise of African Nationalism*, pp. 4–5.

43. Ibid., p. 5.

44. Karis and Carter, eds., *From Protest to Challenge*, pp. 73–74.

45. For details see Charles Buxton, *Memoirs of Sir Thomas Fowell Buxton* (London: John Murray, 1848); John Harris, *A Century of Emancipation* (London: Kennikat Press, 1971); Sir George Stephen, *Anti-Slavery Recollection* (London: Frank Cass, 1971); Howard Temperley, *British Anti-Slavery, 1833–1870* (London: Longman, 1972). See especially, Aborigines Protection Society (APS), *Report of the Parliamentary Select Committee on Aboriginal Tribes* (London: William Ball, Aldine Chambers, Paternoster Row, and Hatchard and Son, 1837), *Extracts*, and *Aborigines' Friend*; John Beecham, *Colonization* (London: Hamilton, Adams, 1838).

46. Buxton, *Memoirs*; APS, *Report of the Parliamentary Select Committee*.

47. Letter, Buxton, chairman of the committee, to Zachary Macaulay, October 1835. Buxton, *Memoirs*, p. 367.

48. See APS, *Report of the Parliamentary Select Committee*, and *Third Annual Report*, June 23, 1840, vol. 3, pp. 1–6; and Buxton, *Memoirs*.

49. APS, *Third Annual Report*, June 23, 1840, vol. 3, p. 2, Res. 4, moved by Dr. Bowning, seconded by George Thompson and passed unanimously.

50. For more details on the anticolonist sentiments of the APS consult *Third Annual Report*, vol. 3, 1840, and *Extracts*, vol. 2, no. 1, January 1841.

51. APS, *Third Annual Report*, p. 10.

52. APS, *Extracts*, vols. 2, 3, April 1841, p. 73.

53. Molema, *The Bantu*, p. 359.

54. Ibid., p. 359. Also Plaatje, *Native Life*, p. 11; and Jabavu, *The Black Problem*.

55. Molema, p. 360.

56. Plaatje, *Native Life*, p. 194.

57. Ibid., p. 227.

58. Ibid.

59. Ibid., p. 228.

60. Ibid., p. 226.

61. Molema, *The Bantu*, p. 7.

62. Ibid.

63. Ibid., p. 5.

64. Ibid., p. 170.

65. Ibid., p. 194.

66. Ibid., p. 2.

67. Ibid., p. 77.

68. Ibid., pp. 80–120.

69. Ibid., p. 120.

70. Rev. John L. Dube, "A Talk upon My Native Land," Doc. 19, in *From Protest to Challenge*, edited by Karis and Carter, p. 68. Also Marable, "John Langalibalele Dube."

71. John Tengo Jabavu, "The South African Race Congress," *Imvo*, April 2, 1912.

72. Jabavu, *The Black Problem,* p. 99.
73. Chalmers, *Tiyo Soga,* p. 140.
74. Molema, *The Bantu,* pp. 97–109.
75. Ibid., pp. 78–79.
76. Shula Marks, *Reluctant Rebellion: The 1906–1908 Disturbances in Natal* (Oxford: Clarendon Press, 1970), pp. 332–34.
77. Molema, *The Bantu,* p. 317.
78. Ibid., pp. 307–17.
79. Ibid., p. 308.
80. Jabavu, *The Black Problem,* p. 16.
81. Molema, *The Bantu,* p. 334.
82. Jabavu, *The Black Problem.*
83. Marable, "John Langalibalele Dube," p. 334.
84. Ibid., pp. 330–31.
85. Kuper, *An African Bourgeoisie,* p. 147.
86. Chalmers, *Tiyo Soga,* p. 444.
87. Ibid., p. 440.
88. Ibid., p. 443.
89. Ibid., p. 430.
90. Ibid., pp. 430–31.
91. Molema, *The Bantu,* pp. 126–32.
92. Ibid., p. 133.
93. Ibid., pp. 133–35.
94. Ibid., p. 126.
95. Pixley Seme, "The Regeneration of Africa," Doc. 20, in *From Protest to Challenge,* edited by Karis and Carter, p. 69.
96. Pixley Seme, quoted in Walshe, *The Rise of African Nationalism,* p. 33.
97. John L. Dube, "Zululand and the Zulus" in *Missionary Review of the World* (June 1898).
98. Jabavu, *The Black Problem,* preface.
99. Ibid., p. 155.
100. Molema, *The Bantu,* pp. 366–67.
101. Karis and Carter, eds., *From Protest to Challenge,* p. 48.
102. Plaatje, *Native Life,* p. 52.
103. Ibid., p. 51.
104. Ibid., p. 161.
105. Molema, *The Bantu,* p. 349.
106. Ibid., p. 242. Also Jabavu, *The Black Problem,* p. 6.
107. Plaatje, *Native Life,* p. 130.
108. Memmi, *Dominated Man,* p. 195.
109. Cesaire, *Discourse on Colonialism,* pp. 17–18.
110. Carter and Karis, eds., *From Protest to Challenge,* Doc. 35, p. 126.
111. Ibid., p. 125.
112. Plaatje, *Native Life,* p. 175.
113. Ibid., p. 176.
114. Ibid., p. 260.
115. Ibid., p. 261.
116. Ibid.
117. Walshe, *The Rise of African Nationalism,* p. 96.
118. Ibid., p. 96.

Chapter 2

African Mind Processing: Colonial Miseducation and Elite Psychological Decolonization

Agrippah T. Mugomba

This chapter addresses itself to the damaging effects upon African elites of colonial miseducation and political socialization, which has so far prevented a genuine revolution throughout the continent.

Education is a potent factor in promoting liberation and revolution. Miseducation has played a vital part in distorting and retarding genuine liberation and revolution in Africa. Colonial miseducation can rightly be held responsible for many of the political, economic, and social ills that afflicted African countries in the past and continue to plague them today.

It is naive and absurd to blame African underdevelopment and its psychological, political, economic, and social consequences on colonial control and exploitation alone. Most African states are now independent, albeit only politically (and even that is doubtful); however, independence has not resolved the numerous inherited problems.

One of the most glaring contradictions of the postcolonial era in Africa is the existence of nominal political independence alongside economic dependency. Those who control the economic empire are also in a position to frustrate the political aspirations of the managers of the political kingdom. Further still, they are able to introduce new forms of dependency, which blunts economic nationalism and consequently renders militant political ideology impotent.

An astute observer of continental Africa, I. William Zartman, has argued that contemporary political developments in Africa can be explained by either of two basic approaches, depending on the particular persuasion of the individual observer: *decolonization* and all that it entails or *dependency*.[1]

These theoretical explanations represent parallel schools of thought which, in recent years, have predominated in the analysis of the international politics of the so-called new states or the grey areas of the international system. In this context, it has been postulated by some that the successor of colonialism is neocolonialism and dependency, while others see what is going on in these societies as a transient phase involving gradual disengagement and the multilateralization of ties to the metropolitan nations. The first group looks suspiciously at the continuing presence of "external controls" (such as continuing political influence, economic domination, cultural conditioning), comparing these with the ideals associated with genuine independence; to them the changes arising out of the formal process of political decolonization are therefore trivial and deceptive. The second group emphasizes actual changes—moves towards genuine independence—and see them as part of a continuing process.[2]

An elaboration of decolonization theory posits that

Euro-African [and other] North-South relationships are caught up in an evolutionary process, as various forms of bilateral, metropolitan influences are replaced with multilateral relations. In the process, political independence is only the "first" step, and the "last" step of complete independence is probably not attainable in an increasingly interdependent world. . . . each layer of colonial influence is supported by the others, and as each is removed, it uncovers and exposes the next underlying one, rendering it not only vulnerable but also untenable. Thus, there is a natural progression to the removal of colonial influence: its speed can be varied by policy and effort, but the direction and evolution are inherent in the process and become extremely difficult to reverse.[3]

The process of political decolonization focuses on the achievement of autonomous development within a broad framework of continuing dependence and underdevelopment. Dependency theory postulates that the recovery of political independence tends to mask and distort the reality of continuing dependence on global and regional economic structures and the constraining impact which external political and economic structures have on the achievement of genuine political independence and autonomous economic development. Basically, the theory is that the

metropolitan countries block African development by co-opting African leaders into an international social structure that serves the world capitalist economy. By training and conditioning the upper layer of African society into Western habits of consumption, reading, vacation, style, and other European values, the dominant politico-economic system removes the need for direct intervention and indirect colonial rule; the more the new elites "develop," the more their expectations rise, the more they become programmed to look North, to think Western, and to alienate themselves from their national society, which is locked into its underdevelopment. Since mass development is such a monumental task in the best of conditions, and since it is even more difficult against the wishes of the dominant capitalists, these alienated, Westernized elites are motivated to repress the spread of development in their society and thus to maintain themselves in power as a political class. The end result is that national development is impossible: foreign predominance is maintained by the co-opted elites, a neocolonial pact as firm as its colonial predecessor was in its time.[4]

The two approaches are not mutually exclusive. In many respects, they represent two sides of the same coin, and the weight assigned to each very much depends on one's perception and interpretation of reality. The decolonization approach draws heavily on dependency theory in analyzing how certain postcolonial relationships have actually operated. But the differences should not be ignored either: dependency theory takes a much narrower view of the process of political decolonization and economic disengagement by maintaining that a vicious circle operates and produces both continuities and discontinuities which are a reflection of altering patterns of dominance-dependence relationships (e.g., from predominantly bilateral forms of colonial dependence to multilateral postcolonial ones). The decolonization process is assumed to have its own internal logic, "wherein each step creates pressures for the next and reduces the possibilities of counteraction by retreating postcolonial forces."[5]

A more realistic analytical approach would accept both theories as valid explanations of continuing decolonization within a framework of dependence and underdevelopment in Africa.[6] No clear contradiction or logical inconsistency is readily apparent in adopting such a perspective. Indeed, the multilateralization of forms and patterns of dependence is a common feature of both the postcolonial state in Africa and those others which are still going through the painful motions of a retarded process of decolonization.

The principal objective of this chapter is to establish dynamic linkages between the colonial education (this writer considers *miseducation* to be the more appropriate term) and political socialization of the foremost African nationalist leaders, and the political economy of dependent development. The argument will be advanced here that there is a direct correlation between education for dependence and servitude, which the colonial school system overly emphasized, on the one hand, and the emergence of neocolonialism resulting in continuing dependency and underdevelopment, on the other. The postcolonial political orientation and behavior of the first generation of African leaders (and, too, the second generation, composed of soldier-politicians) appear to fit into this broad framework.

A comprehensive analysis of the psychological impact of colonial miseducation in Africa in general, and in southern Africa in particular, would need to focus on at least five interacting groups: the political elites, the military establishment, the religious hierarchy, the intellectual community, and the masses (encompassing the uneducated peasantry and the undereducated proletariat). Each group has been profoundly influenced by either formal academic education or informal education, as in the case of the peasants who have absorbed the colonial values of blind faith, docility, servitude, and dependence. While comprehensively analyzing psychological impacts falls outside of the immediate concern of this chapter, it is nevertheless important to recognize the need for such an investigation.

Although the analysis presented in this chapter seeks to explain a wider, continental phenomenon that characterizes politics and society in postcolonial Africa, its relevance to the transient situation in southern Africa is more than obvious: history has been repeating itself in that region, with the possible exception of the former Portuguese colonies. But even there, it is not entirely unlikely that the nascent leaderships might yet encounter the pitfalls which have bedeviled other African political elites throughout the continent.

Admittedly, the chapter raises more questions than it provides answers to. This is because we are calling for a reexamination of the past and the present, in order to understand the continent's deeply rooted problems of dependence and underdevelopment and their impact on a region in which leaders of both recently liberated states and those that are waiting impatiently for their turn, are still groping around for solutions as well as a sense of direction. And in arguing the need for the psychological liberation or decolonization of the political elites, the alienation of the intellectual/academic community in Africa (which is far from being liberated from the same influences of colonial miseducation) is revealed, albeit indirectly. The gulf between the rulers and the ruled is increasingly becoming as wide as it is alarming. There is a very real dilemma here: How can the uneducated majority in Africa be liberated while the educated minority remain locked up in a fantasy world of their own? The converse is, of course, equally true.

Colonial Miseducation and the Political Economy of Dependent Development

The relationship between political decolonization and economic dependence in Africa is a neglected and underdeveloped area of scholarly investigation.[7] And yet, most of independent Africa has learned the hard way, after the initial excitement over the recovery of independence had passed, that political change alone does not alter inherited patterns of dependent economic relationships. Underlying the contemporary issue of political control is the larger and more complex problem of economic sovereignty.

Formal constitutional independence in Africa has not been accompanied by economic independence or autonomy; most African states remain victims of the international capitalist straitjacket. More important, however, is the fact that moderate, "reasonable" regimes have never been known to indulge in policies aimed at an equitable redistribution of national wealth; neither do they champion the cause of socioeconomic revolution. Indeed, their principal source of strength derives from active collaboration with foreign economic interests.[8]

The coexistence of nominal political independence and economic dependence is undoubtedly one of the most profound contradictions characterizing the postcolonial state in Africa.[9] Those who control the economic empire are also in a position to frustrate the political aspirations of the managers of the political kingdom and, furthermore, are able to introduce new forms of dependency. Dependence blunts economic nationalism, which in turn renders militant political ideology impotent, irrelevant, and largely rhetorical.

Towards the end of his postindependence administration in Ghana the late Kwame Nkrumah accurately described neocolonialism as a condition whereby a state possesses all the outward trappings of international sovereignty, but in reality its economy and, consequently, its political policies are controlled and directed by external capitalist forces working in close collaboration with internal elites, especially those in control of the state apparatus.[10] But what Nkrumah did not say is that the development of neocolonialism as a more viable alternative to classical colonialism is closely linked to the colonial psychology deeply rooted in the minds of contemporary African political leaders, a mentality—most noticeable among the "founding fathers"—moulded by complex forces, including the impact of formal colonial education and political socialization processes that took place before, as well as during, the struggle for independence (e.g., the mellowing influences of long periods of incarceration in colonial jails). The rise of the *lumpenmilitariat*[11] as the second generation of postcolonial African leaders has added another link in the chain of neocolonialism and dependency. African soldiers, led by officers trained in Western military academies, have demonstrated an even greater commitment to the defense of the political and economic status quo defined—with minor adjustments to suit local conditions—by imperialist interests, thus introducing potentially more damaging and perhaps longer-lasting forms of dependence because of active collaboration with the metropolitan interests representing international imperialism and capitalism.[12] It is important to recognize how militarism and the accompanying results of militarization on African politics and economics support entrenched neocolonial dependency and perpetuate underdevelopment of native interests.

In retrospect, colonial authorities seem to have had the ability to pierce through the minds of the older generation of African political leaders and to discover that they all had one central characteristic. Although uniformly committed to the destruction of colonial rule, older African leaders were more than willing to cooperate as apparent "equals" with their former rulers in the postindependence era, with few misgivings about past misdeeds and injustices inflicted on them by their erstwhile enemies. Thus, when the struggle for freedom began in earnest after World War II and intensified in the 1950s, a neocolonial solution was seen by the embattled colonial powers as the answer to the rapid growth of nationalist demands in Africa. Although the policy may not have been so consciously designed, neocolonialism became a credible alternative to continuing imperial control as a result of some flaws noticeable in the thrust of African nationalist political thought.

First, African nationalist leaders leaned towards the strategic need to capture the political kingdom first and left other contradictions for later resolution. They believed colonial powers no longer had the will to continue their resistance to decolonization. When European imperial powers changed strategy from formal political control to entrenching economic domination, the emergent African elites did not seem to worry. When the elites more often than not saw political power transferred by constitutional means, they were encouraged to believe that such power would be sufficient to deal with economic problems of underdevelopment and dependence. What happened was simple enough; the colonialists shifted positions by moving from the front seat to the more relaxed one at the back. But because of the central importance of controlling the economic kindgom, they didn't lose their capacity to continue shaping the destiny of the African continent. On the other hand, the African leaders, who had been outsiders all along, now found themselves occupying the front seats (but only as "pseudopilots" lacking decisive navigational skills). The contention here is that the colonial powers never intended to leave Africa at all; what they did, with apparent African collaboration, was to give a face lift to the sagging image of colonization by placing Africans in positions of power while continuing to keep them on a leash. Thus outsiders played the tune to which the Africans danced merrily (albeit with muted grumbles).

Second, having formally captured political power, the new African leaders spent several years consolidating their weak domestic power bases while paying lip service to the inherited problems of underdevelopment and dependency. Meanwhile, external forces used this breathing space to consolidate the economic position they already held. It was a powerful position from which they could not be easily dislodged later in the continuing struggle for genuine liberation. The two sides—new leaders and external manipulators—needed each other, albeit for very different reasons: that "mutual dependence" characterized by unequal partnership created a marriage of convenience as firm as direct colonial control itself.

Third, when the African leaders were engaged in the formal constitutional negotiations for the transfer of power, their overriding desire was to assume political power at whatever cost. As a consequence, the successor elites neglected the various new relationships that were worked out by the "departing" colonial powers, whose interests aimed to perpetuate or strengthen the dependency of these successor elites. When the African leaders finally realized what liabilities they were inheriting, they assumed that the control mechanisms of the colonialists could be tempered and eliminated easily. The more obvious control legacies from the colonialists involved remaining in the franc or sterling currency zones, agreements providing for subsidies to balance national budgets as well as those aimed at encouraging economic investments (under politically safe climates) and setting up "partnerships" in economic ventures with foreign governments and private enterprise, and defense pacts allowing the retention of military bases and foreign troops within the independent states. These control mechanisms reinforced imperial connections: indeed, the French Empire changed into a Francophone community, while the British Empire became the British Commonwealth. Similarly and not surprisingly, in the terminal phases of Portuguese colonialism in Africa, successive administrations in Lisbon touted the idea of a Lusitanian community: its failure can be attributed only to the rebuffs from the nationalist guerrilla forces in the former colonies, who saw through the farce of such an arrangement and recognized the inherent threat to their hard-won freedom.

Fourth, African nationalist leaders readily accepted Western attempts at creating privileged elites who would take over political power. The ultimate survival of these elites, because of their "embourgeoisement," depended on active collaboration with external forces. Large secret accounts were established for some in foreign banks as "security" or "insurance," in case leaders were toppled from power before they had salted away enough funds to live comfortably thereafter; in the majority of cases, locals were recruited and co-opted into the exclusive network of foreign enterprises as board directors with no real power; yet in others the new leaders accepted economic donations (bribes) as token gestures indicating support for (approval of) the policies they were pursuing.

Finally, the supposedly novel idea of state involvement in the local operations of multinational corporations was warmly received by these MNCs and their home governments once the implications were realized: such developments eliminated entrepreneurial as well as political risks, while profits continued to flow in the form of royalties, fees for "technical services" (such as consultancy and provision of managerial skills), use of patents and brand names, and through guaranteed sales and servicing of equipment. Indeed, some corporations offered to be partially nationalized, realizing that they would never go bankrupt once the local government was in partnership with them—nor would they have to worry about trade union strikes, since this would be seen as a challenge to the local government (which by repressing its own workers would be protecting those corporations!).

Admittedly, an analysis of this kind amounts to a frontal attack and an indictment of the "pioneer" generation of African leadership for its partial responsibility in creating conditions leading to the development of neocolonialism in the continent. However, there are more than enough illustrative examples to justify the adoption of such a position. The argument being advanced here is that nationalist perceptions of what decolonization meant and the consequences of that process have been responsible, at least in part, for the entrenchment of international capitalism, which has reinforced the almost total dependency of the continent.

It is therefore no accident of history that the fruits of "freedom" have not been distributed equitably among the citizenry in most African countries. The political elites who challenged colonialism successfully were also seen by the colonialists as the best guardians of capitalist interests: they were therefore cultivated and nurtured to play the unacceptable role of defenders or custodians of foreign interests. By doing so, the colonial powers actually aborted (paradoxically with the connivance of the new elites) the African revolution that had begun after the Second World War; furthermore, colonial forces were able to convert their weak, defensive position into one of comparative advantage. So today, while conventional colonialism has all but disappeared, neocolonialism is the modus operandi on the continent—thanks to the dialectical development of African nationalism itself.

INHERITED COLONIAL LEGACIES

In order to understand the linkages between the rhetorical dimension of African nationalism and the reality of neocolonialism in Africa, it is important to examine the process through which colonial institutions were inherited by the first generation of postcolonial African leaders. Three main stages were involved in the transition from colonial rule to independence. Under colonialism, political and economic structures were firmly controlled by white settler communities. The educated African elites constituted mere appendages in the economic realm. These elites watched from a distance as far as the political kingdom was managed.

The second stage in the takeover process brought in "acceptable" African leaders, who operated alongside settler leaders in a "partnership" arrangement. As the heat of African political demands was felt increasingly by settlers, the intervention of metropolitan colonial governments led to the incorporation of the more "militant" (reformist) African leaders. Often this led to the introduction of "internal self-government" as a prelude to independence. At this stage, then, the more representative African leaders were no longer frustrated observers but apprentices learning the art of governing by direct participation.

The final stage involved the formal African takeover of the political (but not the economic) kingdom. The Africans assumed control over institutions that had never been designed to serve majority interests. Indeed, the rules of procedure in the independence constitutions had been defined by the very interests relinquishing formal political control. Thus were the ascending African elites expected to repeat the processes they had seen in operation during their period of apprenticeship at the terminal stages of colonial rule. No doubt, modifications were introduced in the independence model of government to suit the preferences of the succeeding African elites, but in the majority of cases independence constitutions were modeled on preindependence ones. This expedient arrangement is precisely responsible for the contradictions inherent in the postindependence models of African leadership and government.

To appreciate the monumental impact of these contradictions, it is important to make a series of crucial observations:

(1)   There is no way the colonial model of government could be viewed as democratic. It was heavy-handedly authoritarian and, therefore, totally undemocratic. Authoritarianism and democracy in a colonial context represent irreconcilable opposites. Independence constitutions were supposed to give legitimacy to the illegitimate authoritarian colonial institutions and, thereby, make them serve the interests of the majority (that being the implication of democracy). The experiences of postindependence leaderships in Africa demonstrate that this has been a futile effort.

(2)   Colonial constitutions always aimed at protecting the interests of minorities (predominantly racial, but also extending to the heterogeneous political and economic minority elites). The interests of the majority (racial and other) were never referred to in such legal documents. Independence constitutions also sought to protect minority interests by entrenching "constitutional guarantees." For all practical purposes, bills of rights written into these constitutions were more relevant to minorities than to majorities. Postindependence African lead-

ers have attempted to live up to their commitments, with disastrous consequences. They have found themselves guaranteeing minority interests at the expense of the majority, just as colonial settlers did.[13]

(3) Independence constitutions were supposed to transform colonial institutions that promoted injustice and inequality into ones that would promote justice and equality. Numerous examples can be cited to demonstrate the cosmetic nature of changes from colonial rule to independence: (a) the colonial Government House became State House (or some other variant) following independence, with little more than a change in the racial pigmentation of the occupants; (b) Ministries of Law and Order, Native Education, and Internal Affairs, to name but a few, became overnight Departments of Justice, National Education, and Home Affairs, respectively. The constitutional transfer of power supposedly removed the injustice and miseducation which those institutions had protected or promoted under colonial administration. Similar colonial structures, such as the civil service, army, and police force were also incorporated into the new political order with minimal changes.

(4) Colonial constitutions protected the economic privileges of racial minorities. Independence constitutions have played a similar role throughout the continent: the first generation post-independence leadership, in control of the political kingdom, has found it necessary to co-opt the politically disenfranchised settlers who have retained effective control of the economic empire. That new partnership has proved a more effective and lasting neocolonial control mechanism than classical colonialism itself could ever have been. In this context, just as the strategic allies of the settlers were externally based, those of neocolonial African regimes are also external to the political kingdom. Indeed, African leaders have continued to preside over and stage-manage the economic (and cultural) rape of their own countries. One major consequence of these neocolonial arrangements is that the overwhelming majority of African governments have remained just as distant and alienated (if not more so now) from their own people as colonial regimes were divorced from the masses. Small wonder that the masses have always celebrated the displacement of African regimes: the struggles of the masses and those of the ruling elites have remained poles apart, before and after the transition from colonialism to neocolonialism.[14]

ELITE SOCIALIZATION AND THE
NEOCOLONIAL LEADERSHIP MODEL

An investigation of the inner workings of the colonial consciousness of African political elites needs to focus on four principal issue areas. One is the contribution of colonial miseducation provided in mission schools, where students were taught the virtues of "nobility," "servitude" and absolute respect for authority.[15] In colonial situations, such values promoted a love-hate inferiority complex and acute frustration in the victims of such lopsided education. In the political arena, continuing subordination was clearly dysfunctional. Only defiance and insubordination would attract the attention of colonial authorities. That introduced a second set of issue areas: the need to rebel and the risk of prison. Imprisonment on political grounds was virtuous in its own dialectical way; it was often the road to future political stardom.

Repressive actions such as detention and restriction by colonial authorities had, in numerous instances, the benevolent quality of mellowing the militant attitudes of many a nationalist leader; serving time for "political crimes" provided such individuals the needed opportunity to alter the strategy and tactics of fighting the colonial enemy. Nationalists increasingly shied away from confrontation and edged towards collaboration, while retaining the same objective of capturing power through constitutional rather than unconstitutional means.[16] Colonial authorities were quick to recognize the apparent changes in the attitudes of these leaders; consequently, they proceeded to adapt to the changes and revised their own strategies, especially when they realized their control would have to come to an end sooner or later. Thus the colonial authorities began in earnest to build up the very same individuals they had locked away. Both jailer and prisoner stood to gain from such a change in strategy. Imprisoned nationalists became instant heroes as rallying points for resistance movements. Without imprisonment, such individuals would probably have been displaced from competition by younger generations of radical leaders less inclined to engage in the politics of reformism. And on the other side, the colonial authorities discovered they had something in common with their former enemies, the collective need to prevent the radical elements in the nationalist movement from inheriting the mantle of power from the politically defeated colonialists. Thus, the colonialists found allies in the older generation of nationalists, whom they proceeded to mould and legitimize in preparation for the assumption of political but not economic power. Since those elders of the nationalist movement owed their rise to political office to their former oppressors, it was only natural that they should repay their debt. This often meant disowning the militants or even imprisoning them in order to keep power in their own hands. Even more significantly, the elders surrounded themselves with those lieutenants who had "fought" with them, including their jailmates.

The psychological harm done to many nationalists through long periods of incarceration in colonial prisons made a major contribution to the self-righteousness, the sense of personal destiny, and the monarchical tendencies exhibited in the behavior of the first generation of postindependence African leaders. Political attitudes changed rapidly as the confrontation with colonial forces escalated while the major African political figures were in detention. When they eventually came out, they were totally unprepared for the transformations that had taken place in their absence. Quite often, these leaders were rushed off to attend constitutional conferences designed to transfer power from the minority to the majority. Invariably, the African leaders went to such gatherings with little preparation and were not therefore in a position to fully realize the implications of the agreements they were being persuaded to accept. Serious credibility gaps soon emerged when they realized that what they were willing to accept fell far short of the expectations of those who had watched developments unfold while the leading nationalists were politically quarantined. But since these leaders could not contemplate the prospects of being disowned by their own people, it became necessary to fall back on the former colonial enemy in order to reassert and legitimize their position. Such an expedient alliance pointed in one direction, a neocolonial pact that created a highly artificial relationship between leaders and their followers. Thus political survival under such circumstances depended heavily on collaboration with the politically powerless settlers; the metropolitan connection provided the bond between these unusual partners.[17] At the same time, a reversion to the African tradition of a monarchical political kingdom ushered in the model of imperial presidency that has been firmly established throughout the continent. In addition, there is the messianic character of contemporary African political behavior. As founding fathers of their nations, the African leaders sought to establish a unique position for themselves in the early stages of the history of their individual countries. Thus monuments were erected to commemorate the distinguished achievements of people who were still alive. The imperial life-style itself added weight to this psychological disposition. Every African head of state is effectively a president for life, with a term of office limited only by nature's intervention [death] or a military coup. When some of these leaders were displaced, their statues met the same undignified fate as colonial monuments.

Finally, African leaders have encountered difficulties in maintaining a balance between the expectations of the former colonial powers on the one hand, and the African masses on the other. Once African leaders realized they were about to assume political control, they went out of their way to reassure the defeated colonialists that they, the new rulers, would exercise "moderation" and "pragmatism" in their policies and "maturity" in their political behavior. The principal beneficiaries have not been their followers but the very colonial interests the new elite challenged during the struggle for independence. If colonial authorities and settler communities had anticipated early enough the postindependence benevolence of African political elites, colonialism itself might never have survived as long as it actually did. The overriding desire shown by African leaders to disprove projections of "vengeance" or "retribution" against the former rulers has produced extremely negative results for the masses. Nominal constitutional independence has been a blessing in disguise for metropolitan and settler interests, along with the collaborative African elites, while at the same time constituting daylight robbery for the majority of African citizens. Developed to its logical conclusion, the neocolonial model of African leadership and government spells disaster for those countries in Africa yet to recover independence. The successful installation and stabilization of neocolonial regimes built around the functional model of "stable instability" threatens, paradoxically, to undermine ideologies of both militant African nationalism and white supremacy. Because neocolonialism has so far proved a more effective insurance policy that works in the interests of both metropolitan forces and local African collaborators, political systems based on either leftist or rightist inclinations are both expendable and dispensable. The political Right stands to benefit from the endurance of the neocolonial system, at the expense of both the ideological Left and the majority of the population in every case. The ideological Left and the masses at large have been the principal casualties of that most fundamental of all contradictions in contemporary African political systems, the existence, side by side, of a constitutional and equitable bill of rights and a statutory preventive detention law or its equivalent. Prisons and other forms of detention and confinement in postindependence Africa have been the natural political graveyards for ideological militants and the holding-pens for hordes of ordinary, nonpolitical citizens. In many African countries, more jails have been built after independence than before. This reflects the realities of neocolonial rule and the gross miseducation of African political elites.

CONCLUSION

It is totally unrealistic to expect any wholesale radical change or reorientation, over time, in the psychological profiles of the first (or even the second, military) generation of postindependence African leaders and intellectuals. The dysfunctional colonial education and the accompanying decolonization process constitute effective and perhaps insurmountable barriers. The mental decolonization of the educated elites and of the masses has to run concurrently with formal decolonization; this is not an exercise to be deferred until after constitutional independence has been secured. Since no revolution ever occurred in the overwhelming majority of those countries that recovered independence through constitutional reformist methods, there is no guide to show how the problem of elite psychological decolonization might be tackled. On the other hand, the few African countries to emerge from the colonial womb by way of a caesarian birth represent a different model of the postcolonial state in Africa. Only here have leaders correctly diagnosed the colonial disease of elitism. Curative doses of political education and ideological reorientation are now being administered to the patients, which in these instances means whole populations!

Although it might appear quite meaningless, and probably futile, to suggest possible solutions to the lingering consequences of colonial education in Africa, the African intellectual elites cannot afford to shun the responsibility of recommending corrective measures. A modest attempt in that direction might begin by recognizing three truisms about postcolonial Africa: the neocolonial process and outcome of formal decolonization legitimized what was, in essence, illegitimate; it sought to democratize what was truly undemocratic; and it institutionalized what needed, in retrospect, to be deinstitutionalized. In independent Africa in general, and in transitional southern Africa in particular, there is a desperate need to dismantle colonial institutions and structures in order to foster genuine political, economic, and social changes. New edifices need to be constructed; colonial foundations need not be uprooted and discarded entirely, but a very different set of ideological criteria need to be applied in order to avoid entrapment in the classical model of neocolonialism and the political economy of dependent development as well as the modified versions which can be expected to come out for experimental tests from the ideologically sophisticated laboratories of imperialism. To do that is to stage a real revolution that must affect the psychological, political-ideological, economic, and social aspects of territorial decolonization. Anything short of that will aid the crystalization of the neocolonial model of African leadership and government that has emerged since independence, a model that can best be described as "Afrocracy."[18]

10. See Kwame Nkrumah, *Neo-Colonialism: The Last Stage of Imperialism* (London: Heinemann, 1965), p. ix. Another observer, Fred M. Gottheil, has noted that

> Colonialism, in its broadest sense, is a conglomerate of dominant-subservient relations. It contains power dimensions whose roots are psychological as well as political. . . . [Economic] *colonialism represents a set of structures that are imposed upon a nation by another in order to affect international distributions of income and wealth* [emphasis original].

Gottheil, "On an Economic Theory of Colonialism," *Journal of Economic Issues* 11, no. 1 (March 1977): 85.

11. The term is employed by Ali A. Mazrui to describe "that class of semi-organized, rugged, and semi-literate soldiery which has begun to claim a share of power and influence in what would otherwise have become a heavily privileged meritocracy of the educated" (Mazrui, *Soldiers and Kinsmen in Uganda: The Making of a Military Ethnocracy* [Beverly Hills: Sage Publications, 1977], p. 127). See also Mazrui, "The Lumpen Proletariat and the Lumpen Militariat: African Soldiers as a New Political Class," *Political Studies* 21, no. 1 (March 1973): 1–12.

12. See Samuel Decalo, *Military Coups and Army Rule in Africa* (New Haven: Yale University Press, 1976), pp.5–37, on some of the forces that interact to influence the behavior of African soldiers when they emerge as a political class playing dominant roles in society.

13. In regions such as eastern, central, and southern Africa, a particularly damaging aspect of this "protectionism" was the "special status" accorded the Asian minorities, who served as a strategic buffer between white settler communities and the African majority during the colonial period. The bitter resentment of the disenfranchised and economically exploited majority has often been translated, in the postcolonial era, into deliberate policies designed to frustrate the Asians, who have continued to dominate the middle rungs of the economy, in the hope that they would move out and open the way to African advancement. See D. D. C. Don Nanjira, *The Status of Aliens in East Africa* (New York: Praeger, 1975), and Maria N. Mugomba, "Asians and the Economic Underdevelopment of East Africa" (paper presented at the Annual Convention of the Pacific Coast Asian Studies Association, Anaheim, California, June 9–11, 1978).

14. There are exceptions to this general pattern. Chapter 10 shows the differences in the orientations of states which recovered independence through constitutional negotiations and trade-offs, and those which achieved the same goal via the "caesarian" method of armed struggle.

15. Similar observations are made in Agrippah T. Mugomba, *"Liberation Ecumenicalism and Armed Struggle in Southern Africa"* (paper presented at the first Joint Convention of the Latin American Studies Association and the African Studies Association, Houston, Texas, November 2–5, 1977).

16. Among the representative works reflecting these leadership models are Jomo Kenyatta, *Suffering without Bitterness* (Nairobi: East African Publishing House, 1968); Oginga Odinga, *Not Yet Uhuru* (New York: Hill and Wang, 1967); Bildad Kaggia, *Roots of Freedom 1921–1963* (Nairobi: East African Publishing

House, 1975); Kwame Nkrumah, *Ghana: The Autobiography of Kwame Nkrumah* (Edinburgh: Thomas Nelson and Sons, 1959); Philip Short, *Banda* (London: Routledge and Kegan Paul, 1974); and John C. Hatch, *Two African Statesmen: Kaunda of Zambia and Nyerere of Tanzania* (London: Secker and Warburg, 1976). On the philosophical foundations of contemporary African nationalism, see G. C. M. Mutiso and S. W. Rohio, eds., *Readings in African Political Thought* (London: Heinemann, 1975). See also Basil Davidson, *Can Africa Survive?* esp. ch. 5, and *Let Freedom Come: Africa in Modern History* (Boston: Little, Brown, 1978), esp. pt. 6.

17. Those African states where this marriage of convenience has fully blossomed have not only experienced rapid economic growth—they have also served as conduits or intermediaries promoting both regional neocolonialism and counterrevolution. In this context, it has been noted that

> we must understand the phenomenon of *subimperialism* as an increasingly vital feature of the strategy of counter-revolution in the era of people's wars. It describes the rise and growing importance of some relatively strong and vigorous capitalist countries sited in different areas of the Third World, which are being built up by U.S. and world imperialism as concentrations of economic and military power, as the powerhouses that feed the batteries of "freedom" and "order," i.e., of repression and counterrevolution, in their respective regions. While these regional powers are evidently and of necessity junior partners of U.S. imperialism, it would be a mistake to underestimate that they have a degree of independence as well as expansionist ambitions of their own, or to overlook their periodical conflicts of interest—the occasional "lovers" quarrels—with their chief partner [emphasis original].

Editorial in *Review of African Political Economy*, no. 4 (November 1975): 5.

18. This concept is employed by W. J. Breytenbach, who has observed that

> although the form and philosophy underlying government structures in [one-party African] regimes could be considered to deviate from the accepted form and philosophy of liberal-democratic systems, various democratic values do continue to survive in their institutions and procedures. This could be the final destination of "Afrocracy"—an unprecedented synthesis between traditionalism, Marxism, and the values of the West—culminating in a one-party, one-vote, one-government system. Maybe this will be Africa's major contribution to political philosophy and theory.

Breytenbach, "One-Party Regimes and Majority Rule," *Africa Institute Bulletin* (Pretoria) 15, no. 1–2 (1977): 23.

PART II

Philosophical Foundations of Colonial Education

CHAPTER 3

Apartheid and Second-Class Education in South Africa

MOUGO NYAGGAH

The principal objective of this chapter is to analyze the apartheid (segregated) educational policy and related legislation enacted for the implementation of a distinctly inferior education for Africans in contrast to that provided for whites. The analysis is divided into three parts: the educational system before the present Nationalist regime's accession to power; the earlier Nationalist debates over apartheid educational policy formulations and refinements; and an interpretation of the actual laws proposed and designed by the regime for policy implementation. The conclusion reached here is that the British missionary's liberal education provided to the Africans before 1948 was less than ideal, but was at least better than that provided by the Nationalist regime later. Apartheid education has been part of an overall, well-conceived doctrinaire policy of systematically maintaining white hegemony over the blacks so that the former may perpetually exploit the latter.

Since the summer of 1976, news reports from South Africa have dealt with the Soweto[1] students' revolt against the poor education system designed for blacks under the country's apartheid policy. The immediate catalyst for the conflict looked simple: the African high school students preferred to continue taking all their classes in English, while the government wanted the students to take half of their classes in English and the other half in Afrikaans.[2] This was the beginning of a major and continuing crisis with serious repercussions. Officially, over five hundred Africans have been killed. In addition, the conscience of the world has been aroused. The United Nations Security Council has imposed a mandatory arms embargo against South Africa, two major Western powers (West Germany and the United States) and the Netherlands recalled their ambassadors from South Africa following the death in jail of Steve Biko, the most articulate of the student leaders,[3] and the United States Congress overwhelmingly expressed its disapproval of the inhuman suffering under apartheid policy. At one point, the students stated that they did not want to study Afrikaans because it was the language of their oppressors, the Boers, who dominate the Nationalist party government.

This study will review the initial developments of the apartheid policy and show how the laws enacted to institutionalize that policy since 1948 have resulted in inferior education for blacks. We contend that the present second-class education for blacks is a result of a planned policy aimed at systematically denying Africans educational opportunities equal to those of whites. The larger implications of this policy are the maintenance of the *baaskap* (bossism) policy of white domination and continuation of exploitation of the Africans politically and economically.

PRE-APARTHEID EDUCATION

A careful analysis of government policy toward African education before the coming of the Nationalists into power reveals a relatively progressive education policy similar in many respects to the policy followed by the British in their other African colonies. While it would be naive for any African to say that this education system was ideal for the blacks in South Africa, nevertheless it had the potential for the kind of improvements that occurred elsewhere in Africa after World War II and Sir Winston Churchill's speech "Winds of Change." First, there was steady government support for African education. As early as 1922, the Union government's Financial Relations Fourth Act (no. 5) had passed, empowering the governor-general to allocate funds "to any province for extension and improvement of Native education."[4] Three years later, the Natives Taxation and Development Act (no. 41) of 1925 was passed, imposing a £1.0 tax on all Africans and establishing the special Native Development Account, from which funds could be used, inter alia, "for the maintenance, extension and improvement of educational facilities amongst natives."[5] There were numerous institutions created either to study African education performance and then recommend appropriate action or to advise the provincial and national legislatures and administrations how to improve black education. The Native Economic Committee recommended in 1932 the adoption of an education policy for Africans quite similar to what many newly independent African nations have adopted: an education based on African values and institutions, yet one which would "facilitate effective adaptation to Western civilisation to such a degree as would be necessary and advisable."[6] The *Report of the Interdepartmental Committee on Native Education* (Welsh report) recommended the administrative and financial takeover of African education by the Union government. The committee's educational policy recommendation was similar to that of the Native Economic Committee: to enable the African to understand " . . . his indigenous environment and culture as well as . . . the white man's civilisation."[7] With an education based on this background, together with literacy and technical knowledge, Africans would not be "reduced to inferiority and powerlessness in the face of the complexities of European civilisation."[8] After World War II, the recommendations of this committee were implemented by the enactment of Education Finance Act (no. 29) of 1945. From this period until the coming of the Nationalist party to power, the funding and services towards African education increased markedly.

There were other aspects of pre-apartheid African education that were also important. The missionaries of various denominations had been and continued to be the backbone of African education until most of their schools were taken over by the Nationalist regime in the mid-1950s.[9] The objectives of the missionaries in their African schools were to Christianize the Africans and provide academic and technical education which would enable Africans to get semiskilled jobs after the completion of the primary or secondary school education or, for the very few lucky ones, to continue to University of Fort Hare or overseas for higher education.

The provincial administrations in the Cape and Natal, where the British ideals and culture were more dominant, had a more advanced, well-funded, and well-planned black education system that those in the Boer republics of Transvaal and Orange Free State. Teaching supplies were free to teachers in the Cape, while in the Boer areas they were not.[10] Both the Cape and Natal had comprehensive systems of many state-run or state-aided schools for the Africans. The Cape was also seriously considering free compulsory education for African children.

In this province, primary education was already free for all races in government or government-aided schools. Even in plans for training teachers, it is clear that the English provinces were ahead, for the de Villiers Commission reports: "In the Transvaal and Orange Free State no provision is at present made for training of Native teachers for the Primary Higher Certificate. It would appear that facilities for such training will soon be required for both these Provinces.[11]

The medium of instruction in these schools was one of the African languages in the first two or the first four grades and then English, which the children had been taking as a foreign language since the first grade. There is evidence to indicate that the switch to English was not complete, since teachers encountering difficulties with students not understanding English often used the mother tongue supplementarily. This approach was far superior to the technique adopted during the apartheid period requiring children to use their mother tongue for the first eight years while studying two official languages, instead of just one. In 1966, the minister of Bantu affairs, M. C. Botha, estimated that an African child spends almost one third of his time studying these languages.

However, in the pre-apartheid period unanswered questions remained about education policy toward blacks. These questions centered around the interrelationship between African education and politicoeconomic status of the Africans in the South African society. Although these questions were raised by the education commissions and committees before and after World War II, there was no definite policy taken. These investigative bodies left the impression that their role was to make educational recommendations and leave the political and economic policy decisions to be made elsewhere. These decisions were never made. In the course of their investigations, the commissioners interviewed witnesses who felt that the Africans should be given only a limited education which would keep them in their place, geographically, socially, or both. Other witnesses advocated a more open and less rigid system which would afford the Africans greater educational opportunity and economic mobility as circumstances changed. In general the pre-apartheid commissioners followed the latter group of witnesses, albeit sometimes with reservations.[12] Yet the unanswered questions lingered on until the coming of the Nationalist regime.

NATIONALIST POLICY

When the Nationalist party came to power, one of its major policy decisions centered on these very questions, which fell within the parameters of the all-encompassing policy of apartheid. The Nationalists campaigned for this policy, which largely contributed to the narrow Nationalist victory in 1948. Before we get into the postelection policy debates, we should recapitulate crucial aspects of the Briton-Boer historical conflicts, as well as the general antiblack Boer attitudes, because these factors came to have a direct bearing on policy decisions.

From the slavery days, before emancipation in 1838, and throughout postslavery days, the Boers never believed in the nineteenth-century humanitarian philosophy which was articulated by the British abolitionists and missionaries who thought in terms of extending equal human rights to blacks. The Boers resented British politicians for abolishing the slave trade and slavery and the British missionaries for agitating against slavery and teaching blacks ideas about equality, not only in the nineteenth century but well into this century. The late founder of the Nationalist party, J. B. Hertzog, for several years the prime minister of South Africa and supported at various times by British laborers and industrialists, believed his party represented Boer interests first and those of other whites second. When he deviated from this concept in the 1930s by compromising "too much" with the British, his Boer compatriots who were more to the right than he was politically branded him a traitor and consequently formed the Purified Nationalist party in alliance with the leadership of the Boer secret society, the Broederbond.[13] The Broederbond and the new party were thus dedicated to recapturing control of the South African political, economic, and social institutions and reverting to the days when the Boers controlled their destiny in their republics.

Thus the new questions raised about the politicoeconomic position of the Africans which needed to be answered before a definitive education policy was formulated can be understood within the context of Anglo-Boer conflict instead of resorting to simplistic analyses based on racism alone. The architects of the apartheid policy, who believed in complete segregation between whites and nonwhites,[14] also believed in the domination by the Boers of all the whites.[15] The apartheid policy would therefore have a dual purpose: (1) revision of the progressive or liberal education policy from the British colonial tradition in the Cape and Natal, which would deny the Africans the most significant means for achieving economic mobility in the modern world, provide a rationale for continued discrimination, and perpetuate economic and political exploitation of the blacks; (2) allow control of the educational system by the Boers. This would deny the missionaries their traditional fertile ground for spreading the humanitarian ideas which undermined Boer political authority and questioned the distorted Calvinistic theological interpretations of the Bible by the Dutch Reformed church. The Dutch Reformed church provides the theological rationale for the apartheid policy and vigorously resists criticism from other churches.[16]

The discussions of the African education development policy are found mainly in three primary sources. These are the Eiselen Commission report,[17] the Hansard debates over the Bantu Education Act (no. 47) of 1953,[18] and H. F. Verwoerd's Senate speech of June 7, 1954.[19]

The Eiselen report is a reflection and summary of the ideas the Nationalist party regime wanted to implement rather than a genuine attempt to assess objectively the African needs for education as the previous commissioners and committees had done. Several factors lead to this conclusion. The commission was chosen by a government already committed to implementing the apartheid policy, which the Nationalists stated to be their immediate goal if they were elected. The commission chairman, Dr. Eiselen, formerly a professor of anthropology at Stellenbosch University, was the bastion of conservative Boer intellectuals. Several of these university intellectuals had actively taken interest in developing theoretical justification for apartheid policy as well as for the secret Broederbond as necessary in coordinating overall Boer efforts to gain control of political, social, and economic institutions in South Africa.[20] From the professorship, Eiselen first became the chief inspector for native education in the Transvaal and then the secretary for native affairs, while Verwoerd was the minister for native affairs. Another member of the commission, M. D. C. de Wet Nel, was a strong supporter the founders of the Broederbond in the 1930s. Both de Wet Nel's and Eiselen's fathers were members of the Boer clergy. The Eiselen report was diametrically opposed to the basic educational approach and institutions as they were structured, partly because under the terms of the appointment of the commission an entirely new African educational policy was expected, and partly because under the new philosophy of apartheid the Africans were to be treated as "an independent race, in which their past and present, their inherent racial qualities, their distinctive characteristics and aptitude, and their needs under the ever changing social conditions are taken into consideration."[21] Furthermore, there was a basic Nationalist party assumption that the previous educational system was faulty and should be overhauled to conform to government policy. Thus the commissioners were expected to determine

> the extent to which the existing primary, secondary and vocational educational system for Natives and the training of Native teachers should be modified in respect of the contents and form of syllabuses, in order to conform to the proposed principles and aims, and to prepare Natives more effectively for their future occupations.[22]

The commission was also asked to investigate and recommend on the organization, administration, and financing of the new educational system as well as any other related issues.

Consequently, the commission was highly critical of the existing system. Chapter seven of the report, which dealt with "the criticism of the present system," was so scathing and subjective that A. H. Murray, one of the commissioners, dissociated himself from the views expressed in that chapter. His dissenting view is important because it challenges the credibility of the entire commission and shows that the commission was an official attempt to legitimize racist policy by pretending that the new educational policy was based on an objective investigation. Thus Murray, in his dissent, reveals that the criticism was based more on the opinion of commissioners than on the evidence presented to the commission:

> A good many of the points of criticism brought forward in Chapter VII were not raised in evidence during the inquiry and embody the personal experience and views of members of the Commission who have had to do with Bantu education.[23]

He also disagrees with the criticism leveled against the education department and the inspectors in chapter seven.

The recommendations termed by the commissioners "extraordinary steps for the improvement of the Bantu education" eventually came to be repeated regularly by the minister for native affairs and his Nationalist party cohorts in parliamentary debates or in public speeches outside of Parliament in the next decades. The commission recommended centralized Union government control, maintenance, and management of African education rather than control by the provincial administrations; it prescribed the objectives for a distinctly inferior education for blacks, aimed at giving them what the Nationalist regime considered an adequate education useful for blacks in their "own community"; it stated the proposed reorganization plans for African education, a new structure for the school system, a rigid pattern for recruiting and controlling the staff and teachers; and finally, it outlined the anticipated relationship between educational institutions and other institutions.[24]

The second source for African education policy is the Hansard parliamentary debates in the fall of 1953. Following the Eiselen report, the minister for native affairs, H. F. Verwoerd, introduced the Bantu Education Bill in Parliament in September 1953. The acrimonious debate that ensued over this issue revealed numerous interesting facts about the apartheid policy as a whole and the role played by this issue in the old triangle conflict between Briton, Boer, and African. Initially, the minister for native affairs clarified the objectives of the education policy within the overall apartheid policy. This policy was the Nationalist solution to the previous racial tensions between whites and blacks which the minister argued resulted from the educated Afrcans' frustrations about not getting jobs in the white areas. He contended that the policy would be better because it would not "create people who are trained for professions not open to them."[25] He criticized the previous educators' liberal education as wrong because "good racial relations are spoiled when the correct education is given under the control of people who create wrong impressions on the part of the Native himself, if such people believe in a policy of equality. . . ."[26] This, as it appears later on in the debate, was aimed at missionary education and other forms of liberal education in the Cape and Natal provinces. Furthermore, Verwoerd argued, education for blacks had to be carefully coordinated and "controlled in such a way that it should be in accord with the policy of State."[27] The initial premise on which apartheid policy is based, that "education should prepare one to render services to one's own community," was articulated fairly early in the debate.[28]

The minister then continued that this control rightly belonged to the Union government because it paid for African education. This argument was spurious, since the Union government funded free education for whites with even larger sums and yet left the control of white education to the provincial administrators. Verwoerd's centralization plan for African education was to achieve the implementation of an overall national policy which the government feared the provincial administrations might sabotage. This policy was also based on the assumption that under Verwoerd's ministry the government would be able to establish a policy which would be used to determine the number of blacks to be educated for semiskilled or professional jobs and the number to be left uneducated for manual work. Thus in extolling the advantages of common policy, Verwoerd comes to the point clearly:

> Instead of the various provinces following various policies, one can
> have a central policy here, a clear policy which can be tested in the
> general interests of the country. . . . With a common policy we can see to
> it that education will be suitable for those who will become industrial
> workers in the country and . . . agricultural . . . [and] higher
> professionals. . . ."[29]

And the education of blacks was going to be clearly different from that of Europeans, as he revealed in his retort to those who believed that black students should be taught the same mathematics as Europeans: "What is the use of teaching the Bantu child mathematics when it cannot use it in practice? That is quite absurd."[30]

Finally, as he pleaded for placing African education in his department, because he knew best what opportunities would be available for the Africans, he stated what he considered a "very important fact," that the African "education policy should not clash with Government policy." He went on to define a very bleak future for Africans in a stratified state by reminding " . . . the honorable members that if the Native in South Africa to-day in any kind of school in existence is being taught he will live his adult life under a policy of equal rights, he is making a big mistake."[31] As he urged the United party to support this bill, Verwoerd made no secret that this opposition to any equality with the Africans was the Nationalist party's official policy:

> Honorable members always profess not to be in favour of equal rights, and therefore they should now support me in principle in what I am saying. If they, like we on this side, are not in favour of equal rights, and if they are, like we are, in favour of the Native's development within his own sphere and in the service of his people, then such a person should be reared in that idea right from the start.[32]

When the minister finished and the debate started, there were other aspects of the policy that were clarified. The government subsidy plan for missionary schools was temporary and the ultimate expectations were that they would eventually disappear.[33] The Orange Free State and Transvaal Boers, who were opposed to a centralized education policy during the Smuts (Prime Minister Jan C. Smuts) government, were not supporters of that policy.[34]

In speaking for the bill, a Nationalist party member of Parliament, Maree, provided an in-depth view of the apartheid policy. He observed that there were only two directions that the important "Native policy" could take in South Africa:

> One is the trend of liberalism, which means uniform development. On the other hand there is the trend adopted by the Nationalists, which means development in their own sphere. On the one hand one has liberalism which means nothing but intermingling; on the other hand, one has nationalism which means segregation. These different trends in policy are not only of importance when we are dealing with residential segregation or labour arrangements and such matters, but it is of the utmost importance when we are dealing with education.[35]

The main difference between the liberalistic and nationalistic approaches in education is that the former supports education for an individual while the latter supports education for society. This difference goes back to the nineteenth century as Maree saw it:

> As a result of the fact that the liberalistic outlook has always, since the days Van der Kemp and Read and Philips formed the basis for the education of the Natives of South Africa, we have the position to-day that the Native education in no way forms an integral part of any planned socio-economic trend of development . . . Native education is at present nothing less than an instrument in the hands of liberalism.[36]

This is probably as close as we can get to a synthesis of the old triangle conflict with the new apartheid policy. Maree was so articulate in stating the philosophical basis of the new apartheid policy that another parliamentary member noted the difference between the old Nationalist party led by Hertzog and the new leadership: "In other words, what we have heard to-day is a restatement of the policy of apartheid in more rigid terms than even Gen. Hertzog ever gave to it in his early days."[37]

There were also disagreements over this policy which were articulated by the United party members and other members of the opposition. The tenor of the opposition tended to follow the arguments similar to those articulated by pre-apartheid commissioners. One member, in seconding the motion to defeat the bill, said "people must realise that the basic principles of education must be the same for all races."[38] He added, "I say that this Bill will be resented by the Native people as a whole throughout the country, and I say that it is the most ill-advised step to take. . . . " He correctly warned the government that "the problems of a multiracial community are far more complex and stubborn than the Government's apartheid policy will ever be able to meet. . . ."[39] Another member noted that the differentiation made between the liberal education policy and Nationalist education policy was "crude" and lacked a sophisticated grasp of the meaning of education. More quotations along these lines can be found throughout the debates, but the few quoted here should establish the basis of policy differences between the Nationalists and the Eiselen Commission on one hand, and the United party members along the ideas of the pre-apartheid era progressive liberal education policies dealt with in our discussion of the earlier committee and commission reports.

So far, it is apparent from the evidence culled from the parliamentary debates, particularly from Verwoerd's important quotations, that the new education system for Africans was going to be distinctly inferior to that for Europeans. There was no attempt by the Nationalists to hide their attitudes about their racial superiority to the blacks. In this case, Maree's statement about the evils of liberal education, which prevailed in South Africa before the introduction of the Bantu Education Act (No. 47) of 1953, is most apt. Africans were going to be given an education designed to do what some of the witnesses told the Welsh Committee that education should do for Africans: keep them in their place. The Nationalist apartheid policy was going to achieve this end, both geographically and socially.

If there are any doubts left as to the meaning of the apartheid education policy, these should be removed by looking into the ideas put forth by Verwoerd in 1954. By this time, two of the most important architects of the policy were in the Ministry of Native Affairs, Verwoerd as the minister and Eiselen as his ministerial secretary.[40] Verwoerd criticized "Native Education under the old system," particularly under the missionaries "who were not sympathetic to the country's policy." He also criticized the curriculum, which,

> ... by ignoring the segregation or "apartheid" policy, was unable to prepare [blacks] for service within the Bantu community. By blindly producing pupils trained on a European model, the vain hope was created among Natives that they could occupy [positions] within the European community despite the country's policy of "apartheid." This is what is meant by the creation of unhealthy "White collar ideals" and the causation of widespread frustration among the so-called educated Natives.[41]

The government planned to take over the missionary schools, including full control over the training of teachers. The government alleged that "for decades the churches have used the training of teachers for the furtherance of their own particular interests."[42] This was presumably to teach liberal ideals. The function of the newly acquired schools was to enable the African to acquire the knowledge "to meet the demands which the economic life of South Africa will impose on him."[43] One of the important functions the new schools serve is to teach Africans the two official languages. This makes the Africans better servants for Europeans because, as Verwoerd aptly put it, "the economic structure of our country, of course, results in large numbers of Natives having to earn their living in the service of the Europeans."[44] Also the new schools were ordered to start teaching Afrikaans immediately in the Cape and Natal provinces, where it had been practically ignored in the past.[45] Verwoerd ended his speech with a long paragraph which is a very good summary of his department's policy and its implications in South Africa during implementation.

> My department's policy is that education should stand with both feet in the reserves and have its roots in the spirit and being of Bantu society. There Bantu education must be able to give itself complete expression and there it will be called upon to perform its real service. The Bantu must be guided to serve his own community in all respects. There is no place for him in the European community above the level of certain forms of labour. Within his own community, however, all doors are open. For that reason it is of no avail for him to receive a training which has as its aim absorption in the European community, where he cannot be absorbed. Until now he has been subjected to a school system which drew him away from his own community and misled him by showing him the green pastures of European society in which he was not allowed to graze. This attitude is not only uneconomic because money is spent for an education which has no specific aim but it is also dishonest to continue it. The effect on the Bantu community we find in the much discussed frustration of educated Natives who can find no employment which is acceptable to them. It is abundantly clear that unplanned education creates many problems, disrupting the community life of the Bantu and endangering the community life of the European.[46]

APARTHEID LAWS

Since the entire apartheid policy is based on the premise that blacks should develop separately in their "own areas or communities," a logical beginning in analyzing apartheid laws is the Bantu Authorities Act (no. 68) of 1951. This was the major law enacted by the Nationalists to establish African authorities (tribal authorities, regional authorities, or territorial authorities) with defined functions and powers to make limited legislation affecting the Africans living under their jurisdiction.[47] These areas were mainly within the 13 percent of the South African land reserved for Africans, as delineated by the Land Act (no. 27) of 1913, Native Land and Trust Act (no. 18) of 1936 and related amendments. The remaining 87 percent of the land in South Africa (except for small sections in the urban areas where the Asians and coloreds live) is classified as the "white" area. These percentages are very important in assessing the impact of apartheid: the policy is based on the wrong assumption that the 18.6 million Africans can enjoy full political, economic, and social rights only in "their" 13 percent of South African land, and that they do not have any rights in the 87 percent of the land where 4.2 million whites live.

The Bantu Authorities Act also abolished the Natives Representative Council, instituted by the Representation of Natives Act (no. 12) of 1936,[48] which had acted as liaison between the blacks and the government since 1936. Under the new legislation, the "tribal, regional, or territorial" authorities were expected to perform functions similar to the old Natives Representative Council: they could advise the minister on matters affecting the Africans in their respective jurisdictions. In education, for example, we find that according to section 5 these authorities shall have the power to provide for "the establishment, maintenance, management and conduct of educational institutions, and the advancement of scholastic and other education." This clause, as with so many clauses in apartheid laws, has an aura of good intentions until one finds supplementary clauses which severely limit what these African authorities can do "subject to the provisions of any regulations, and *to the directions of the Minister*" [emphasis added], or another limiting clause like "provided that no such by-law shall have any force or effect until it has been *approved by the Governor-General*" [emphasis added]. The significant point here is quite clear: the African authorities in the 13 percent of the land did not have any real power to make laws or develop policy either in education or in any other field without the express approval of the government. So, the premise that the Africans could be responsible for their "own areas" is senseless.

There are three other related legislative items which were passed in the next two decades. The Promotion of Bantu Self-Government Act (no. 46) of 1959 was passed to amend the Bantu Authorities Act, Native Land and Trust Act, and the Native Administration Act (no. 38) of 1927[49] and to provide for "gradual development of self-governing Bantu national units and for direct consultation between the Government of the Union and the said national units in regard to matters affecting the interests of such units."[50] This legislation consolidated and divided the earlier African authorities into eight national units— North-Sotho, South-Sotho, Swazi, Tsonga, Tswana, Venda, Xhosa, and Zulu, with the larger of them under a commisoner-general to coordinate government policy with the "national" or "territorial" authority.[51] In the following year, the Bantu Homelands Citizenship Act (no. 26) of 1970, with sections 2 and 3 providing that each African shall be registered as a citizen of his homeland (determined on the basis of his place of birth or that of one or both of his parents, language ability, or social identification) and that as a citizen he "shall exercise such rights in that area and enjoy all other rights, privileges and benefits and be subject to all duties, obligations and responsibilities of a citizen of that territorial authority area as are accorded or imposed upon him in terms of any law."

The third piece of legislation is the Bantu Homelands Constitution Act (no. 21) of 1971, as amended through 1976, which amended the Bantu Authorities Act and parts of the Bantu Homelands Act. Since this is the law that is designed to be the ultimate statute before final granting of "independence"[52] to the so-called homeland nations, it is noteworthy that it was intended

> to provide for the establishment of legislative assemblies and executive
> councils in Bantu areas, the powers, functions and duties of such
> assemblies and council, the disestablishment of territorial authorities
> upon the establishment of executive councils, the declaration as
> self-governing territories of areas for which legislative assemblies have
> been established, and the constitution of Cabinets for such territories.[53]

These three pieces of legislation are important for political analysis of apartheid education policy for several reasons. Both the Promotion of Bantu Self-Government Act (no. 46, 1959) and the Bantu Homelands Constitution Act (no. 21, 1971) provide that the homeland authorities or assemblies can play a leading role and offer help in, inter alia, educational interests of the Africans under their jurisdiction.[54] One notion in the provisions of the Citizen Act is that an African whose educational opportunities were limited in the white area could enjoy full opportunities and rights in his homeland. But if this figurative African's homeland were to decide to build more technical or science high schools, the power to make this decision could be withdrawn by the governor-general or the minister because these two officials had the right to withdraw from the homeland any powers previously granted.[55]

More important, these two officials could repeal any enactment by the homelands. Furthermore, the African of this example would be disappointed to discover that the Bantu Homelands Constitution Act specifically provides that "study and training courses, syllabuses, teaching methods, medium of instruction and public examinations prescribed in terms of any law shall be prescribed in consultation with the Minister." Finally, he would be dismayed to find that university education was completely out of the jurisdiction of the homelands.[56]

Consequently, it has been politically frustrating for Africans to change the apartheid education policy in the homelands since the enactment of the Bantu Authorities Act in 1951. We are not discussing radical changes here because the African bureaucrats in the homelands, through whom are channeled demands for policy change to the Union government, are appointed by the government and can be removed at any time without any recourse. Although there have been elections in some of these homelands, the winners are predictable because the Union government controls all the important institutions in these areas. The Africans have no effective means of applying pressure on the Union government short of violence, and the government can continue doling out education as it sees fit.[57] Within these politicolegal constraints, it becomes abundantly clear that the education legislation passed by the Nationalist regime for African education is merely a blueprint for inferior education.

The Bantu Education Act of 1953 was the first major law passed for implementing the new education policy. Its impact, together with related statutes, on preuniversity education was disastrous in many respects. The student enrollment doubled in the primary and secondary schools within two decades, but the quality of education deteriorated because the teacher-student ratio went up from around one to forty-five to one to sixty;[58] students could not take the textbooks home for studying or doing homework. Most of the new primary school teachers were primary graduates who came back after a three-year training period, and most of the high school teachers did not have university education.[59] The salaries of the teachers were very low,[60] and the teachers were generally dissatisfied with working conditions and especially with the rigid rules which denied them the most fundamental rights, like free speech.[61] The new funding system also caused adverse effects because it replaced the Native Education Finance Act (no. 29) of 1945, under which the education budget was voted by Parliament annually, with a system based on the Exchequer and Audit Amendment Act (no. 7) of 1955, under which the fixed amount of R13 million [62] was paid annually by the Union government towards African education. When the new plan failed to generate enough revenue, it was augmented by the Native Taxation and Development Account Act (no. 38) of 1958, which raised the African poll tax from R2 to R3.50 annually and also introduced a new income tax for all African men and women.

Another undesirable result of the Bantu Education Act was a general decline in academic standards due to unreasonable new language requirements. A new regulation required the medium of instruction to be mother tongue from first grade through eighth grade instead of through second or fourth grade, as it was previously. Also, instead of taking one official language, generally English, the students were required to take both English and Afrikaans. In contrast, the white students used their mother tongue, one of the official languages, and took the other one by choice. The situation was even worse for Africans, since many African teachers did not know Afrikaans or were not trained to teach it. African children spent almost one-third of their time studying languages. The African contribution to policy formation under the new school committees was negligible because the committee members owed their offices to the chiefs and headmen, who were in turn either appointed or nominated by parents to be appointed by the secretary for native affairs.[63] While the quantity of African education ostensibly improved, the quality deteriorated due to dwindling funds, poor teachers and staff, poor working conditions, unsympathetic Nationalist bureaucracy, and lack of enthusiastic support from the Africans.

A few examples will illustrate the worsening conditions in the African preuniversity education. The schools are structured like a pyramid—many lower primary schools, with the majority of students at the bottom, and few senior high schools, with very few students at the top—and most of the students are filtered, by examinations or by apartheid constraints at various stages. Only an extremely few finish senior high school.[64] For example, taking the first grade figures as the basis for comparing the number of students in the other levels we find that in 1955 the number of students in the first grade was 282,910, in the fourth grade 113,499, in the fifth grade 90,948, in the eighth grade 34,667, in the ninth grade 16,122, and in the twelfth grade 1,392. From these figures, we can calculate the percentages of the students in the other grades, taking the first grade as 100 percent. We therefore find that the fourth grade students were 40.1 percent of the first grade, fifth grade 32.1 percent, and the other grades 12.1 percent, 5.7 percent, and 0.5 percent for eighth, ninth, and twelfth grades respectively. The figures and percentages for 1965 and 1973 are indicated and contrasted with the 1955 figures in the following table:

Table 1. Attrition Rate of African Students, Grades 1–12.[65]

	1955	%	1965	%	1973	%
Grade 1	282,910	100.0	515,449	100.0	728,772	100.0
Grade 4	113,499	40.1	228,480	44.3	383,026	52.6
Grade 5	90,948	32.1	176,827	34.3	320,606	44.0
Grade 8	34,667	12.3	86,311	16.7	181,455	24.9
Grade 9	16,122	5.7	29,565	5.7	70,711	9.7
Grade 12	1,392	0.5	2,852	0.6	11,344	1.6

It is apparent from the percentages indicated in Table 1 that between 1955 and 1973 only 40.1 percent to 52.6 percent of the students who started school were able to reach the fourth grade, 32.1 percent to 44.0 percent the fifth grade, 12.3 percent to 24.9 percent the eighth grade, 5.7 percent to 9.7 percent the ninth grade, and 0.5 percent to 1.6 percent the twelfth grade. In short, about half of the blacks got only a fourth grade education, under one quarter an eighth grade education, and fewer than two out of one hundred finished high school. I. B. Tabata characterized apartheid education in South Africa as "education for barbarism" because of such bleak figures in so wealthy a country as South Africa. When the Bantu Education Act was proposed, the National Executive Committee of the African National Congress called it a "Devil's piece of legislation" and urged a united effort for defeat.[66] These South African blacks were not exaggerating how poor education for Africans was. When the de Villiers Commission was investigating education after World War II, it noted that eighth grade education was inadequate for the modern world:

> . . . the Commission believes that in order to feel at home in his world the modern boy of 15 years requires more general knowledge than his great-great-grandfather would have possessed 50 years ago. No matter what he wishes to become, he will have to acquire literally thousands of specific skills. . . . A hundred years ago a person who possessed the general knowledge of the average Standard VI pupil to-day would have been regarded as well-informed and "well-educated"; today his general knowledge [Standard VI] is regarded as *hopelessly inadequate for any kind of existence in the modern world* [emphasis added].[67]

The inadequate financing of African education was recognized by this commission in 1948 and even more recently by the minister for Bantu education, Van Zyl, when he admitted that much more money was spent on white education than on that of blacks. Changing the funding plan under the 1945 Native Education Finance Act by the Nationalists was the worst prescription for preuniversity African education. Muriel Horrell, in Rhoodie's *South African Dialogue*, summarizes this dilemma aptly:

> There has been very large growth in school enrollment; but for every 100 white children in secondary classes there are still only 73 Indians, 34 Coloured children, and 13 Africans.

For every R100 spent annually on the education of white pupils roughly R28 is spent on Indians, R26 on Coloured pupils, and R6 on Africans.[68]

Beyond the primary and high schools and teacher training institutions, the apartheid education policy was guided by the Extension of University Education Act (no. 45) of 1959, which gave the minister for native affairs power to establish, maintain, and manage universities for blacks and other nonwhites. As a result of this bill, the University College of Fort Hare Transfer Act (no. 64) of 1959 was enacted, to transfer the maintenance, control, and management of University College of Fort Hare to the Union government, under the minister for native affairs. Ten years later, three other pieces of legislation were passed, one to modify the University of Fort Hare administration,[69] the others to establish two new black universities—the University of Zululand[70] and the University of the North.[71] These three laws introduced further discrimination based on ethnic grounds in admissions: the University of Fort Hare was to be for only Xhosa students, the University of Zululand for only Zulu and Swazi students, and the University of the North for only students from the North-Sotho, South-Sotho, Tsonga, and Venda areas, as referred to in section 2 (1) of the Promotion of Bantu Self-Government Act of 1959.

Again these universities and the new laws governing them fit very well within the education for apartheid policy for numerous reasons. The admission is strictly controlled; under the Extension of University Education Act of 1959, white students are inadmissible to nonwhite universities.[72] This provision was included in the laws establishing the two new black universities and elevating Fort Hare to a university.[73] There is further discrimination against black students within these universities because no African can attend a university outside his "national unit" without the consent of the minister.[74] The implication of these provisions is the furtherance of "divide and rule" tactics of the Nationalist regime to stifle the development of a unified Azania[75] nationalism. With the establishment of these universities, African students can no longer be admitted to either of the two "open" universities (University of Cape Town and University of Witwatersrand) to study any courses available at the black campuses. Theoretically, the minister could give consent for Africans to attend white universities to pursue courses not available in the black universities, but available statistics of African students in white universities indicate that the minister's consent is not easily granted. Out of 190 African students applying for permission in 1960, the minister approved only four.[76] In fact, the number of African students in the two "open" universities has dwindled steadily: from 113 students in 1959 (39 at Cape Town and 74 at Witwatersrand) to 7 students in 1968 (3 at Cape Town and 4 at Witwatersrand).[77]

The rigid control of the black universities likewise fits well within the designed official policy. Under the 1959 Transfer Act, all the powers, rights, duties, and functions hitherto enjoyed by Fort Hare were transferred to the minister.[78] From that time, the minister delegated some of these powers to the individuals or institutions created to help him administer the university: a rector, university council, advisory council, a senate, advisory senate, or any other body he might establish.[79] For the next ten years, the university was run like a government department. The powers delegated by the minister could be withdrawn at his discretion; he had to be consulted before any changes could be made; he or the council set working conditions for staff and faculty; and he controlled the funding as well as student affairs directly or indirectly. Under section 35 of this act, he was given wide powers to make any rules or regulations for the university, including regulations for different races in the university. Thus, part of this section stipulated that "different regulations may be made in respect of different persons, groups of classes of persons or races employed." The minister used his power to dismiss faculty or students from the university for political reasons and to make rigid regulations against political activities by students.[80]

Although under the three university acts in 1969 some of the minister's powers were given to the university councils, he still maintained a strong controlling influence over the universities. For example, sections 18 of all three acts give the minister nearly absolute powers for dismissing any staff through the council because he could order the council to institute any inquiry on personnel charges and then make recommendations which he could approve or reject. Generally, the chances of any disagreement arising between the council members and the minister over matters concerning blacks were minimal since the council (and senate) members were white and appointed either by the state president[81] or by the minister directly or indirectly. Probably the most dangerous power that the minister has over the black universities is over curriculum development. Sections 27 of these laws provide for the departments and courses to be offered and then stipulate categorically: "The council may not without the prior approval of the Minister establish any department or course for a degree, diploma or certificate or in a subject, for which express authority to the university college did not exist under any law immediately prior to the fixed date." In contrast, the minister of national education does not have such sweeping powers over the white universities which fall under his ministry, as we can determine from the consolidated University Act (no. 61) of 1965, as amended through 1975, which defines the relationship between these universities and the government.[82] As illustration will suffice to show why the minister's power to stifle curriculum development is so detestable to Africans and so valuable to advocates of apartheid. The government does not want technical fields like engineering or architecture established in black universities for two reasons: first, to make the homelands dependent on the republic for skilled technicians, and second, to minimize the Africans' ability to compete for jobs with whites in the 87 percent of South African land appropriated as "white" area. None of the seventeen black students at the University of Cape Town in 1952 or the seventy-five students at the University of Witwatersrand in 1953 were studying in either of these two fields.[83] Certainly when we consider this situation together with the earlier statistics of only seven African students in the "open" universities in 1968, the minister's opposition to the initiation of these technical courses at the African universities, and the stated official goals for apartheid, the conclusion is abundantly clear: black education under apartheid policy is for maintaining white superiority, the *baaskap*.

But this should not come as a surprise. Verwoerd knew this quite well when he said, as he was introducing the Bantu Education Act in 1953, "I just want to add that if my department controls Native education it will know for which type of higher profession the Native can be trained. . . ."[84] The figures on the training of African doctors are equally appalling. As recently as 1971, the Minister for Bantu education, Van Zyl, recounted the progress made by his department with an aura of satisfaction. But when we look at the figures for medical students, there is not much to boast about, particularly in view of the fact that there are 18.6 million blacks, but substantially larger numbers of white medical students or graduates each year for the 4.2 million whites. Van Zyl writes, "there are at present 154 Bantu students undergoing medical training. An average of 10 to 12 qualify each year."[85] Several African countries with smaller black populations and significantly less wealth, such as Kenya or Ghana, graduate more black doctors annually!

To sum up, before the Nationalist party regime took over in 1948 the education policy was partially guided by the missionary and humanitarian liberal philosophy which was similar to the British education policies in the other parts of Africa. Although this education was not ideal for the Africans, mainly because it emphasized their Westernization, it was relatively more progressive in the opportunities for academic and professional advancement it offered Africans as compared to the new apartheid-based education after 1948. The Nationalists radically changed the old education system and passed many laws to bring African education into conformity with the apartheid national policy under which whites dominated all the institutions. Since the multitude of laws passed to implement this policy became steadily more unbearable to Africans and peaceful opposition proved futile, the Africans finally resorted to violence. This is the violence we have been reading about since the summer of 1976. In conclusion, educational opportunities for the Africans were relatively better before the Nationalists came to power in 1948. The debates and discussions of education for apartheid in the early 1950s together with subsequent laws enacted to enforce it indicate quite clearly that the resulting inferior education for blacks was systematically planned.

Notes

1. Soweto is an acronym for southwestern town. Little known beyond South African borders before 1976, the town has approximately 1.25 million Africans and is about fifteen miles from Johannesburg.

2. These are the two official languages in South Africa. Afrikaans is an Africanized Dutch patois spoken in South Africa by the Boers, descendants of the seventeenth- and early eighteenth-century Dutch settlers in the Cape Province. The Boers also call themselves Afrikaners.

3. A subsequent autopsy report by a South African government pathologist indicated that death was due to severe brain damage, raising questions about the circumstances surrounding Biko's death.

4. *Report of the Commission on Technical and Vocational Education* (de Villiers report), U.G. 65/1948 (Pretoria, 1948) p. 232; *Report of the Interdepartmental Committee on Native Education* (Welsh report), U.G. 29/1936 (Pretoria, 1936), pp. 44–45.

5. Secs. 12, 13(a).

6. de Villiers report, p. 237

7. Welsh report, p. 107

8. Ibid.

9. The Catholic and Seventh-Day Adventist churches refused to surrender their schools. Instead they decided to forego any government aid.

10. Welsh report, p. 74.

11. de Villiers report, p. 239.

12. Welsh report, pp. 53-54.

13. Hertzog's "mistake" was his close working relationship with the United party, which was dominated by the British, whom the Boers remembered bitterly as enemies of everything that the Boers stood for since the time of the Napoleonic Wars. The memories of the deaths of Boer women and children in concentration camps during the Anglo-Boer War of 1899–1902 were still fresh.

14. There are two other nonwhite minorities in South Africa: the Asians and the coloreds, people of mixed parentage.

15. William H. Vatcher, *White Laager: The Rise of Afrikaner Nationalism* (New York, 1965), pp. 75–80; and Appendix I.

16. For an analysis of the relationship between the Dutch Reformed church and the Nationalist party, see a chapter by the Roman Catholic bishop of Durban, Denis E. Hurley, "The Church and Race Relations," in *South African Dialogue: Contrasts in South African Thinking on Basic Issues,* edited by Nicholas Rhoodie (Philadelphia, 1972), pp. 458–478. The head of the Dutch Reformed church is Dr. J. D. Vorster, the brother of former Primer Minister Vorster.

17. *Report of the Commission on Native Education, 1949–1951* (Eiselen report), U.G. 52/1951 (Pretoria, 1951).

18. *Debates of the House Assembly*, 1st Session, 11th Parliament, 1953, vol. 83 (Cape Town, 1953), cols. 3575–672, 4041–132, 4267–347 (hereafter cited as Hansard).

19. H. F. Verwoerd, *Bantu Education: Policy for the Immediate Future* (Pretoria, Information Service of the Department of Bantu Administration and Development, June 7, 1954).

20. Brian Bunting, *The Rise of the South African Reich* (London: Penguin 1969).

21. Eiselen report, p. 181.

22. Ibid.

23. Ibid., p. 169.

24. Ibid., pp. 129–64.

25. Hansard, col. 3576.

26. Ibid.

27. Ibid.

28. Ibid., col. 3577.

29. Ibid., col. 3580.

30. Ibid., col. 3585.

31. Ibid., cols. 3585-86.

32. Ibid.

33. Ibid., col. 3589.

34. Smuts' close association with British humanitarian liberal traditions toward the Africans made him suspect in the minds of the Boers who did not wish implementation of government subsidies for missionary education in their republics. However, under the Nationalist party government and the new apartheid policy, the Boers had nothing to fear. It could be reasonably hypothesized here that the new education policy was in a sense the victory of the restrictive antiblack education policies followed in the two Boer republics.

35. Hansard, cols. 3611–12.

36. Ibid., col. 3611

37. Ibid., col. 3620

38. Ibid., col. 3591.

39. Ibid., col. 3598.

40. Verwoerd's picture appears on page 4 and Eiselen's on page 10 in the pamphlet referred to above (note 19) on Bantu education.

41. Ibid., p. 7.

42. Ibid., p. 12.

43. Ibid., p. 15.

44. Ibid., p. 18.

45. This was also one of the roots of the Anglo-Boer conflicts. The Boers felt that the British liberal education perpetuated the inferiority of Afrikaans in the two predominantly English provinces by neglecting it in curricula. With centralization of African education, the Boers could demand equal instruction in the two official languages.

46. Verwoerd, *Bantu Education*, p. 23–24.

47. Secs. 2–8.

48. In 1936, African voters were removed from the common voters' roll. Since that time, the Africans were restricted to voting for only seven whites to represent them in the Senate and House of Assembly and to electing twelve

blacks to a twenty-two member council until the 1950s, when changes were made.

49. This act set up a bureaucracy consisting of white officers in the upper and middle levels and Africans in the lower level as chiefs or headmen, to administer the African reserves.

50. See the preamble to the statute.

51. Secs. 2–3.

52. Transkei, the first national unit to get self-government, became the first "independent" nation under this plan in October 1976, although none of the members of the United Nations has recognized it diplomatically. BophuthaTswana, the second homeland, got her "independence" in December 1977. In reality these areas are totally dependent on South Africa.

53. See the preamble to the statute.

54. Act no. 46, sec. 12, and act no. 21, sec. 3.

55. Ibid. sec. 2.

56. Ibid.

57. In both Transkei and BophuthaTswana—the "independent" home-lands—all the elected members support the apartheid policy.

58. H. J. Van Zyl, "Bantu Education," in *South African Dialogue,* edited by Rhoodie, pp. 511–12; Chris van Rensburg, ed., *Education for South Africa's Black, Coloured and Indian Peoples* (Johannesburg, 1975). p. 64, tabs. 18, 19.

59. In contrast, according to the new National Educational Policy Act (no. 39) of 1967, sec. 1, the white primary school teachers were to be trained at the university.

60. When the Africans asked for a higher salary or for equal pay with the whites, Verwoerd informed them that the African teachers' salary scales were not determined on the basis of qualifications but on the basis of the standard of living in the black community (Verwoerd, *Bantu Education*, p. 19).

61. No criticism of government officials or policy was allowed. Teachers were also strictly forbidden from making any statements to the press or writing letters to the editor of a newspaper. See Government Notice no. 841, "Regulations Governing Conditions of Appointment, Service and Discipline of Bantu Teachers in Government Bantu Schools," April 22, 1955, sec. 16.

62. One rand (R) is approximately $1.15.

63. In Natal, parents elected the members to the school committee (Welsh report, p. 36), while the the Cape Province most of the mission-aided schools were under the management of sympathetic African ministers appointed by the missionaries, who favored liberal education, unlike the Boers.

64. The schools are divided into lower primary (grades 1–4, higher primary (grades 5–7), junior high school (grades 8–10), and senior high school (grades 11–12). See Kgware in *Trends and Challenges,* edited by Duminy, pp. 56–57.

65. Figures adapted from tabs. 7, p. 26, and 11, p. 30, in Rensburg, ed., *Education for South Africa's Peoples*.

66. I. B. Tabata, *Education for Barbarism* (Durban: Prometheus, 1959), p. 9; Thomas Karis and Gwendolyn M. Carter, eds., *From Protest to Challenge: A*

Documentary History of African Politics in South Africa 1882–1964 (Stanford: Hoover Institution Press, 1972–), vol. 2, *Hope and Challenge 1935–1952*, by Thomas Karis (1973), p. 152.

67. de Villiers report, p. 33. Note that this "hopelessly inadequate" education is the norm for blacks.

68. Rhoodie, p. 496.

69. University of Fort Hare Transfer Act (no. 40), 1969.

70. Act no. 43, 1969.

71. Act no. 47, 1969.

72. Sec. 17.

73. University of the North, act no. 47, 1969, sec. 21; University of Zululand, act no. 43, 1969, sec. 21; Fort Hare Transfer Act, (no. 40), 1969, sec. 21. These provisions in the three laws are nearly identical, and secs. 3–43 and sec. 1 of each, dealing with definitions, are also the same. The differences in the other sections of these laws are negligible.

74. See secs. 2, 22 of Fort Hare Transfer Act (no. 40), 43, and 47 of 1969.

75. This is the name that South African leaders of the ten black organizations banned recently by the Nationalists, and other nationalists use to refer to South Africa. It will presumably be used in the future under the black majority rule government.

76. Muriel Horrell, *Bantu Education to 1968* (Johannesburg: South African Institute of Race Relations, 1968), p. 113.

77. Ibid., p. 116. The figures for students at the University of Natal and University of South Africa are higher because the latter is a correspondence institution and medical students from the segregated nonwhite section in Natal are included in the university totals.

78. Sec. 2.

79. Ibid. sec. 6.

80. Muriel Horrel, *A Decade of Bantu Education* (Johannesburg, South African Institute of Race Relations, 1964), pp. 136–38, 148–51.

81. This term replaced *governor-general* after the Union of South Africa became a republic in 1961, following the union's withdrawal from the British Commonwealth over the issue of apartheid.

82. The black universities are specifically excluded from provisions of this act. They are simply excluded from the definition of *university* in sec. 1.

83. Michael C. O'Dowd. *The African in the Universities* (Cape Town, 1954), pp. 12–13.

84. Hansard, col. 3585.

85. Van Zyl, "Bantu Education," in *South African Dialogue,* edited by Rhoodie, p. 507.

CHAPTER 4

Producing the "Good African": South Carolina's Penn School as a Guide for African Education in South Africa

RICHARD HUNT DAVIS, JR.

After World War I, the topic of what constituted the proper course of education for blacks became a focal point of revived interest among educators and others concerned with black welfare in Africa, Britain, and North America. The debate involved both whites and blacks on all three continents. Blacks generally lacked access to political power and therefore were unable to bring much influence to bear on eudcational policy decisions; thus the control of black education rested mostly in the hands of whites. This was especially true for South Africa, where there existed a major effort to give new directions to African education. Those involved in this effort looked outside the boundaries of their own country, especially to the American South, for examples and guidance.

The major concern of white South Africans involved with the process of educating Africans was how to provide the necessary level and degree of schooling while at the same time maintaining the proper amount of social control. The answer to this dilemma seemed to rest in the rural-oriented black educational institutions of the southern United States. Penn School in South Carolina assumed a prominent role in the efforts of the white authorities to develop a so-called proper education for Africans. An examination of the attempted use of Penn School as a model serves, as this study attempts to show, to illuminate much about the nature of African education in South Africa during the years between World War I and World War II.

> I believe I've found what I came to America to get—a community centre with its head in God's heaven but with its feet firmly planted in the good and bad of this Earth. I wanted something to translate into African conditions. This is the nearest approach to our African situation that I have seen. With a thousand Penns we could transform

Africa. Will Penn help us and allow us to send our officials, missionaries and social workers, white and black, to this wonderful fount of inspiration. Thank God, it will. We have forged links today that will last long after we have gone back to Africa.[1]

C. T. Loram
Penn School Guest Book
October 13–14, 1926

In the period following World War I, white educational authorities in southern Africa cast about for a type of education they deemed suitable for Africans. Their search led them to the southern United States, where there was a type of education they considered applicable to African conditions. It was a caste education,[2] based on industrial education (i.e., manual training), designed to fit blacks into a subordinate position in white-dominated society where they would serve white needs but not challenge white control. Such schooling seemed to these white educators ideal for the settler societies of southern Africa.

The best-known black educational institutions in the American South and the ones which attracted the most foreign attention were Hampton and Tuskegee institutes. But, it was the smaller and less well-known Penn School on St. Helena Island off the South Carolina coast which certain key educators came to regard as the most suitable American model for African education in southern Africa. South Africa's leading white "expert" on African education, Charles Templeman Loram, considered Penn School to be more relevant to African educational needs than any other black American school.[3] In emphasizing the significance of Penn School as a guide for African education, Loram was following the lead of the American educator, Thomas Jesse Jones, who was to have such a major impact on the theory and practice of African education in the British colonies and in South Africa during the interwar period.[4] What, then, was the Penn School, and why did it receive such favorable attention from white officials responsible for the education of Africans in southern Africa? How did Africans view education along the lines of Penn School? An investigation of these questions will shed considerable light on the conditions of African schooling in the southern part of the continent during the interwar era.

THREE MAJOR THEMES IN AFRICAN AND BLACK AMERICAN EDUCATION

Penn School engendered a high degree of enthusiasm among Loram, Jones, and other whites concerned with African education in southern Africa largely because it exemplified some of the major themes then current in the schooling of blacks both in Africa and in the American

South. Kenneth J. King recently pinpointed three of these as being of particular importance: the development of a special education separate from that for whites and adapted specifically to the supposed needs and peculiarities of blacks; the unfolding of black schooling that served as an "education for life"; the assumption that the dual school system of the southern United States was relevant to the needs of African education.[5]

The early education of blacks in the United States and in Africa generally had not differentiated between schooling for whites and for blacks. When differentiation existed it was along supposed class lines, with blacks being lumped together with others belonging to the "lower classes." Beginning in the mid-nineteenth century, however, a new policy of adapting schooling to meet the imagined special needs and characteristics of the so-called black race gradually emerged as a result of the growth of pseudoscientific racism and the "new" imperialism. It was asserted that the schooling of blacks should cease to be an "imitation" of that for whites. Among the first to expound a fully developed educational philosophy along these lines was Samuel Chapman Armstrong, who had emerged to educational prominence as the founder of Hampton Institute. In his first annual report to Hampton's trustees, Armstrong set forth the basic arguments for differentiating black education from that for whites: the central question facing his school concerned the proper nature of an educational institution devoted to meeting the needs of an ignorant people possessing serious character deficiencies. Educated blacks heretofore had been misfits because their literary education had given them an overestimation of themselves and had not trained them to meet the real wants of their people. What blacks needed instead were teachers of "moral strength as well as mental culture" and the introduction of manual labor as a cure for their poverty.

Hampton was to "become a drill ground for the future" and to send "men and women rather than scholars into the world."[6] The institute would thus produce leaders for a stable, literate, and semi-skilled community that would remain in a state of permanent economic, political, and social subordination to the dominant, white sector of southern society.

Such a paternalistic and essentially static view of blacks and the related assertion of the need for a differentiated education became increasingly characteristic of those whites—missionaries, government officials, and philanthropists—on both sides of the Atlantic who were concerned with black welfare and in particular with black education. In South Africa during the 1880s, Principal James Stewart of Lovedale (a long-established institution in the eastern Cape Colony sometimes compared with Hampton) was at work transforming a Scottish-based

curriculum into one adapted to what he defined as African requirements.[7] The most famous exponent of adaptation, however, was not a
white but rather Booker T. Washington, who as Louis Harlan comments in his biography of Washington, had come under the very
powerful influence of Armstrong at a critical stage in his life.[8] Washington's educational and social philosophy possessed a degree of ambiva-
lence that did not necessarily lend itself to an acceptance of black
subservience and subordination.[9]

After Washington's death, Thomas Jesse Jones, educational director of the Phelps-Stokes Fund, emerged as the most outspoken exponent of educational adaptation. His formula consisted of four "simples"
or fundamentals: "first, sanitation and health; second, agriculture and
simple industry; third, the decencies and safeties of the home; and
fourth, healthful recreations."[10] Here again, as with Armstrong, we
find an educational philosophy that attempted through the school to
cope with the problems facing the common people. At the same time, it
neglected to provide for their legitimate aspirations beyond an elementary, though perhaps improved, mode of existence. Furthermore, it
rejected the concept of providing schooling that would produce an
educated elite.

Closely related to the theme of adaptation was "education for life,"
based on the presupposition that Africans and black Americans were
and should remain a predominantly rural people. Thus, "the educational diet was to be limited and defined by the most pressing needs of
the backward rural communities."[11] Hampton and Tuskegee were the
foremost institutions promoting this form of education. They stood as
models for other schools in both the United States and Africa that were,
in the parlance of the times, community-minded in purpose. The white
South African Maurice S. Evans, on a visit to the United States in 1912,
wrote of the pleasure he had in visiting these two institutions, where he
found the educational process linked to life. At Hampton, "a spirit of
social helpfulness was present; they were training themselves [through
trades courses, agriculture, and manual training for males; housekeep-
ing, gardening, and hygiene for females] to help their own people. . . .
it is clear that the great majority [of students] carried the spirit of
Hampton into the world of life." To Evans, the atmosphere of Tuskegee
was one that dwelled not on social and political disabilities but rather on
what had to be done: "So the tone was a hopeful one, much had been
achieved, very much more was to be accomplished in the future."[12]

Evans had pinpointed the principal elements of "education for
life" in his observations of Hampton and Tuskegee. First, its purpose
was to provide an elementary level of schooling which would focus on
the supposedly basic needs of economically backward, socially isolated,

and politically disenfranchised communities. Second, to the extent that it produced leaders, they were to work in a spirit of cooperation with and deference to philanthropically minded whites—hence the abstinence from discussion of political and social problems, since the probing of such topics was not conducive to a spirit of cooperation. India, where an educated nationalist leadership was posing a serious challenge to continued British rule, served as an example of what to avoid to white supremacists, who blamed much of the unrest in that country on schools that had failed to inculcate values in their pupils consonant with their position as a colonial people.[13] Thomas Jesse Jones expressed the position bluntly when he argued that what had to be avoided in Africa and in the southern United States as far as possible was the "disease" of an educational system like that of India "that overstocks the market with clerks, talkers, and writers." Otherwise there would be a recurrence in these areas of the troubles that plagued British authority in India.[14] "Education for life" along Hampton-Tuskegee lines offered a positive alternative. In its industrial education format it had all the components for keeping blacks socially inferior, economically weak, and politically impotent for a long time to come.

The assumption that Africa should follow the lead of the southern United States in educational matters, which constituted King's third theme, gained wide currency in colonial education circles and among those Americans involved in black schooling. This development has recently attracted the attention of a number of scholars,[15] but it was also readily apparent to observers of the African education scene at the time. As the British scholar and perceptive critic of African education A. Victor Murray noted in 1929:

> One of the most important factors in African education to-day is the influence of America, both black and white. The educated Native is beginning to be conscious of his kinship with the Negro people across the Atlantic and they in turn are showing an increased awareness of him. At the same time the white Americans have come to feel that their experience of the black and white "problem" in the Southern States is something which may help to the solution of a similar problem in Africa. They have also experimented a good deal in education, and the trustees of the various educational funds which are in existence have shown a generous willingness to finance schemes for Native education. In British territory the authorities have facilitated American research, and have also been willing to co-operate in plans put forward by the educationists. America, therefore, cannot be neglected if we would have a true view of the position of African education.[16]

Murray thus brings out many of the basic elements of King's third theme. First, the influence of American education stemmed from both blacks and whites, though, as with Murray, the concern of the present paper is with the influence of white Americans.[17] Second, white Americans believed they had found in certain forms of education the key to solving the so-called race problem, and that the southern "solution" was transferable to Africa. Third, American philanthropic organizations, in particular the Carnegie Corporation and the Phelps-Stokes Fund, were willing to fund educational experiments and ventures in Africa along American lines. Finally, colonial authorities (including South African officials) cooperated in introducing American educational philosophy and practices into Africa schools.

South African educators were among the first to see something of value for the schools under their control in the black educational institutions of the American South. In 1903, the prominent missionary educator, James Stewart, busy with plans to reconstruct Lovedale, decided on a special trip to the United States in order to confer with Booker T. Washington and to visit Tuskegee.[18] Eleven years later, Charles T. Loram, then a student at Teachers College, Columbia University, wrote to Washington that because his chief interest lay with African education he was anxious to visit Tuskegee in order "to have an opportunity of seeing what you have been able to accomplish for a branch of the same people in this country."[19]

In the early years, trips of visitors from Africa to black schools in the American South assumed no institutionalized form. The visitors were already in the United States for other purposes, as Loram was, or else travelled to the South for the specific purpose of visiting the black schools, as Stewart did. About 1923, these visits began to adhere to a more established format under the guiding hand of Thomas Jesse Jones and the Phelps-Stokes Fund. Jones wished to provide overseas visitors with exposure only to certain aspects of the black American experience, for he was at odds with those elements represented by W. E. B. DuBois. The Phelps-Stokes Fund started issuing invitations, backed up with travel grants, to persons involved in African education to visit the United States. The standard itinerary for such individuals consisted of sojourns at Hampton, Tuskegee, Penn, and Calhoun School, a study of the Jeanes system of visiting teachers, and, if time permitted, a stop in Atlanta to meet John Hope, president of Atlanta University, and to view the work of the Commission on Inter-racial Cooperation.[20] A few years later, the Agricultural Missions Foundation and the Visitors' Grants Committee of the Carnegie Corporation joined the Phelps-Stokes Fund in bringing African educators to study American black education.[21] Several hundred visitors participated in these programs, almost all of them white.[22]

Other forms of direct action for transplanting American ideas on black education to Africa went hand in hand with the program of bringing African educators to the United States. The two Phelps-

Stokes African education commissions constituted the most prominent and far-reaching examples of this effort. The first (1920–1921) visited west Africa, west-central Africa, and South Africa, while the itinerary of the second, in 1924, included east and central Africa and South Africa. The commission reports emphasized adaptation and community consciousness for African schools just as they did with black education in the States. Jones was the principal author of both reports and wrote them in a manner that closely resembled his 1917 survey of Negro education.[23]

In order to promote further adaptation and community consciousness, Jones and like-minded individuals on both sides of the Atlantic collaborated in establishing schools in Africa that would embody these principles in their curricula. One project was to transplant the American system of Jeanes teachers to Africa. The Jeanes plan involved a network of visiting teachers for rural schools who would aid local teachers in making their schools focal points for the transformation of their communities. Jeanes teachers emphasized the so-called practical things in education.[24] "The outstanding characteristic of the Jeanes work . . . [was] its concentration on the needs of rural schools and rural communities."[25] When transferred to Africa, the Jeanes programs for the training of Jeanes teachers were established in existing institutions, first at Kabete, Kenya, in 1924, and then elsewhere in eastern and southern Africa.[26] Another notable example of this general effort to transfer American ideas to Africa was the construction of the Booker Washington Agricultural and Industrial Institution in Liberia in 1929. Its specific purpose was to be an African Tuskegee.[27]

The concern of white educational authorities and philanthropic foundations largely lay with impressing their views of black education on other whites, but during the colonial era, Africans also journeyed to the United States to visit and learn from the black institutions of the South. Against the background of a general lack of educational opportunities in their own countries, the Africans were usually impressed with the range and extent of education available to black Americans. Most came as individuals on their own initiative or under the sponsorship of various black organizations. In certain instances, as in the case of John L. Dube of Natal, they returned to found schools of their own patterned after an American model.[28] Others came under white philanthropic sponsorship to imbibe certain aspects of the black American experience. It turned out to be impossible, however, as will be seen in a case involving Penn School, for the philanthropists to control the range of contacts these students had with black Americans. In part, at least, this rose out of a fundamental misunderstanding on the part of Jones and others about the nature of the black American community.[29]

Expression of the Three Themes
at Penn School

Hampton and Tuskegee were the schools that most clearly stood for the principles of adaptation and "education for life." They also attracted the most attention from those who were looking to the southern United States for models for African education. For many, these institutions were the giants of black education institutions. Penn School, however, possessed characteristics that made it appear particularly relevant to visitors from South Africa and elsewhere on the continent.[30] Loram's endorsement of Penn was one of several. A special appeal of Penn for visitors from Africa was its isolation. This made it seem to approximate more closely African conditions than did Hampton or Tuskegee. Located off the South Carolina mainland, the island school and its surrounding community of six thousand or so rural blacks only three or four generations removed from Africa, and with but a handful of whites, was at least partially insulated from the dominant currents of American life. Until the construction of a bridge to the mainland in the mid-1920s, the only way to reach the island was by means of a rather primitive ferry.[31] Over the course of time, however, St. Helena's isolation became more apparent than real:

> The arrival of the bridge and the emergence of the New Negro had already conspired to undermine . . . [the] cultural hegemony of St. Helena Island. The unyielding boll weevil had obliterated the economic basis of the islanders' lives, and then the disastrous failure of the white potato crop had prostrated those farmers who had . . . [adopted this new crop]. By the end of the Twenties, St. Helena Island had already been suffering from a severe agricultural depression for ten years, and the efforts to find a new cash crop had been entirely without success.[32]

If the setting of Penn School seemed to approximate African educational conditions of isolated whites directing the work of African assistants in schools serving a rural and supposedly backward population, it was the conduct of the school itself that caused it to be a model for African education. Under the principalship of Rossa B. Cooley, assisted by her long-time coworker Grace B. House, Penn School embodied the concepts of adaptation and "education for life." The charm and romance of two dedicated white ladies working for the "uplift" of blacks undoubtedly contributed further to the appeal of Penn School. The crucial element, however, was, to use Cooley's terminology, the dual revolution in school-keeping at Penn that had taken place under her principalship. The first revolution was the transition from "the limitations of purely academic education" to the "principles of vocational education developed at Hampton Institute" and the bringing of the farms to the school. The second revolution amounted to "carrying out an experiment . . . bringing the school to the farms, and making this oldest of Negro schools in a sense the newest—an all-island school, an all-the-year-round school, merging school and community into a common adventure."[33] Intertwined in both of these so-called revolutions were the concepts of adaptation and "education for life."

For Cooley, House, and their supporters, the proper environment of St. Helena's blacks was agricultural. They asserted that a real career for blacks existed in agriculture. Following it, blacks could become an asset to their country and prove their ability to develop as valuable citizens.[34] The city was the enemy. It was the source of venereal diseases that added yet another burden to the islanders' health problems, of fancy clothing fashions ill-suited to demands of practical island life, and of the lure of ill-founded dreams and illusions that pulled young islanders away from their heritage of the land. All too frequently, young islanders became "lost in the tide that carried many a boy to Savannah."[35] In order to retain the young on their family farms and to counteract the pull of the cities, "the main object of the school therefore . . . [was] to fit the boys and girls for these home farms, and to do all the extension work possible to create an interest in and give an education to secure better farms, better health, and better homes."[36] Penn graduates should be "capable of dealing effectively with the problems of a rural community." If, perchance, they were to leave the island for further education at Tuskegee, Hampton, or on rare occasions Howard, they then should have been imbued at Penn with the realization that a life of service to their fellow islanders was the way to the truest happiness and the fullest life.[37] At Penn School, therefore, adaptation meant vocational agricultural education, and "education for life" meant education for rural living.

Principal Cooley considered Penn to be an educational laboratory where experimentation took place on the linkage between schooling and improving the quality of rural life.[38] Of course, Penn primarily focused on southern blacks, but Cooley and others associated with the school also began to promote Penn's relevance to African educational needs. And educators in Africa were receptive, for they had a predominantly rural and agricultural orientation. As the report of the second Phelps-Stokes commission noted: "It is imperative that schools shall cease to give the impression that knowledge of the three R's and of the subjects usually in the curriculum is of more importance than agricultural knowledge."[39] Such a message clearly represented the mainstream of thinking on African educational matters among colonial officials and missionaries alike. There had emerged what King has called the "agricultural syllogism"—Africa is predominantly rural, therefore it will continue as such.[40]

Penn School, with its emphasis on rural life and its rejection of the urban environment, was in an ideal position to attract the attention of those responsible for education in colonial Africa, but before this position could be exploited a major promotional effort was needed. Spearheading this drive was the highly influential Thomas Jesse Jones, who had already touted Penn's educational philosophy and policies as highly suitable for black needs. As early as 1922, he began to draw attention to Penn's applicability to African educational problems.[41] Over the following years, he continued to push Penn School as an ideal model for Africa. Cooley's own efforts at publicizing her school, such as her *Homes of the Freed*, provided Jones with additional ammunition for pushing Penn's relevance to African educational needs. Upon receipt of this book, Jones wrote to Cooley: "I feel certain that your vivid presentation of the significant [sic.] work in the Islands will stimulate and guide many others in similar work. Especially will this be the case in Africa."[42] With this type of encouragement, Penn began actively to stress its role in pointing African education in the proper direction. The principal's report for 1927-1928 noted that eighty-six missionaries and government officials from Africa had visited St. Helena Island to date. It also quoted a letter from Loram stating that educators in southern Africa were using *Homes of the Freed* as a textbook.[43] Penn's policy of promoting its relevance for Africa (and for other areas of the colonial world such as India and the Middle East) was partially a fund-raising device,[44] but it was more than a matter of simple expedience. The assumption that the central concepts of adaptation and "education for life" were also suited to African needs blossomed into an article of faith at Penn School.

MANIFESTATION OF THE THREE THEMES IN SOUTH AFRICA

By the mid-1920s, when Penn School came to the attention of South Africans concerned with African education, there already existed in that country strong manifestations of the themes of adaptation, "education for life," and the relevance of the American example to African conditions. This was also true for other areas of the continent, but conditions in South Africa, with its substantial white settler population, seemed more clearly to approximate the American South than anywhere else on the continent.[45] Educational theory regarding African schooling first swung heavily in the direction of emphasizing adaptation and "education for life" in the years centering on World War I. In the Cape Province, the newly appointed superintendent-general of education, W. J. Viljoen, noted in his 1918 report that the principal occupation of Africans was farming and that the schools should therefore be involved in improving agricultural methods. "What must be done is to provide non-European schools with a curriculum suited to their needs, and not the least of these is to equip them for their future lives as agriculturalists and artisans."[46] The following year, the Cape provincial Commission on Native Education recommended that while there should be no lowering of the standard of African education in comparison with that for Europeans, yet it was necessary to supplant the existing "overstress of scholasticism in the curriculum" with more vocational and practical training, especially in the areas of agriculture and domestic science. In this way the schools could have a "more practical bearing on future life and work of the pupil," which was to be found more in farming and skilled and semiskilled occupations than in clerical or teaching occupations.[47] Similarly, the prominent missionary educator Father Bernard Huss was taking the position that the improvement of agriculture among Africans was one of the principal problems facing South Africa. Hence, it was necessary to divert African education from its "bookish" orientation to an emphasis on agriculture.[48] Clearly, then, an agriculturally oriented, antiurban attitude constituted a dominant trend in African education. In South Africa as elsewhere on the continent, the agricultural syllogism prevailed.

As the concepts of adaptation and "education for life" gained increased currency in South Africa, the visits of persons concerned with African education to the United States also grew. During the second decade of the twentieth century, key figures who travelled to the South to observe and learn from black educational practices included Maurice Evans, D. D. T. Jabavu, and Loram. Jabavu, who spent the summer of 1913 at Tuskegee studying its education methods in preparation for taking up a teaching position at the South African Native College at Fort Hare, was only one of a handful of Africans who toured the South.[49] The number of such visitors grew rapidly in the 1920s and 1930s, so that ultimately nearly every South African with a decisive voice in determining the course of African education had visited the United States. The activities in South Africa of missionaries from the African Methodist Episcopal church, the American Board of Commissioners for Foreign Missions, and similar bodies further heightened the penetration of American ideas concerning the schooling of blacks.

The congruence of these themes are well-illustrated in the life of a single individual, Charles Templeman Loram. Through his career as an official in the Natal education department and of the Union government, his membership and participation in crucial international education commissions and conferences, his position as a leading spokesman of so-called South African liberals, his association with the Phelps-Stokes Fund and the Carnegie Corporation, through which he became, together with J. H. Oldham of the International Missionary Council and Thomas Jesse Jones, part of the triumverate on African education during the interwar years, and finally as a professor at Yale, Loram influenced the course of African education in southern Africa more than any other single individual prior to World War II.[50] Loram's educational ideas developed in large part during 1914 to 1916, when he studied for a doctorate at Teachers College, Columbia University, although nearly a decade of previous work as an inspector of schools in Natal provided him with practical experience. South African writers on the so-called race question, such as Dudley Kidd and Maurice Evans, also had an impact on his thinking. His dissertation, which was published in 1917 as *The Education of the South African Native*, presents an integrated expression of the central nature of all three of the themes which we have been discussing.[51] For Loram, as indeed for Jones with the so-called Negro problem, "the proper education of the Native" held the greatest promise for the settlement of the "Native Question." To determine the content of a proper education, Loram relied extensively on his first-hand observations at Hampton, Tuskegee, Virginia Union University, and a variety of other black schools in Virginia, Alabama, and Maryland.[52] The main body of his study consists of a review and a critique of the existing system of African education in South Africa and proposals for a restructured African school system centered on the themes of adaptation and "education for life" and built around an African curriculum that was differentiated from that for whites and was designed to prepare Africans for an agricultural way of life. Maintenance of the proper social order required Africans to be educated to work and Europeans educated to command.[53] Africans were to be steered away from towns, which "belonged" to the whites, and into farming, which was most in keeping with the Africans' nature and view of life and was where they would not compete economically with Europeans.[54]

SPECIFIC USES OF THE PENN MODEL IN SOUTH AFRICA

The educational philosophy and practice of Penn School found ready acceptance in African education circles in South Africa. Its size and setting in particular made it appear a suitable example for South Africa, as it did for other parts of the continent. Loram's 1926 visit to St. Helena Island set in motion a number of specific, though interrelated, steps to apply the Penn School experience to African, and especially southern African, conditions. Behind Loram in this effort was the Phelps-Stokes Fund. Thomas Jesse Jones had already called attention to Penn School's relevance to Africa and had helped arrange visits of some educators to Penn prior to 1926.[55] Furthermore, the fund, which considered Loram the leading authority on African education, had specifically urged him to visit Penn and had provided the necessary financial assistance.[56] Loram's enthusiasm for Penn was immediate and genuine.[57] He considered it the most outstanding of all the black institutions in the United States he had visited,"not only for its own worth but as a help to foreign students seeking guidance and inspiration in the United States":

(1) The administration is well thought out and while easy is yet sufficiently firm.

(2) The class instruction in academic subjects was the best I have seen in this country.

(3) The relating of all the school work to the needs of the community is in conformity with the best theories of education. It is that feature in particular which makes the school a model and an inspiration to teachers from overseas.

(4) The extra curricula activities such as the "home acre", the boys and girls clubs, the classes for grown up men and women, the splendid luncheon system, the "sales room", the farm, the shops are altogether admirable.

(5) The spirit of religion expressing itself in community service is an aspect of Christianity which appeals strongly to me.[58]

Loram quickly set in motion efforts to make Africa part of Penn's extension work. He secured the agreement of the Phelps-Stokes Fund to support the travel of two experienced African women teachers to Penn, where they would spend the academic year as part of the regular staff. They would thus imbibe Penn's methods through practical experience to carry back to South Africa and adapt to local conditions. A summer at Tuskegee or Hampton also was to constitute part of their proposed training before their return to South Africa.[59] The intention was for the two women to work at a rural black school which operated under relatively simple circumstances. This type of experience would best equip the two teachers to meet the educational and community demands they would face at home. Nor were they supposed to experience American urban conditions, which would have little bearing on their projected work in rural areas where they were to serve essentially as Jeanes teachers. Loram argued that Tuskegee and Hampton were of a larger size and greater complexity than was necessary for the bulk of the proposed training. Penn, however, was ideal.[60] Not only was it the correct size and located in a remote rural area, but it was also under white leadership. Loram thought in terms of the Penn trainees returning to South Africa to work in the countryside under white supervision. They were, so to speak, to assume positions as junior partners in the firm.[61]

The two women who came to Penn, Violet Sibusisiwe Makanya and Amelia Njongwana, had notions that differed from those of their sponsors. The resultant clash illustrates the divergent perceptions black and white South Africans could hold of Penn and the approach to education it represented. In part, it also helps explain why African education in South Africa could never successfully be reconstituted along Penn School lines.[62]

Makanya and Njongwana arrived in the United States in August 1927 for stays of three and two years, respectively.[63] They made substantial changes in the plan of training that Loram and the Phelps-Stokes Fund had laid out for them and also came to disagree between themselves.[64] Both women were experienced teachers, and both had forceful personalities.[65] Beyond this, little else is available about Njongwana, perhaps because ill-health forced her to cease working shortly after her return to South Africa.[66] Makanya started teaching in 1912 at a small rural school and then in 1915 joined the staff at Inanda, Natal's leading African girl's boarding school. She left this position in 1923 to enter the previously untried field of social work among Africans. It was, according to one source, "a supreme venture of faith"; she was abandoning a successful career in teaching for a new one without funds and without backing. By the time Makanya came to the United States, her second career was already a success.[67] She resumed it with new insights gained from her American sojourn upon her return to Natal in 1930.[68]

If for Loram, Jones, and Stokes, Penn School offered the ideal American training ground to fit their concept of African development in South Africa,[69] for Makanya and Njongwana the school quickly proved to offer intellectual training far below what they sought. They considered Penn ill-prepared to provide them with any regular guidance in either its fundamental principles or the particular practices they were supposed to study.[70] To Jones, their attitude suggested that they "were not sufficiently educated to appreciate the practical extensions of education, culture, and religion at Penn and they concluded that they were being kept in a secondary school."[71] Makanya, on the other hand, informed her friends "that there was nothing to be gained there which she had not already had before coming to America."[72] In March 1928, Makanya and Njongwana left Penn for Tuskegee, where the Phelps-Stokes Fund was willing to support them for the summer and an additional academic year.[73] Attempting to hold the women to Loram's original purpose, the fund's president admonished them:

> it is the spirit and quality of the work (at Tuskegee), not its size or large
> material equipment, that is the most important thing. The glory of
> Hampton and Tuskegee is that their graduates have been willing in
> such large numbers to go back into humble surroundings and work
> with simple tools and inadequate equipment, to try to fit other
> members of their race for the battle of life through the work of head,
> heart, and hand.[74]

Makanya and Njongwana considered Tuskegee more beneficial

than Penn, but they found it wanting and expressed a desire to move on to urban social work. This was completely out of keeping with the purpose the Phelps-Stokes Fund officials had in mind, and they pressured them to remain at Tuskegee. Principal Moton, however, was unwilling to coerce them into remaining at his school and helped arrange for study elsewhere.[75] Njongwana gained admission to the Atlanta School of Social Work and took her room and board at Spelman College. The Phelps-Stokes Fund funded her for a year's study, and she ended up relatively satisfied with the education she received.[76] Acting upon the advice of Congregationalist friends, Makanya entered the Schauffler Training School, "a small bible training school [in Cleveland] with some interest in the social phases of religion as applied to urban conditions," where she seemingly studied for a year. With this step she severed her financial ties with the Phelps-Stokes Fund, though it continued to assist her with her visa.[77] She then took a year's course work at Teachers College, Columbia University, where Mabel Carney a specialist in rural education, was on of her principal teachers.

The rejection of Makanya and Njongwana of the program set forth for them constituted a severe blow to the Phelps-Stokes Fund's hopes for training a cadre of "good Africans" in the United States, that is Africans who would work for educational and societal goals defined by whites to serve white ends.[78] Moreover, it showed the essential bankruptcy of Loram's dreams for transforming Africa with "a thousand Penns." Penn was unacceptable as a model to those Africans on whom the task would rest. Perhaps most significantly, the episode demonstrated the inability and unwillingness of whites in key positions of authority on educational matters to consult with and upon occasion to defer to the wishes of Africans on issues of fundamental importance. Jones's and Loram's insistence that they and their fellow white educational authorities and not Africans were the proper individuals to decide the correct course of African schooling was evident in their reaction to the two teachers' actions. Jones expressed considerable disappointment over the failure of Makanya and Njongwana to heed the fund's advice.[79] He even went so far as to suggest a conspiracy: "I am inclined to believe that considerable effort is being made to influence such Africans away from the Tuskegee conception of education and life."[80] Loram's reactions were even stronger. Speaking about defection, the destruction of his plans, and his terrible disappointment, he suggested that the fund require Makanya to repay the money she had received (the fund's president considered this too vindictive). Flattery from certain white Americans, he argued, had turned Makanya and Njongwana away from participating in his scheme for restructuring African education in South Africa.[81] An alternative explanation for the women's shift in plans came from one of Makanya's newly found American supporters: "I have a feeling that Miss Makanya, having already been engaged in social work among her own people for a number of years, should be given the privilege of at least advising with the Fund as to what course she shall take."[82] But this neither Loram nor Jones could tolerate

With the failure of the Penn School training project, Loram and the Phelps-Stokes Fund concluded that white instead of African teachers were required for such experiments.[83] In their efforts to utilize Africans in key positions for restructuring African education, they had encountered problems similar to those connected with attempts to incorporate black Americans into African educational reform—ideally this seemed the correct approach but in practice it proved impossible to implement.[84] Efforts continued, however, to promote Penn as a model for African schooling in southern Africa. These fell into two major categories: spreading the Penn idea within southern Africa and bringing visitors from that area to Penn. Support came not only from the Phelps-Stokes Fund but from other quarters as well. There thus emerged a relatively broad-based interest in transplanting Penn School concepts to southern Africa.

Concurrent with the proposal for bringing African teachers to St. Helena Island was Loram's scheme for distributing one hundred copies of Cooley's *Homes of the Freed* and Penn School's catalog to educators and government officials in southern and east Africa. The Phelps-Stokes Fund financed the distribution, as did one of Penn's chief benefactors, George Foster Peabody, on a later occasion.[85] Accompanying each copy of *Homes of the Freed* was a pamphlet by Loram which compared and contrasted the circumstances of black Americans and black South Africans and then emphasized the adaptability of the community-oriented core in Penn's education.[86] Loram also arranged for (and perhaps wrote) reviews of Cooley's book in South African newspapers and journals, such as the *Cape Times*, which highlighted for its predominately white readership the pertinence of Penn School to South Africa:

> ... like all the schools started immediately after emancipation, it
> failed to teach just those things that were neces[s]ary for the newly
> liberated negroes. These people, who know not even the elements of
> home building and of the industrial arts, were taught to run before
> they could walk, instead of learning how to cook, sew, cultivate their
> gardens, and build adequate houses, their education was strictly
> academic.[87]

Instituting Jeanes teacher training programs constituted a second way for spreading the Penn idea within southern Africa. Loram wrote to Rossa Cooley in 1927 that, thanks to Carnegie Corporation support, "we shall have two imitations (feeble perhaps but real) of Penn School in 1928 and three or four in 1929."[88] The Carnegie Corporation of New York had pledged matching funds to establish Jeanes teacher training programs (the "imitations" of Penn) at existing African schools for the purpose of raising the community through education.[89] Loram had initiated the idea at the 1926 Phelps-Stokes dinner in his honor with his plea for American assistance in establishing twenty Jeanes schools in Africa. He foresaw the implementation of the program within five years, predicting that five schools, to be located in southern Africa, in addition to the existing Jeanes school at Kabete could get going within twelve months.[90] One thousand Penns never came into existence, nor even twenty. The total number of Jeanes training centers reached only eight: Kenya (one), Northern Rhodesia (two), Southern Rhodesia (two), Nyasaland (one), Zanzibar (one), and Mozambique (one). Between 1929 and 1938, the Carnegie Corporation granted £191,000 to the first seven and the Phelps-Stokes Fund supported the program in Mozambique.[91] Despite the availability of Carnegie funds, there never was a Jeanes school in the Union of South Africa. Inanda in Natal appeared to be a likely candidate for several years, but by 1932 it no longer seemed a feasible location. Though there was some suggestion about the Jeanes school in neighboring Swaziland, another site was never chosen.[92]

The Union of South Africa did not, however, go completely without Jeanes teacher training. During the years 1928, 1930, and 1931, Loram conducted Jeanes vacation courses for white and black teachers in African schools. The thrust of these courses was the Jeanes principle of adaptation.[93] Yet, the courses amounted to only a limited implementation of the Penn/Jeanes set of ideas when placed against the promise that Loram had seen in these ideas for the solution of South Africa's so-called native problem. The promise foundered on the reality of Makanya's and Njongwana's determination to plan their own education and careers, the failure of the Inanda scheme, the opposition of some education officials for a variety of reasons, and other obstacles.[94]

The program of having visitors from South Africa and elsewhere on the continent spend a few days on St. Helena Island as part of personal tours to study black education and interracial work in the American South also received funding from the Phelps-Stokes Fund and the Carnegie Corporation Visitors' Grants Committee. Loram again was involved, particularly with the Carnegie Corporation through its service as chairman of its South African-based Visitors' Grants Committee.[95] Most of these white visitors to Penn came away with a great enthusiasm for the school. For example, a teacher at a Cape boarding school declared that "Penn ways will be our model!"[96] A Durban attorney noted that while he had found Tuskegee most interesting, "nowhere except at Penn did I find anything so close to our S. African conditions. . . ."[97] And the director for African development in Southern Rhodesia promoted Penn as a model for his country:

> Perhaps the closest approach to African conditions may be found at Penn School, St. Helena Island, South Carolina . . . . It is in a scheme similar to this, adapted to African conditions, that the ideal for Native education in Africa, in a country such as Southern Rhodesia, would seem to lie.[98]

Occasionally, a visitor with a more critical eye would, while expressing appreciation for Penn's achievements, suggest that the school was an inappropriate model for African conditions:

> Viewed from the dispassionate standpoint of the educational administrator of a public system of schools . . . Penn School with all its success is no more than a beautiful vision. A complete educational system for an African Province, built up on the model of Penn, might possibly revolutionize the life of the entire Native population; but the system would necessitate expenditure on a scale quite beyond the range of practicability. The fact that the striking example of Penn has scarcely in the slightest affected the Negro public schools of South Carolina—they are reputed to be amongst the most backward in the States—is in itself proof of the impracticability of adopting the Penn model for any large system of public education.[99]

Loram continued to suggest names of visitors to the Phelps-Stokes Fund and the Carnegie Corporation after taking up the race relations faculty position at Yale. He also started bringing students from Africa, including some Africans, to study under him. His connections with the Phelps-Stokes Fund and the Carnegie Corporation helped fund a number of these students.[100] This marked the first time since his sponsorship of Makanya and Njongwana that Loram was directly involved in bringing Africans to the United States. While continuing to oppose African undergraduate education in the United States, he thought that he could properly guide Africans through a special course of postgraduate study at Yale which would emphasize "the gospel of the Four Essentials."[101] Beginning in 1932, Loram's students accompanied him on an annual spring tour of the South for a firsthand study of culture contacts and race relations. Penn School formed an important part of the itinerary, for Loram continued to emphasize its relevance to Africa. On at least one occasion, Loram also arranged for Principal Cooley to speak to his seminar in New Haven.[102]

Loram's approach to African training had changed. Though still extolling Penn's virtues, he was no longer proposing that students spend a year at Penn learning by doing, so to speak, in order that they might return home as skilled workers in the mold of the "good African." Instead, they attended a major university to earn advanced degrees. As he wrote to Thomas Jesse Jones, it had become necessary to give superior training to Africans and to secure their cooperation in this manner. Missionary societies were curtailing their work in South Africa, which meant that Africans would soon have to take over the management of their educational, agricultural, and social work.[103] Thus, the opportunity appeared for an individual of the stature of Z. K. Matthews to earn a Ph.D. at Yale and return to a distinguished career as an educator in South Africa and ultimately as Botswana's ambassador to the United Nations. He took with him carefully nurtured impressions of certain forms of black American education, but the process of implanting a "proper" educational philosophy had become far more complex and sophisticated than the rather simplistic approach to the training of Makanya and Njongwana less than a decade earlier.[104]

CONCLUSION

A high degree of interest in a certain type of black American education and in Penn School as a particularly suitable example of this form of education emerged among South African educators, especially whites, during the period between World War I and World War II. The great interest and even enthusiasm for Penn caused considerable energy to be devoted to adapting Penn's methods to South Africa in order to produce the "good African." Spearheading this effort was Charles T. Loram, South Africa's leading so-called expert on the native. Support from the Phelps-Stokes Fund and the Carnegie Corporation also was significant both in the United States and in Africa.

The idea of Penn School as a guide for African education in South Africa remained largely an ideal with little in the way of concrete implementation. For one thing, Penn had become an outmoded model by the time it came to the attention of South Africans. As Burns has noted, Cooley's "conception of the functions of rural education had changed very little over the years." Her commitment was to the assumptions of an earlier age.[105] The economic and social conditions of blacks changed in the 1920s and 1930s; so did their political aspirations. If Penn had earlier ministered adequately to the needs of St. Helena islanders, and this is debatable, it no longer did so. Likewise, in South Africa the increasing economic dependence of Africans on the cities undercut the basic premises for introducing schooling along the lines of Penn.[106] Much of the African future lay in the growing industrial sector. Furthermore, the 1936 disfranchisement of Cape African voters helped produce a mood of growing political militancy that ran counter to the political course of action which "good Africans" supposedly espoused.

Also militating against Penn as an effective model was a second factor: the educational environment of South Africa differed significantly from that of the American South. For instance, the Cape Province, long the pacesetter for African schooling, had a strong tradition of academic education for Africans that found continued acceptance despite the growing popularity of the concepts of adaptation and "education for life." Also, educating people for an agricultural way of life presupposed that the recipients had land to farm. St. Helena's residents owned their land and could, at least until the boll weevil struck, make a living from it. In South Africa, where Africans possessed only 7 percent of the land, few had adequate acreage to secure a decent livelihood as farmers. True, there were similarities between black Americans and black South Africans: both peoples lived under white domination; both were of African origin; both still resided primarily in rural areas; both suffered legal and social disabilities. By choosing to stress these similarities, however, Loram, Jones, and others underplayed what a contemporary critic noted: "In more fundamental matters the South African Native problem is *sui generis*, and altogether different from the Negro problem of the United States."[107]

The third and perhaps most crucial factor in preventing the full implementation of the Penn idea was African opposition. An individual such as Albert Luthuli might temporarily support Loram's schemes (an endorsement he later disavowed),[108] or the African National Congress might in 1924 resolve "that system of native education is desirable which would be better adapted to the peculiar and practical needs of the Bantu people."[109] But when Makanya and Njongwana resisted the notion that Penn School represented the epitome of educational achievement suitable for Africans, they anticipated the direction most African thinking would take on the issue of differentiated education. For instance, Rev. J. A. Calata, president of the Cape African Congress, said Africans understood the need for an education with a practical value, but they also rejected the notion that it had to be segregated from that of other races.[110] The "Bill of Rights" in the 1943 Africans' Claims in South Africa was even more explicit:

> We reject the conception that there is any need of a special type of
> education for Africans as such, and therefore we demand that the
> African must be given the type of education which will enable him to
> meet on equal terms with other peoples the conditions of the modern
> world.[111]

Africans thus soon realized what Penn School represented: an educational philosophy that, at its heart, asserted black subordination. As such, it expressed educational components of the colonial relationship, which was why it appealed to Loram, Jones, and so many other whites. This was also why it failed to find favor among Africans.

Though Bantu education lay in the future, the debate in the 1920s and 1930s over differentiated education and the notion ot the "good African" had prepared Africans to confront what were in many ways the same issues when they appeared in the guise of apartheid in the early 1950s.

The research for this paper was made possible by grants from the National Endowment for the Humanities, the University of Florida Humanities Council, and the American Council of Learned Societies.

Notes

1. Hampton House Guest Book, Penn School, University of North Carolina Library, Manuscripts Department, Southern Historical Collection, Penn School Papers (hereafter cited as PSP), box 46, vol. 651/2.

2. Kenneth J. King, *Pan-Africanism and Education: A Study of Race Philanthropy and Education in the Southern States of America and East Africa* (Oxford: Clarendon Press, 1971), p. 21.

3. Letter, C. T. Loram to George Foster Peabody, October 29, 1926, PSP, box 5, file 42; Letter, Loram to Anson Phelps Stokes, October 16, 1926, Yale University, Sterling Memorial Library, Anson Phelps Stokes Family Papers (hereafter cited as APS), box 31, folder 510. I am indebted to Elizabeth Jacoway Burns for providing me with the letter from the Penn School Papers, along with some of the other material from this collection.

4. Thomas Jesse Jones, *Education in Africa: A Study of West, South, and Equatorial Africa by the African Education Commission, under the Auspices of the Phelps-Stokes Fund and the Foreign Mission Societies of North America and Europe* (New York: Phelps-Stokes Fund, 1922), pp. 34–35.

5. King, *Pan-Africanism and Education*, pp. 252–59.

6. Suzanne Catharine Carson, "Samuel Chapman Armstrong: Missionary to the South" (Ph.D. dissertation, Johns Hopkins University, 1952), pp. 89–91. See also Louis R. Harlan, *Booker T. Washington: The Making of a Black Leader, 1856–91.* (New York: Oxford University Press, 1972), pp. 61–62; August Meier, *Negro Thought in America, 1880–1915: Racial Ideologies in the Age of Booker T. Washington* (Ann Arbor: University of Michigan Press, 1966), pp. 88–89.

7. R. Hunt Davis, Jr., "Nineteenth-Century African Education in the Cape Colony: A Historical Analysis" (Ph.D. dissertation, University of Wisconsin, 1969), pp. 183–87. See also James Stewart, "What is Education?" *Christian Express*, June 1884, reprinted in *Outlook on a Century*, edited by Francis Wilson and Dominique Perrot (Lovedale, S. A.: Lovedale Press, 1973), pp. 65–76.

8. Harlan, *Booker T. Washington*, p. 52.

9. Ibid.

10. Draft of a speech by Dr. Jesse Jones at a dinner given by His Majesty's Government, London, March 26, 1925, APS, box 179, folder 110. A full exposition of Jones's educational philosophy appears in his *Four Essentials of Education* (New York: Charles Scribner's Sons, 1926). For detailed critiques of Jones's educational philosophy, see King, *Pan-Africanism and Education*, esp. pp. 21–43; Edward Henry Berman, "Education in Africa and America: A History of the Phelps-Stokes Fund, 1911–1945" (Ph.D. dissertation, Teachers College, Columbia University, 1969), pp. 69–88.

11. King, *Pan-Africanism and Education*, p. 37.

12. Maurice S. Evans, *Black and White in the Southern States: A Study of the Race Problem in the United States from a South African Point of View* (London: Longmans, Green, 1915), pp. 131–39. In an earlier work, *Black and White in Southeast Africa: A Study in Sociology* (London: Longmans, Green, 1911 [reprinted New York: Negro Universities Press, 1969], pp. 112–25, Evans advo-

cated an education for Africans that would "build up character, not necessarily on our lines, but on what may prove to be the best method of conserving what is best in their race character, and working up from that." The principal ingredients in this education would be agricultural and industrial training.

13. King, *Pan-Africanism and Education*, pp. 155–56, 215.

14. Letter, Thomas Jesse Jones to Lionel Curtis, August 2, 1922, APS, box 27, folder 434.

15. In addition to King, *Pan-Africanism and Education*, see Berman, "Education in Africa and America"; Richard D. Heyman, "The Role of the Carnegie Corporation in African Education, 1925–1960" (Ph.D. dissertation, Teachers College, Columbia University, 1970); Charles H. Lyons, *To Wash an Aethiop White: British Ideas about Black African Educability, 1530–1960* (New York: Teachers College Press, 1975), pp. 150–62; R. Hunt Davis, Jr., "Charles T. Loram and an American Model for African Education in South Africa," *African Studies Review* 19, no. 2 (September 1976): 87–99.

16. A. Victor Murray, *The School in the Bush: A Critical Study of the Theory and Practice of Native Education in Africa*, 2d ed. (London: Longmans, Green, 1938), p. 291.

17. Ibid.

18. Personal communication, November 7, 1973, from Shelia Brock, University of Edinburgh. Brock has written "James Stewart and Lovedale: A Reappraisal of Missionary Attitudes and African Response in the Eastern Cape, South Africa" (Ph.D. dissertation, University of Edinburgh, 1974). Stewart had made an earlier tour of the United States, in 1893, and had included Fisk, Atlanta University, and Clark College in his itinerary.

19. Letter, C. T. Loram to Booker T. Washington, September 28, 1914, Library of Congress, Booker T. Washington Papers, box 508.

20. King, *Pan-Africanism and Education*, pp. 177–87. See also Berman, "Education in Africa and America, " pp. 268–71.

21. For the Agricultural Missions Foundation, see King, *Pan-Africanism and Education*, pp. 202–06. Heyman, "The Role of the Carnegie Corporation," pp. 95–101, provides information on the Visitors' Grants Committee. Only a minority of these visitors came to study black schools. List of visitors as of May 1936, Carnegie Corporation of New York (hereafter cited as CC) Carnegie Corporation Visitors' Grants Committee through 1936 folder.

22. In a letter, May 2, 1932, to Thomas Jesse Jones, Anson Phelps Stokes noted that he hoped that "there is some other African native that we can name as among the visitors . . . . At any rate I fear someone would criticize it, and with some justice, if we state that we have had over 200 visitors and only give the name of one native." Jones, in his reply, dated May 7, stated that there had been three Africans among the visitors, to which Stokes, May 9, responded, "I am glad that you . . . have added a few Native Africans to our lists of visitors." All in APS, box 70, folder 1169.

23. Berman, "Education in Africa and America," pp. 121–59; King, *Pan-Africanism and Education*, pp. 95–127.

24. Jackson, Davis, *The Jeanes Visiting Teachers* (New York: Carnegie Corporation, 1936), p. 13.

25. Lance G. E. Jones, *The Jeanes Teacher in the United States, 1908–1933* (Chapel Hill: University of North Carolina Press, 1937), p. 108.

26. For the Jeanes schools, see Richard D. Heyman, "The Initial Years of the Jeanes School in Kenya, 1924–31," in *Essays in the History of African Education*, edited by Vincent M. Battle and Charles H. Lyons (New York: Teachers College Press, 1970), pp. 105–23; King, *Pan-Africanism and Education*, pp. 150–76.

27. Berman, "Education in Africa and America," pp. 194–229, discusses the Booker Washington Institute. See also his "Tuskegee-in-Africa," *Journal of Negro Education* 40, no. 2 (1972): 99–112.

28. Louis R. Harlan, "Booker T. Washington and the White Man's Burden," *American Historical Review* 71, no. 2 (January 1966): 441–67, illustrates something of the great interest that Africans had in Washington's work and ideas. For Dube, see R. Hunt Davis, Jr., "John L. Dube: A South African Exponent of Booker T. Washington," *Journal of African Studies* 2, no. 4 (Winter 1975–76): 497–529; Manning Marable, "A Black School in South Africa," *Negro History Bulletin* 37, (June-July 1974): 258–61.

29. King, *Pan-Africanism and Education*, pp. 212–51; Berman, "Education in Africa and America," pp. 279–86. For a more extended discussion of African students in the United States, see Richard D. Ralston, "A Second Middle Passage: African Student Sojourns in the United States during the Colonial Period and Their Influence upon the Character of African Leadership" (Ph.D. dissertation, University of California, Los Angeles, 1972).

30. Elizabeth J. Burns, "The Industrial Education Myth: Character-Building at Penn School, 1900–1948" (Ph.D. dissertation, University of North Carolina, 1974), serves as the basis for what follows on Penn School. I am also indebted to Dr. Burns for additional information that she provided me through personal conversations and through the loan of some of her notes.

31. J. E. Davis, "A Unique People's School," reprint of an article from the *Southern Workman* (April 1914), PSP, box 57, provides a highly romanticized view of Penn's isolation.

32. Burns, "The Industrial Education Myth," pp. 388–89.

33. Rossa B. Cooley, *School Acres: An Adventure in Rural Education* (New Haven: Yale University Press, 1930), pp. 4–5.

34. Rossa B. Cooley, "The Negro in His Own Environment," *Vassar Quarterly* (May 1920): 178. Off-print located in PSP, box 57.

35. Rossa B. Cooley, *Homes of the Freed* (New York: New Republic, 1926), p. 45.

36. Penn School, *Report of the Principal, 1915–1916*, p. 1, from notes by E. J. Burns on material originally in PSP.

37. Penn School, *Report of the Principal, 1927–1928*, p. 6, from notes by E. J. Burns on material originally in PSP. In *Homes of the Freed*, pp. 151–54, Cooley provides a sketch of Dr. York Bailey, who, as a trained medical doctor returned to his boyhood community, provided a prominent example of a life dedicated to the service of the island community.

38. Cooley, "The Negro in His Own Environment," pp. 180–81; Cooley, *School Acres*, p. 89; Paul U. Kellog, memorandum [1925], PSP box 4, folder 36. See also Burns, "The Industrial Education Myth," pp. 370–71.

39. Thomas Jesse Jones, *Education in East Africa: A Study of East, Central and South Africa by the Second African Education Commission, under the Auspices of the Phelps-Stokes Fund in Cooperation with the International Education Board* (New York: Phelps-Stokes Fund, 1925), p. 37.

40. King, *Pan-Africanism and Education*, 206. See also Lyons, *To Wash an Aethiop White*, p. 148.

41. Jones, *Education in East Africa*, pp. 34–35.

42. Letter, Jones to Cooley, December 22, 1926, PSP, box 5, folder 44. See also letter, Jones to Paul U. Kellog, November 15, 1920, PSP, box 6, folder 60, concerning Jones's enthusiasm for *School Acres*; letter, Jones to Anson Phelps Stokes, June 28, 1935, APS, box 71, folder 1177, reflecting his continued interest in Penn's well-being.

43. Penn School, *Report of the Principal, 1927–1928*, pp. 29–30. The report contained a photograph of a map of Africa with pins representing the place of origin of each of the visitors. The largest cluster was from southern Africa. Loram made arrangements for the distribution of one hundred copies of *Homes of the Freed* among educators, missionaries, and government officials, principally those in southern Africa. See "Minutes of Annual Meeting of Phelps-Stokes Fund, November 17, 1926," APS, box 177, folder 50. In a letter, August 26, 1930, to George Foster Peabody, PSP, box 6, folder 59, Loram was attempting to arrange the distribution in South Africa of fifty copies of *School Acres*.

44. Letter, L. Hollingsworth Wood to General Education Board, January 12, 1927, PSP, box 5, folder 40; letter, Jones to Isabella Curtis, May 4, 1926, PSP, box 5, folder 40, concerning the fund-raising pamphlet entitled "How Penn School Serves Africa." Wood was vice-chairman of the Penn trustees; Curtis was an active fund-raiser for the school. For a full discussion of Penn's use of its African connections for fund-raising purposes, see Burns, "The Industrial Education Myth," pp. 311–23.

45. See Thomas Jesse Jones, *The Two U.S.A.'s: Some Aspects of the Race Question* (Johannesburg: South African Institute of Race Relations, [1931].

46. Cape of Good Hope, Department of Public Education, *Report of the Superintendent-General of Education for . . . 1918* [C.P. 5-'19] (Cape Town: Government Printers, 1919), p. 15.

47. *Report of the Commission on Native Education*, in Cape of Good Hope, Department of Public Education, *Report of the Superintendent-General of Education for . . . 1919* [C.P. 4-'20] (Cape Town: Government Printers, 1920), pp. 67–68. Similar sentiment for establishing education to meet the particular needs and capabilities of Africans runs throughout provincial and Union governmental education reports of this period.

48. Bernard Huss, "Agriculture amongst the Natives of South Africa," *International Review of Missions* 11 (April 1922): 260–69.

49. For accounts of Jabavu's stay, see *The Tuskegee Student* 25, nos. 14 (July 26), 17 (August 23), 19 (September 20), and 20 (October 4, 1913).

50. For more on Loram's career, see Richard D. Heyman, "C. T. Loram: A South African Liberal in Race Relations," *International Journal of African Historical Studies* 5, no. 1 (1972): 41–50; Davis, "Charles T. Loram." On the

triumverate, see King, *Pan-Africanism and Education*, p. 52

51. Charles T. Loram, *The Education of the South African Native* (London: Longmans, Green, 1917).

52. Ibid., pp. vii–xi.

53. Ibid., pp. 51–52.

54. Ibid., pp. 234–38

55. Jones, *Education in Africa*, pp. 34–35. Two South African educators who, with Phelps-Stokes Fund assistance, were early visitors to Penn School were Alexander Kerr, principal of the South African Native College at Fort Hare, and D. McK. Malcolm, chief inspector of native education for Natal. See entry, April 26–30, 1922, Hampton House Guest Book, Penn School, PSP, box 46, vol. 651/2.

56. Jones, *Education in East Africa*, p. xxi. Loram's position as one of the three foreign representatives of the fund was a further endorsement of his work. For the Penn visit, see Stokes to Jones, July 24, 1926, APS, box 27, folder 439; Loram to Stokes, October 16, 1926, APS, Box 31, Folder 510.

57. In addition to his comment in the Hampton House Guest Book, Loram's letters brimmed over with enthusiasm for the school. To Cooley, October 30, 1926, PSP, box 2, folder 14, he wrote: "My visit to Penn was the most wonderful and helpful experience I had in the United States." A letter to Stokes, October 16, 1926, APS, box 31, folder 510, was in the same vein: "For us in Africa it is the most significant work I have seen in the United States." And, at a dinner in his honor, he stated: "At Penn School, South Carolina, I believe I have found the ideal school and the model for African education." *Address by Dr. C. T. Loram . . . on the Occasion of a Dinner Given in his Honour by the Phelps-Stokes Fund* (New York: Phelps-Stokes Fund [1926]), p. 4.

58. Letter, Loram to George Foster Peabody, October 29, 1926, PSP, box 5, folder 42.

59. Letters, Loram to Cooley, October 30, 1926, PSP, box 2, folder 14; Loram to Peabody, October 29, 1926, PSP, box 5, folder 42; Maragret McCulloch to S. M. Colgate, December 2, 1927, PSP, box 5, folder 50. The Phelps-Stokes Fund initially appropriated $800 for their travel. "Minutes of Annual Meeting of Phelps-Stokes Fund, November 17, 1926," APS, box 177, folder 50.

60. Letters, Jones to Stokes, November 29, 1927, and to V. S. Makanya, July 25, 1928, both in Phelps-Stokes Fund Archives, New York (hereafter cited as PSF), file B-4, folder Misc. M's (letter of July 25, 1928, also in APS, box 27, folder 446); letter, Loram to Stokes, January 10, 1929, APS, box 31, folder 512. See also letter, Stokes to Makanya, June 29, 1928, APS, box 32, folder 519.

61. The full phrase was: "Take the Native into the firm of South Africa Limited, European, Christian, civilized purchasers and consumers, and train him for a junior partnership in business." See letter, Stokes to Loram, June 21, 1928, APS, box 31, folder 511. Also, letters, Stokes to Frederick P. Keppel, June 21, 1928, and Keppel to Stokes, July 18, 1928, APS, box 28, folder 465. Keppel was president of the Carnegie Corporation of New York.

62. King, *Pan-Africanism and Education*, pp. 227–28, discusses Makanya and Njongwana and places them in the context of other African students who came to the United States under the fund's auspices.

63. Letters, Clark Foreman, P-S Fund, to Jessie W. Coombs, August 26, 1927, and Jones to Njongwana and Makanya, June 11, 1928, PSF, file B-4, folder Misc. M's; Jones to Stokes, December 7, 1928, APS, box 27, folder 446; Jones to Stokes, February 9, 1929, APS, box 28, folder 447; L. A. Roy, P-S Fund, to U.S. Commissioner of Immigration, June 19, 1930, PSF, file B-4, folder Misc. M's.

64. Letter, Jones to Stokes, October 22, 1928, APS, box 27, folder 446.

65. The correspondence with regard to Makanya and Njongwana attests to the strength of their personalities and character. See, for instance, letter, Georgina A. Gollock to Stokes, August 15, 1927, APS, box 23, folder 361. Gollock was coeditor of the *International Review of Missions*, London.

66. Letter, D. D. T. Jabavu to Stokes, April 26, 1932, APS, box 69, folder 1155.

67. "Sketch of Miss Sibusisiwe V. Makanya" (1931), unidentified typescript, PSF, file B-4, folder Misc. M's.

68. Violet Sibusisiwe Makanya, "The Problem of the Zulu Girl," *Native Teachers' Journal* (Natal) 10, no. 3 (April 1931): 116–20; Makanya, "Social Needs of Modern Native Life," *South African Outlook* 61 (September 1931): 167–70; letters, Stokes to Jones, September 6 and October 1, 1932, APS, box 70, folder 1170.

69. Letter, Jones to John R. Lyons, August 16, 1928, APS, box 27, folder 446; letter, Jones to Ernest W. Riggs, September 22, 1928, APS, box 32, folder 519. Riggs was secretary of the American Board of Commissioners for Foreign Missions. Lyons was pastor of a church in Claremont, California.

70. Memorandum, Foreman to Jones re Makanya and Njongwana, n.d., PSP, file B-4, folder Misc. M's; letters, Stokes to Loram, April 10 and June 29, 1928, APS, box 31, folder 511. There was also a hint of personal tension with members of Penn's staff. See letter, Jones to Stokes, June 15, 1928, APS, box 27, folder 445.

71. Letter, Jones to Lyons, August 16, 1928, APS, box 27, folder 446.

72. Letter, Ernest E. Lightner to Stokes, September 6, 1928, APS, box 32, folder 519, and PSF, file B-4, folder Misc. M's. Lightner was a Congregational minister in Los Angeles.

73. Letter, Jones (?) to Makanya, February 6, 1928, PSF, file B-4, folder Misc. M's; "Minutes of Meeting of the Trustees of the Phelps-Stokes Fund, June 6, 1928," and letter, Stokes to Makanya, June 29, 1928, both APS, box 32, folder 519.

74. Letter, Stokes to Makanya, June 29, 1928, APS, box 32, folder 519.

75. Letter, L. A. Roy to Jones, July 20, 1928, APS, box 27, folder 445; letter, Lightner to Jones, September 6, 1928, APS, box 32, folder 519, and PSF, file B-4, Misc. M's; letter, Stokes to Makanya, July 25, 1928, APS, box 27, folder 446, and PSF, file B-4, Misc. M's; letter, R. R. Moton to Jones, September 24, 1928, APS, box 32, folder 519, and PSF, file B-4, folder Misc. M's.

76. Letter, Moton to Jones, September 24, 1928, APS, box 32, folder 519, and PSF, file B-4, folder misc. M's; letter, Jones to Florence Read, October 2, 1928, and memorandum, Jones to Stokes, December 26, 1928, both in APS, box 27, folder 446; letter, Jones to Stokes, February 9, 1929, APS, box 28, folder 447. Read was president of Spelman College.

77. Letter, Roy to Jones, July 20, 1928, APS, box 27, folder 445; letter, Makanya to Stokes, September 4, 1928, APS, box 32, folder 519; Jones, "Memorandum as to Miss Makanya and Miss Njongwana," October 10, 1928, "Sketch of Miss Sibusisiwe V. Makanya," and letter, Roy to Harry E. Hull, April 7, 1930, all in PSF, file B-4, folder Misc. M's. Hull was commissioner-general, U.S. Bureau of Immigration.

78. For Loram and Jones on the "good African," see King, *Pan-Africanism and Education*, pp. 157, 232.

79. Letter, Jones to Stokes, July 24, 1928, APS, box 27, folder 445; letter, Jones to Stokes, October 3, 1928, APS, box 27, folder 446.

80. Letter, Jones to Stokes, July 24, 1928, APS, box 27, folder 445.

81. Letters, Stokes to Loram, April 10, 1928, Loram to Stokes, November 25, 1928, both in APS, box 31, folder 511; letters, January 10, 1929, Loram to Stokes, and Stokes to Loram, February 14, 1929, APS, box 31, folder 512.

82. Letter, Lightner to Stokes, September 6, 1928, APS, box 32, folder 519.

83. Letter, Stokes to Loram, April 10, 1928, APS, box 31, folder 511, referring to a letter that Loram had written to Makanya and Njongwana.

84. See King, *Pan-Africanism and Education*, pp. 79–94, for a discussion of efforts to recruit black Americans with the "Tuskegee Spirit" for work in Africa.

85. Letter, Loram to Stokes, October 16, 1926, APS, box 31, folder 510; "Minutes of Annual Meeting of Phelps-Stokes Fund, November 17, 1926," APS, box 177, folder 50; letter, Loram to Cooley, October 30, 1926, PSP, box 2, folder 14; letter, Roy to Cooley, October 18, 1929, PSP, box 6, folder 57; letter, Peabody to Loram, May 18, 1927, PSP, box 5, folder 47; letter, Loram to Peabody, August 26, 1930, PSP, box 6, folder 59. The last letter referred to the distribution of Thomas J. Woofter's *Black Yeomanry: Life on St. Helena Island* (New York: Henry Holt, 1930). The Carnegie Corporation also seemingly funded distribution of Penn material. See form letter, Loram to Dear Sir/Madam, September 17, 1930, CC folder C. T. Loram '30, which accompanied copies of Penn's *Sixty-seventh Annual Report*.

86. C. T. Loram. *Adaptation of the Penn School Methods to Education in South Africa* (New York: Phelps-Stokes Fund, 1927).

87. Letter, Peabody to J. K. Walbridge, May 18, 1927, and newspaper clipping of the review, PSP, box 5, folder 47. Walbridge was editor of *The Saratogian* (Saratoga, N.Y.). See also *Native Teacher's Journal* 6, (July 1927): 231–33, for another review of *Homes of the Freed*.

88. Letter, Loram to Cooley, November 17, 1927, PSP, box 5, folder 49. In a letter of November 15, 1926, to Stokes, APS, box 31, folder 510, Loram had suggested the possibility of four or five Jeanes schools in operation during 1927.

89. Letter to F. P. Keppel, May 16, 1928, CC, folder C. T. Loram '27–'28. Keppel was president of the Carnegie Corporation.

90. *Address by Dr. C. T. Loram,* p. 8. In listing suggested sites, Loram came up with an actual total of twenty-two schools in the following countries: Kenya (the one already in existence), South Africa (four), Southern Rhodesia (two), Nigeria (two), and one each in Basutoland or Bechanaland, South-West Africa, Northern Rhodesia, Nyasaland, Mozambique, Angola, Uganda, Tanganyika, the Belgian Congo, Gold Coast, Sierra Leone, and Liberia.

91. Memorandum re Jeanes schools, November 28, 1932, CC, folder Jeanes Schools—Misc.; memorandum, J. M. Russell to Keppel, December 15, 1938, CC, folder Jeanes Schools—Nyasaland; letter, Jones to T. G. Benson (August), 1932, APS, box 70, folder 1170. Benson was principal of the Jeanes school in Kenya.

92. Memorandum re Jeanes schools, November 28, 1932, CC, folder Jeanes Schools—Misc.; letter, Loram to Keppel, July 23, 1928, CC, folder C. T. Loram '27–28; letter, Loram to Keppel, April 20, 1930, CC, folder C. T. Loram '30; memorandum of interviews, Keppel and Loram, January 16 and May 8, 1932, CC, folder Loram '32–'33.

93. Letter, Loram to Keppel, April 11, 1928, CC, folder Jeanes Schools—Misc.; letter, Loram to Keppel, July 13, 1930, CC, folder C. T. Loram '30; letter, Loram to Keppel, July 8, 1931, CC, folder C. T. Loram '31.

94. For example, in a letter to Keppel, March 23, 1938, CC, folder C. T. Loram '27–'28, Loram wrote that the Cape "does not appreciate the value of Jeanes work." He also noted that the lack of Union government authority in African education (each province held responsibility) hindered central planning.

95. For an example of Loram's involvement with the Phelps-Stokes Fund, see letter, Stokes to Le Roux van Niekerk, October 28, 1927, APS, box 31, folder 511. Van Niekerk was a South African legislator. For Loram's connections with the Carnegie Corporation, see letter, Loram to Keppel, April 11, 1928, CC, folder CC Visitors' Grants Committee through 1936, and other correspondence in this and the subsequent (1937–1945) folder.

96. Letter, Joanna H. Elder to Grace House, August 6, 1933, PSP, box 8, folder 70.

97. Letter, Leif Egeland to House, October 24, 1930, PSP, box 6, folder 59. In the Hampton House Guest Book, entry dated October 7, 1930, he fully endorsed Loram's entry of October 13, 1926.

98. W. H. Seatonn *Schools in Travail: A Short Study of the One-Teacher Negro Rural School of the Southern States with Some Application to African Conditions* (New York: Carnegie Corporation Visitors' Grants Committee, 1932), p. 45.

99. G. H. Welsh, *The Black Man's Schools: Some Impressions of American Education, with Special Reference to the Negro in the United States, and to Desirable Improvements in the Education of the South African Bantu* (Pretoria: Carnegie Corporation Visitors' Grants Committee [1932]), p. 36. Welsh held the position of chief inspector for native education in the Cape Province. His position on Penn and on the relevance of black American education in general for South Africa was somewhat ironic, since Loram had attached great importance to his coming to the United States. See letter, Loram to F. P. Keppel, April 14, 1931, CC, folder CC Visitors' Grants Committee through 1936.

100. See, for example, letter, Loram to Jones, September 27, 1934, APS, box 75, folder 1238; letter, Loram to Keppel, September 25, 1935, CC, folder Primitive Peoples, Education of—through 1939.

101. Letter, Loram to the editor, *Umteteli wa Bantu*, January 25, 1935, APS, box 75, folder 1238. This paper, published in Johannesburg, had a predominantly African readership. Letter, Loram to Jones, September 27, 1934, APS, box 75, folder 1238. See also, letter, Jones to Stokes, March 19, 1937, APS, box 71, folder 1181, re Loram's success with African students under his auspices as

opposed to the general disappointment that the fund had experienced with such persons.

102. Yale University Department of Race Relations Southern Tour, 1936, APS, box 75, folder 1238; letters, Loram to Cooley, March 11 and March 28, 1932, and program for Yale party, March 27–28, 1934, PSP, box 8, folder 72.

103. Letter, Loram to Jones, September 27, 1934, APS, box 75, folder 1238.

104. Matthews was the first of four Africans from the Union of South Africa that Loram brought to Yale. Stokes had met him while on a tour of South Africa and considered him to be "the soundest and wisest Native that I had met anywhere in South Africa" (letter, Stokes to Jones, September 22, 1932, APS, box 70, folder 1170). Matthews visited Penn as part of the 1934 Yale tour and formed a favorable impression of the school. See his "Impressions of Negro Education in the Southern States," *Native Teachers' Journal* 13, no. 4 (July 1934): 159–63.

105. Burns, "The Industrial Education Myth," pp. 447–48.

106. For the increasing urbanization, see David Welsh, "The Growth of Towns," in *The Oxford History of South Africa*, vol. 2, edited by Monica Wilson and Leonard Thompson (London: Oxford University Press, 1971), pp. 172–243.

107. Welsh, *The Black Man's Schools,* p. 41.

108. Albert Luthuli, *Let My People Go* (New York: Meridian Books, 1962), p. 36.

109. Thomas Karis and Gwendolen M. Carter, eds., *From Protest to Challenge: A Documentary History of African Politics in South Africa 1882–1964* (Stanford: Hoover Institution Press, 1972–), vol. 1, *Protest and Hope*, by Sheridan Johns III (1972).

110. Ibid., vol. 2, *Hope and Challenge 1935–1952*, by Thomas Karis (1973), p. 149.

111. Ibid., p. 220.

CHAPTER 5

John L. Dube and the Politics of Segregated Education in South Africa

MANNING MARABLE

This detailed case study of Ohlange Institute in Natal and the life and impact of its founder and long-time principal, John Dube, "documents the character of that school, its educational structure and personnel, especially during the period 1917–1929, when Dube had largely divorced himself from the problems of the nascent African National Congress." Dube's life-long career at Ohlange manifests his American educational background at Oberlin College, his close association with the ideas of his mentor, Booker T. Washington, his concept of what the Africans needed (industrial education) to survive in South African racist society, which was in many ways similar to America at the time, and finally, his tact in handling both whites and Africans. Dube founded Ohlange with limited funds, a problem which never improved; he made industrial education the main thrust of his Institute (as Booker T. Washington had done at Tuskegee), pioneered liberal education at Ohlange, maintained strong discipline among the students and faculty, and continued to make appeals for funds and teaching staff assistance from the local whites as well as from America. There was a reservoir of goodwill and desire to help among liberal whites because Ohlange's educational orientation was not a threat to the status quo of white domination over blacks, with whites occupying all the skilled positions while blacks remained largely unskilled laborers.

John Langalibalele Dube, the "Booker T. Washington of South Africa," is best known as the first president of the South African Native National Congress, which subsequently became the African National Congress. Dube was a leader of a black deputation of Great Britain to denounce the Natives' Land Act of 1913, the first major legislative step down the long historic road toward *apartheid*. Dube lived in the United States between 1887 and 1892 and 1896 and 1899, was educated at Oberlin, and became somewhat famous as a popular lecturer and author. Like his intellectual mentor, Booker T. Washington, he was an advocate of industrial education, "self help," and tacit segregation of the races. Late in life he became the object of fierce criticism from younger, more militant black intellectuals in his country. Dube had received the King George V Silver Jubilee Medal and in 1936 became the first black to receive an honorary Ph.D. degree from the University of South Africa. Toward the end of his life, black nationalists and members of the Communist party called him a traitor, a sickly looking "Uncle Tom." He never tired of cautioning South African blacks from confronting white state power and civil society.

Dube's career as a politician and writer stemmed from a single source, the existence of Ohlange Institute, a small black school situated on the north coast near Durban, Natal. Established in 1900 with the financial assistance of an American committee of white advisers and friends, the Zulu Christian Industrial School, as it was then called, became the first black-directed and -controlled educational institution on the Tuskegee Institute model in South Africa. The mature Dube was a masterful politician who attempted continually to maintain complete control over his educational institution. He came to view Ohlange Institute as a symbol of black academic achievement in the face of white oppression. His relationship with the members of the paternalistic Anti-Slavery and Aborigines Protection Society, South African white liberals, and philanthropists illustrates his immensely difficult task. The history of John L. Dube and Ohlange Institute reveals much about the character of African educational institutions within a colonial society and something more about the politics of white racism.

During the socially and politically volatile 1920s, South African liberals and white educators began to voice their support for Ohlange Institute, although few influential whites trusted its principal. C. A. Wheelwright, chief inspector of native education and director of the Department of Native Affairs in Natal, applauded Dube's efforts at maintaining his institution without substantial European assistance. Wheelwright observed privately in March 1922 that Ohlange Institute "is, so far as I am aware, the only purely Native Institution on a large scale in the Union, and it endeavors to serve in a small way very much the same purpose as Tuskegee in the United States."[1] On the request of John H. Harris, correspondence secretary for the Anti-Slavery and Aborigines Protection Society, Howard Pim, a Johannesburg public accountant and a member of the Johannesburg Joint Council of Europeans and Natives, investigated Ohlange and its director favorably, with some important reservations. "John Dube is a man who does not altogether inspire confidence," Pim wrote referring to Dube's long record of political agitation. Despite his recognition that Dube "has really accomplished much in running his school at Ohlange for a number of years," Pim believed "his brother Charles who has helped him, is more dependable."[2] In December 1923, after visiting Ohlange, Pim observed that Ohlange's curriculum "could not compete with white establishments." He emphasized, however, that it was excellent for "*a native school with native standards.*" [emphasis added].[3] In both England and South Africa, Dube continued to maintain the confidence of most white liberals. Mrs. Rheinallt Jones wrote to Harris in March 1928 that Ohlange's conservative demeanor and course offerings were quite impressive. "The Institution is to my mind quite as efficient as most Institutions in Natal which have European control—not as good as the best but a *very great deal better than the worst*" [emphasis added].[4] The rhetoric of Ohlange, which by the 1920s connoted partial or complete black political acquiescence, limited industrial and agricultural training, and primary level educational opportunities in the social sciences and humanities, reinforced the Europeans' faith in a sometimes subservient, sometimes militant black principal.

Dube continued to use his speeches and public appeals to reinforce the image of Ohlange as a battleground for Calvinist salvation and proletarian training with some success. Dube published *The Zulu's Appeal for Light* in summer 1914 in England while he was protesting the adoption of the South African Natives' Land Act of 1913. The 1914 *Appeal* listed in considerable detail needs of the school and its pupils. "The aim of our Institution is to give our Native youths, of every denomination, as well as heathen, a Christian and industrial training to form them into good and useful citizens," Dube wrote. The pamphlet provided a brief critique of the relationship between the rise of capitalism and Christianity as much as an advertisement for the school. "You will know the better than I the history of the heathen world, and how the evolution and redemption of the heathen nations has been worked and accomplished," Dube noted; "first comes the trader with his Bible, and finally the policeman with his big stick." The missionary was "not only the precursor of Christ, but also the pioneer of civilization." The essence of Christian thought was largely manifested in the manner in which the African's material reality changed after colonial rule. Christianity "has instilled the noblest of principles into our lives," Dube stated. Yet, it has also "shown us how we should live, what we should live for, why life is worth living." Dube argued that Christianity would ultimately prove its true worth in the material world. "There is, and must be, a certain visible reflection of all these inward workings in the individual's eternal life," Dube observed. "And when this is taken in conjunction with those more material blessings of mental and social improvement with which the missionary has combined it, we get something tangible to form a judgment on." John Dube's faith was only as righteous as it could promote competition in Natal's primitive marketplace.[5]

The 1914 *Appeal*, like its predecessor, *The Zulu's Appeal for Light and England's Duty* (1910), illustrated graphically the large size of the student body and faculty and the specific needs and Christian achievements of Ohlange Institute. The school had 220 pupils in the beginning of 1914. The students paid £6 to attend classes for the nine-month school year, although they were required to work on the premises three hours each day. The staff of Ohlange that year consisted of Adelaide Dube, wife of Charles Dube, who served as teacher in standard 7; Robert Fredericks, teacher of standard 6; K. Blackburn, instructor of courses in commercial training and the Bible; David Opperman, teacher of the first division, standard 5; Merian Opperman, teacher of the first division, standard 4; Nikani Ngcobo, teacher of the second division, standard 5; J. Cele, teacher of second division, standard 4; L. Mtembu, teacher of standard 3; and M. Mapumlo, instructor of standard 2. In the industrial education department, Ohlange employed seven instructors: J. Mcunu in carpentry, J. Nswelling in shoemaking and leatherwork, V. Mootho and C. Tshabalala directed the printing shop and trained students to work on the institute's newspaper, W. Dimba in agriculture, J. Mseleku in masonry and building, and K. Kanoo in blacksmithing. Nokutela Dube instructed classes in music and assisted her husband in running the school, as did Charles Dube, who served as a teacher and headmaster. All were dedicated to teaching the Zulu man to "go out to his fields" and sell his "produce at the market"; the woman learned to cook, use the sewing machine and only occasionally assist her husband in farming. "In such ways" and with a capable faculty, Dube wrote, "is Christianity knocking heathenism out of our people's lives."[6]

A continued problem which jeopardized Ohlange's existence was Dube's personality—his brusque temper, his aggressiveness, and genuine distaste for any white interference or guidance. John Reuling, an American instructor at Adams Institute during the 1920s and 1930s, recalls Dube as a generous and truly progressive man. During the 1920s, many of Ohlange's and Adams's Kholwa teachers "were the sharpest critics" of education which stressed the arts, humanities, and classical languages. "Dube understood the concerns of the African teachers," Reuling states, "but he encouraged me to work for something broader." Pupils thought of Dube as "such a very strong character, widely known, of tremendous capacity."[7] Gideon Mdode Sivetye remembers the principal as "often quoting B. Washington—his patron saint," setting an example of ceaseless work and independence for his students.[8] Other white instructors who were associated intimately with Dube were sometimes offended and angered at that spirit of independence. William Wells, a white teacher who had previously established a small school in Johannesburg, was asked by Charles T. Loram, the superintendent of education in South Africa, to take a position at Ohlange in 1924. Wells assumed the position of headmaster that school year and was quickly frustrated with Dube's narrow ideas and with Ohlange's inefficient management. One particularly irritating aspect of "the bad system in vogue at Ohlange" was the fact that most instructors were not paid on a regular basis. Nellie Wells, the wife of the headmaster, complained to John Harris that Dube's mismanagement "disabled us from completing monthly payments and necessitated the sale of certain effects to cover deficit." Dube refused to give William Wells his check for four months' work, so "we put the matter into the hands of lawyers who failed to derive anything, because we could not go up to Johannesburg ourselves; and we lost all, and have been loaded with debts which we pay off monthly," she lamented.[9] Travers Buxton, secretary of the Anti-Slavery and Aborigines Protection Society, wrote Pim that Mrs. Wells's letter described her "[falling] out with John Dube, in reference to whom she drops a somewhat unpleasant innuendo."[10] Pim responded critically that, according to Charles T. Loram, "Dube is a man who does not get along with everybody."[11]

The central, ongoing concern of Ohlange and its founder was the lack of sufficient operating funds. The institution's student fs could scarcely begin to pay for the hiring of additional faculty, dormitories, additional lands for cultivation, and other essential expenses. After thirteen years of operation, the physical plant did not have plumbing nor running water because Dube had determined that the cost, approximately £300, was out of reach. The industrial department was perhaps not in full operation during several years because of the paucity of tools in the shoemaking, blacksmith, and carpentry shops. A sharp rise in the student body between 1909 and 1914 meant there were not enough sewing machines with which to train new female students. In the 1914 *Appeal*, Dube asked his readers to contribute generously: Ohlange needed to purchase two hundred beds, new books for classroom use and for the library, and timber to make furniture for the newly constructed school building and the chapel.[12]

The difficulty of Dube's fiscal position was that he could not receive enough money from his American supporters and South African friends to operate the school adequately, yet he was fiercely opposed to putting the direction of Ohlange under government control. In 1909, Dube placed his school under the supervision of a rather inactive board of advisers, chaired by his old supporter Marshall Campbell, Victoria County sugar cane planter and Natal senator. Charles Dube was designated headmaster and was given by the advisory board a certain amount of supervisory responsibility. During this period, up to the eve of World War I, Ohlange expanded greatly, and a number of white instructors were hired. During the war, Dube increased his involvement in politics, Ohlange's student population dropped off slightly again, the European instructors left their positions, and Ohlange faced large debts. Pim wrote to John Harris that during the war "the Natal government proposed to take the place over as a state institution" and to assume responsibility for the debts incurred under Dube's management. With characteristic subtlety Dube rejected the offer without refusing outright. Pim noted that Dube "pointed out there were difficulties in the way, and he would have to obtain the consent of the people in America who had originally backed him." The Natal government's educators replied that Ohlange be directed by a committee consisting of Dube and Wheelwright, the chief inspector of native education in Natal. Dube carefully neglected to reply to the offer, despite the mounting fiscal problems he had in keeping Ohlange in operation. Pim remarked in January 1922 that Dube's sole aim was that "he wants support without definite control."[13]

Despite Dube's efforts, Ohlange had deteriorated to the status of a struggling mission school by the early and middle 1920s. Pim's visit to Ohlange in December 1923 revealed the acute shortcomings of the physical plant. Approximately 190 students were in the primary school and over 100 were in the upper standard levels. Accompanying Dube to the shoemaker's shop, Pim "asked to see some of their own work and was shown a pair of boots roughly put together, the stitching of which was distinctly careless." The institute's carpentry shop produced "very roughly made furniture," which local Africans purchased for their kraals. Pim complained: "Again here the workmanship seemed to me careless and not up to the standard of a European School." The lack of sufficient funds had prohibited Dube from purchasing adequate carpentry tools, and Pim admitted, "the hones were also so worn in the middle that it would be quite impossible to sharpen any tool on them properly." The dining room, a large shed constructed of waffle and daub covered partially by cement, was beginning to crack in places. Several water tanks, no longer in service, sat thirty or forty feet above the dining hall "although Dube spoke of an engine he had intended installing in place of the windmill," Pim added. A number of buildings made of brick or stone, including the teachers' living quarters and printing office were "reasonably clean, although the want of water was obvious."[14]

Pim's account stressed the lack of physical orderliness and funds to run Ohlange properly. Dube introduced Pim to William and Nellie Wells, and Pim noted critically "it did not seem to me that they were sufficiently alive to the importance of cleanliness and good order." The kitchen was "a miserable shed"; other surrounding buildings "were also not too tidy"; the roofs were in bad order and the guttering in many places defective. Pim observed condescendingly, "it seems to me that this Institution cannot be judged by European standards, and that those I have talked to about it are agreed that it is really wonderful that Dube has kept it going all these years." Ohlange's reputation among Africans was high and Europeans in the area generally approved of what they knew of the institute's industrial and manual labor curriculum. Pim's chief criticism of Ohlange was not surprisingly of Dube himself: the principal "is a puzzling creature. I should say he was strong-willed and a great egotist; but his effect on me was curiously neutral. . . . Apparently, the people who get on with him do so by the aid of a little flattery."[15]

Beyond the criticisms of Pim, the rhetoric of conformity and compliance which was such a part of Ohlange's image seldom mirrored the school's realities. From the founding of the school, Dube was determined to maintain a strong curriculum in literature and the creative arts. He probably thought of himself as a man of letters—his *The Zulu's Appeal for Light and England's Duty* (1910) and the 1914 *Appeal* were both written in a florid, sweeping style. He encouraged the students who contributed to his newspaper and those who attended Ohlange to appreciate literature, music, and the arts. Dube confided to Reuling during the late 1920s that most of the coastal Kholwa ministers did not fully appreciate "the need to develop qualities of leadership, self-reliance and so forth in the boys and young men." Reuling states that Dube was sympathetic with the social and cultural conservativism of the black ministry, "but he also [understood] the need for community leadership which would have a great degree of training and more of the social vision" than the preceding Kholwa generations. Dube understood that a proper challenge of European hegemony connoted cultural and economic self-improvement, a task which precipitated the creation of independent Kholwa intellectuals.[16]

Dube slowly transformed what was proposed originally to be an industrial training center into an exciting, although oftentimes poorly financed, institute for higher education. The African educator gradually improved the quality of his staff and his mandatory curriculum. As early as 1909, Ohlange offered its student body courses in the social sciences, literature, and music, as well as training in carpentry and blacksmithing.[17] In 1929, a typical Ohlange student took humanities and social science courses which prepared him for the Junior Certificate examination of the University of South Africa, a certificate equivalent to a tenth grade diploma, which could also serve as an entrance qualification into the black university of Fort Hare, located in Cape Province. Students studied for three years after achieving standard 7 level. Courses for the Junior Certificate students included English language skills, English literature, vernacular (Sesuto or Zulu), mathematics, Latin, arithmetic, science, history, bookkeeping, shorthand, typing, and geography. Students in standards 7 and 8 also were required to take "scripture" and "a manual subject"—either carpentry, tailoring, or shoemaking. However, these Junior Certificate students, the largest class of pupils within the institution, were not unskilled laborers. Such training equipped black students with academic skills and bourgeois attitudes.[18]

The commercial department students prepared for the National Commercial Examinations of the Union of South Africa Department of Education. The two basic courses within the commercial studies major were the preliminary commercial course, a two-year full-time course "following the completion of the Intermediate School Code [standard 6]," and the National Junior Certificate in Commerce course, a one-year training period to "fit the student for the National Junior Certificate in Commerce after the Preliminary." Students in both programs took English literature, English language drills, commercial arithmetic, bookkeeping, commerce, history, shorthand, and typing.[19]

Ohlange trained its students in its industrial department not only in specific skills, but gave them general preparation in the skills of becoming independent, small businessmen. Industrial students received three years instruction in carpentry, shoemaking, and/or tailoring. Ohlange Institute's *Prospectus* of 1929 noted that "many of our students who have completed the full course in each of the above trades have found good employment in many parts of the Union."[20] In spite of Dube's rhetoric, such training was not the focal point of campus life. One local American teacher at Inanda recalls that at Ohlange all of "the Industrial pupils took a bit of 'academic work.'" Despite the powerful reputation of the school's commercial renown, Reuling now observes that "the work at Ohlange was more academic than the curriculum of Tuskegee." Although white Natal citizens believed Dube's students were tutored in servile positions, even Ohlange's industrial graduates learned literature, commercial skills such as typing and shorthand, and even Latin.[21]

Throughout this period, "Dr. Dube recognized the value of industrial education and pursued it," Reuling states. "But he himself had had an overseas university education, helped and encouraged many young people to get [and] stood strongly for the rights of African students to pursue any kind of education that they wanted."[22] In 1917 a girl's dormitory opened on campus, and the school instituted a teacher-training course, primarily for the women students. The effort was short-lived, not for a lack of student interest, but "on account of the mounting expenses of running the school." In 1924, the Natal Department of Education "recognized" Ohlange for the purposes of financial assistance and began to subsidize teachers' salaries. According to D. G. S. M'timkulu, Ohlange's second principal, this new support "marked the decline of the Industrial Departments. . . . It became obvious that industrial training was only useful in those trades where the trainee could set up shop for himself, rather than seek employment." Industrial education at Ohlange had been "reduced to Carpentry and Building and Leatherwork," although a tailoring course began in 1926. At a time when Natal whites generally viewed Ohlange as "industrial," the school was producing markedly self-employable individuals: tailors, carpenters, and craftsmen who engaged in private enterprise.[23]

Ohlange was a "pioneer" in liberal education. In 1918 "they were the first, and for some years the only, school" offering a "Cape Junior" curriculum—later called the Junior Certificate course. Ohlange "spurred on the Natal Education Department to open high school courses in Natal," M'timkulu writes. During these years the American Board schools, Inanda and Adams, and other mission schools mimicked Dube's blend of industrial and agricultural training with liberal arts. Adams's students began to take courses in agricultural training in the early 1920s. Marianhill, the Roman Catholic mission school, specialized in carpentry and cabinetmaking. As these other schools became more like Ohlange, Ohlange continually stressed more liberal academic aspects of education among its students. During the early 1930s, the Natal government opened provincial agricultural institutes under the supervision of the Native Department of Education, to produce the agrarian-type laborers which formed a part of the Dube rhetoric. Ohlange in reality continued to produce independent-minded Kholwa entrepreneurs and white-collar workers.[24]

The typical routine which evolved at Ohlange was more spartan and puritanical than at other mission schools. Work for Ohlange students began before dawn and the heat of the morning. The young men slept in breezy, brick dormitories whose doors and windows were usually kept open to cool the stuffy rooms during the night. Students slowly gathered themselves out of their cots, which were packed close together in every room. They walked first to the pit latrines, which were a prudent distance from the main buildings, and then they took cold, communal showers. Classes usually began at 6:30. Some students, especially those who needed to earn extra money to pay their tuition, herded and milked the cows, scrubbed the kitchen and dining room, and tended the garden. Of course, each student was responsible for contributing several hours of labor toward the school's maintenance either two or three days a week, depending on the student's grade. All students worked at assigned tasks on Saturday mornings.[25]

After three classes, students converged into the dining room for breakfast. Kitchen helpers dished rations out of huge, steaming pots over wood fires. To the orderly trestle tables and benches young men carried enameled plates and spoons which they washed in cold water after eating. The diet of the students was always a concern for Dube; Ohlange, Amanzimtoti, and other schools could scarcely afford to spend more than twenty cents per day per pupil for food. Ohlange students were never surprised from meal to meal—corn meal porridge, mealies, some fruit and vegetables, and meat twice a week was the rule for over thirty years. At nine thirty or so, students met at the school chapel and listened to Dube's daily invocational and morning directives. Then followed a series of four classes lasting roughly forty-five minutes each, divided by a recess period. After the sun passed midday, students once again met in the dining room, for lunch. After the meal, most students went to work in the fields or in shops until after four o'clock. Between the end of classroom hours and dinner, students' hours were open for recreational activities, debating, reading, or other forms of "self-improvement." After the evening meal, Ohlange men sat for two hours of study in preparation for the next day's assignments. Darkness extinguished most strictly academic endeavors, since the campus did not have electric power for some years. But students and faculty did often talk to each other about their hopes, their aspirations, and life beyond the boundaries of segregated Natal. Returning to their dormitories, students and faculty usually collapsed into sleep, only to awaken before the dawn of the next day.[26]

Only a strong-willed, dedicated individual could survive the rigors of Ohlange. Reuling noted that many Kholwa youth seemed to feel ready for its challenges. "In an area where there was no literacy at all, it fell to those who reached the third grade level, to teach those who couldn't read at all." There was an overriding sense of urgency in the Ohlange mentality—to learn as much as possible, to succeed in the white man's world, not only for oneself, but for one's people. Every school year closed with the dreaded final examinations for all classes, when students and faculty alike hoped for the former's success. Of Ohlange's and Adams's efforts Reuling says, "[We] gave a great deal of attention toward the externally set departmental examinations... [but] at the same time, we attempted to use all possible ways of humanizing the work, broadening it beyond the strict limited areas that would be covered by the examinations...." Students soon learned to ask their instructors to isolate only potential examination problems. "[At Adams], many times I have been asked, developing or pointing out some interesting fact or other, or suggesting that a certain book be read, or a certain article in a magazine, 'Sir, will we have a question of that in the examination?'" In spite of their fears of failure, "a gratifyingly large number of students did broaden their horizons ... [and] did take up the habit of reading ...." For "Ohlange's unsophisticated simple 'country boys,'" away from home and family for the first time, reading an impossible and perplexing alphabet, speaking in an alien tongue during classes, and imitating the life-styles of those who had conquered your homeland, was perhaps the biggest test of all.[27]

American education in Natal attempted to cultivate late Victorian tastes in its pupils. Dube, the American mission principals, and their staffs knowingly reorganized the social behavior of their students in various ways. One basic purpose for Ohlange, Dube explained to a *New York Herald* reporter in 1899, was the "education of his people in manual labor pursuits, [so that] oxen instead of women could labor in the fields."[28] In examinations at Adams, primary and lower secondary grade students gave individual demonstrations of tasks they had learned; young men spoke on oral English, blackboard drawing, map-making, art work, agriculture, and woodworking; the young women discussed some of the academic subjects, but carefully demonstrated their cooking skills and sewing techniques. Women should serve men; they should be seen but not tampered with. Ohlange men only visited Inanda for concerts or school plays, but visits were "heavily chaperoned." Such irregular trips were "a big feature" in the social life of Ohlange. But particularly here, Dube's notion on the proper life-style of a prospective black bourgeoisie bore on his school's institutional attitudes toward black women and their role in society. Dube's incredible desires to scrupulously safeguard the morality of his students implies the values that he believed were essential for an educated, commercial black elite to have.[29]

The Ohlange instructor and his associates at the nearby American schools struggled with what they felt was an almost impossible task. Reuling recalls that "most staff members were on duty or call from six A.M. until six P.M. on all weekdays, with a great many evenings, week ends, and holiday assignments." Teachers at the institution were "interested, concerned, good team workers and completely dedicated." And they had to be, "working as they did with minimal equipment, overcrowded facilities, [and with] a terrible and continual financial problem. . . ." Teachers sought to make their students independent individuals. The Natal Department of Education inspectors noted that "in going out to the Institution at Fort Hare and out into life in the teaching field . . . our people on the whole showed much more self reliance, and ability to discuss and to decide." Official inspections of all classes limited the amount of freedom teachers had in setting their own courses. "Several times a year," educational inspectors visited Ohlange to monitor the classroom activities of full-time faculty members "for the purposes of evaluating and rating the work of the individual teachers . . . or evaluating the work of the institution as a whole." Adams had "plenty of rules," like Ohlange, which were "archaic and old fashioned, moralistic and strict." Although Ohlange's industrial educational image pleased many, Reuling states, "in infrequent conversations with those missionaries of some other church groups I gathered that there were those who thought that Dube's activities were unfitting for a man who had been ordained to the Christian ministry and that . . . he was 'pushing' too hard." In a hostile environment, with few tools, Dube's teachers believed that they could not afford to push themselves or their students any less hard.[30]

John Dube, more than any single factor, set Ohlange's mood. The principal dominated the campus as Booker Washington had dominated Tuskegee. In Ohlange's formative years Dube tended to use his own physical resources to coerce students into what he considered a proper role. After the 1902 revival, Dube wrote, "the boys are behaving better, [however] we had to send away two boys who . . . were caught with some bad girls in the village." Like his Alabama mentor, Dube was markedly conservative on his students' activities with the opposite sex. "Five lashes for the boy who sends a note to a girl, and the same for the girl if she receives it without reporting it," declared Dube, "nips the amorous correspondence in the bud. . . ." One article on Ohlange students noted that "[Dube's] muscular arm and two hundred pounds avoirdupois is held in wholesome respect."[31] Even during the 1910s, when Dube became active in the African National Congress, and in subsequent years when his health grew worse, the strict regulations still tended to reflect the man's own personality. In the 1920s and 1930s, students were not allowed to leave the school grounds without his permission. "Profane language, drinking intoxicants, [and] use of tobacco in any form are strictly forbidden. . . . Students who write letters to girls while attending this Institute [could be subject to] expulsion without notice."[32] To develop a Western-oriented African middle class, Dube reasoned, his students had to share his own values. And generally, Ohlange's program was quite successful in accomplishing this.

Yet even during the late 1920s, Dube's image to Natal whites and to American teachers at nearby Inanda and Adams continued to be conservative, and even servile. "The white people—those who knew about Ohlange—mostly quite approved of what they thought Dr. Dube was trying to do," an American Inanda teacher now recalls, "as they thought of the school as purely industrial." Ohlange was "considered very suitable for the African," because its curriculum consisted of "industrial work . . . not anything that would compete with the whites."[33] Dube's personal magnetism, his ingratiating remarks to a hostile white community, encouraged them to believe the myth that Ohlange was apolitical and not a threat to white economic superiority. "We always thought . . . [that Dube] tried very hard to keep out of politics," the American instructor from Inanda suggests, and that the students in his school did likewise.[34] Whites could well afford to be "tolerant and admiring of an occasional 'freak' like Dube," Reuling notes. They were convinced that, "obviously, [blacks] had low intelligence, could never do the things that Europeans could do, and were generally inferior." At best, Ohlange provided the province with obedient servants, and at worst, Ohlange and the American Board schools "were a good thing because they would provide some leadership for the 'natives' and provide a safety valve."[35] Because "there was a vast ignorance on the part of whites not only about the capabilities of the Africans but also about their aspirations and their view of the white community," Reuling writes, no one "regarded" Dube or American Board teachers as "subversive."[36]

Dube's image as a modern African—businesslike, politically active, an associate with influential whites, "an earnest Christian [and] comparatively wealthy" person—carved an irresistible picture in the minds of his students. Dube "influenced people by his speaking and by what he accomplished," the Inanda teacher observes. He was a thoroughly modern man who "felt that there was good in some of the old Zulu customs." His home on Ohlange's campus was "quite modern according to standards in rural Natal." The Dube home in 1930 had seven rooms, a large veranda and the luxury of running water. By his last years, he had acquired "considerable land," and "one of [his] projects had been to settle people on part of his land" who had been urban unemployed workers or who had been unable to obtain farmland.[37] Dube was no revolutionary, and neither was his school system, nor ultimately were most of his students. Employing the rhetoric of "self help" and political accommodation, Ohlange sought to uplift blacks into a stable, conservative middle class.

Dube's personal political activism encouraged Ohlange and even Adams staff members and students to support conservative civil rights measures. "All staff members of any of these institutions, whether African or white, were keenly aware of all developments in the political field," Reuling recalls. Dube and Adams graduates made frequent political visits. "There were active discussions of political movements on an inter-racial basis" among Adams faculty, and student had "an increasing awareness" of the Nationalist party's efforts to deprive black people of their remaining civil and political rights. The curriculum of liberal arts training at both institutions added to such interest. Students discussed political theory and issues in history and government classes; quite often, students made "some very vehement comments in school debates. . . . I also remember a feeling of relief that we were twenty miles from the city of Durban and no government officials around," Reuling states. The students "were proud of the African National Congress, and frustrated at the things it couldn't do." Although Ohlange, Adams, and Inanda officially discouraged outright political organizations, many "students after leaving did become politically active," Reuling states. "It is one of my joys and one of my sorrows that many of my former students did pay rather heavy prices in trials and imprisonment for being politically active."[38]

The legacy of Ohlange was a bittersweet mixture of accommodation and hope. Dube's school functioned for several decades as the only example of an autonomous, black-directed educational institution. Its continued existence depended upon a rather fragile entente between South African businessmen and planters, white liberals and ministers, and the Kholwa elite of Natal. To survive the swiftly changing political climate which followed the South African War and the granting of the Union government in 1910, Dube relied heavily upon his American Committee for financial support and upon the rhetoric of accommodation. Unlike his counterpart in the American South, Dube would ultimately learn that there was a cruel price to pay for the power he so rapidly obtained. His Kholwa intellectuals who had graduated from Ohlange, and he himself, would be forced into compromising positions from which they could not escape. The Kholwas' increasing successes as an educated, critically self-conscious class did not allow them to fully understand the violent and rapidly changed characteristics of white South African society.

This essay is adapted from chapter five of my doctoral dissertation, "African Nationalist: The Life of John L. Dube" (University of Maryland, 1976). An early article that I wrote on Ohlange Institute was published in *Negro History Bulletin* 37 (June-July 1974): 258–61. Much of the research in this chapter comes from the archives of the Anti-Slavery and Aborigines Protection Society, Rhodes House, Oxford University, England.

NOTES

1. C. A. Wheelwright to Howard Pim, March 17, 1922, enclosed in Pim to John Harris, March 20, 1922, container G 191, Anti-Slavery and Aborigines Protection Society, Rhodes House, Oxford University, England. Further correspondence from the Anti-Slavery and Aborigines Protection Society will be designated by box number and initial AAPS.

2. Pim to Harris, January 31, 1922, AAPS, G 191. Dube had been corresponding with Harris as early as 1914 in connection with the 1913 Natives' Land Act. Pim, a white paternalist and political liberal, was a close associate of both Travers Buxton (secretary of the Anti-Slavery and Aborigines Protection Society) and John H. Harris.

3. Pim to Harris, December 17, 1923, AAPS, G 191.

4. Mrs. Rheinallt Jones to Harris, March 10, 1928, AAPS, G 192.

5. John L. Dube, *The Zulu's Appeal for Light* (London, 1914), pp. 4, 13.

6. Ibid., pp. 2, 16.

7. John Reuling, former Natal missionary/educator, written interview with the author, October 23, 1973.

8. Letter, Gideon Mdode Sivetye to author, December 13, 1973.

9. Nellie Wells, to the Anti-Slavery and Aborigines Protection Society, April 20, 1925, AAPS, G 193.

10. Travers Buxton to Pim, May 19, 1925, AAPS, G 191.

11. Pim to Harris, January 24, 1922, AAPS, G 191.

12. Dube, *The Zulu's Appeal for Light*, p. 3.

13. Pim to Harris, January 31, 1922, AAPS, G 191.

14. Pim to Harris, December 5, 1922, AAPS, G 191.

15. Ibid.

16. John L. Dube, *The Zulu's Appeal for Light and England's Duty* (Durban, Natal, 1910). Copy in the Missionary Research Library, Union Theological Seminary, New York; Dube, *The Zulu's Appeal for Light*.

17. *Prospectus: Ohlange Institute* (Phoenix, Natal, 1929), pp. 2–5.

18. Ibid., pp. 3–4.

19. Ibid.

20. Ibid., p. 5.

21. An American teacher at Inanda Seminary, Inanda, Natal, to author, July 30, 1973. The teacher has requested to be anonymous. Letter, John Reuling to author, August 30, 1973.

22. Reuling, taped interview with author, October 23, 1973.

23. D. G. S. M'timkulu, "Ohlange Institute," *Native Teachers' Journal* (Natal) 29, no. 2 (January 1950): 22–23. Copy in Government Archives, Department of Education, Pietermaritzburg, Natal, South Africa.

24. Ibid., p. 23; Reuling interview, October 23, 1973.

25. Letter, John Reuling to author, July 26, 1973; letter, Reuling to author, August 30, 1973.

26. Ibid.

27. Ibid.; Reuling interview, October 23, 1973.

28. Clipping from *New York Herald,* March 1, 1899, Booker T. Washington

Scrapbook, 1898–99, Tuskegee Institute Archives, Tuskegee Institute, Alabama.

29. Letter, Reuling to author, October 23, 1973.

30. Ibid.

31. William C. Wilcox, "A Tuskegee Institute in Africa: The Zulu Christian Industrial School in Natal," *Missionary Review of the World* 26 (March 1903): 213–17; Wilcox, "Dube's Industrial School," *Missionary Review of the World* 25 (July 1902): 556. Copies are located at the Library of Congress, Washington, D.C.

32. *Prospectus*, p. 4.

33. Letter, Inanda teacher to author, July 30, 1973.

34. Letter, Inanda teacher to author, July 6, 1973.

35. Letter, Reuling to author, August 30, 1973.

36. Ibid.

37. Letter, Inanda teacher to author, July 30, 1973.

38. Reuling interview, October 23, 1973; John L. Dube, *A Familiar Talk upon My Native Land and Things Found There* (Rochester, New York, 1891).

PART III

Comparative Perspectives on Colonial Education

CHAPTER 6

A History of Colonial Education for Africans in Malawi

BRIDGLAL PACHAI

The major influence on African education during the colonial period was the European Christian missions. The colonial administration had an effect on African education that was not intended, and African Christians, traditional leaders, civil servants, and politicians also had some influence. Of these, the European Christian influence was the most pervasive and had the greatest impact, even though it was often divided, acrimonious, and competitive. The colonial administration was overly concerned with maintaining law and order and, within this framework, the promotion of British commerical interests. African education ranked low in priority. It was left to African initiatives to agitate for more and better schools, and through successful performance and persistent demands, to finally overcome considerable odds. The foundations were thus laid for a quality and quantity of education which remained unsurpassed in central Africa in the colonial period.

Certain features of the colonial history of Nyasaland (1891–1964)* had an important bearing on the quality, patterns, and priorities of education in that period. Colonial rule was preceded by sixteen years of solid pioneering work by permanent Scottish missions in the country (1875–1891), followed by permanent missions of the Anglican church (1885), the Dutch Reformed church (1889), the Zambezi Industrial Mission (1892) and the Catholic church (1901), among the leading Christian missions with headquarters in the West. These missions and churches ranked as the first and most durable external Western influence in education. The next tier of influence rested with the colonial administration, not for what it offered or attempted in education but for its neglect of African education for most of the colonial period. The third influence on education was the tremendous interest shown in Western education by large numbers of the indigenous population, both as products of Western Christian education and as progenitors of indigenous initiatives, often in the face of considerable odds.

These three factors constitute a useful framework for a discussion of education in Nyasaland in the colonial period. Together they point to three main conclusions: (1) for its limited size (about 45,000 square miles) and land area (36,000 square miles), Nyasaland led the way in the quality and quantity of Western education during most of the colonial period in many parts of east and central Africa; (2) educated Nyasas (as the migrant population was popularly referred to) worked in near and distant countries in greater numbers than representatives from any other country in east, central, and southern Africa based on population; (3) African education initiatives through independent churches, private schools, voluntary associations, and the Nyasaland African Congress (and its successor the Malawi Congress party) made a powerful contribution to the growth and calibre of education in the colonial era. When a 1924 Phelps-Stokes report, commenting on the products of Nyasaland education, stated, "other Colonies they are serving, but their own people they cannot serve,"[1] it was alluding to the overall colonial features which placed Nyasaland as the most neglected of all the British colonies in Africa.[2]

WESTERN CHRISTIAN INFLUENCE
AND AFRICAN EDUCATION

For the first sixteen years in the colonial history of Nyasaland (1891–1907), the entire cost of education was borne by the Christian missions and churches, which were all under European control. There was no uniform program in the nature of an educational code until 1905, and even when one existed the Anglican church, through the Universities' Mission to Central Africa (UMCA), refused to subscribe to it. The

* Named Malawi since July 6, 1964.

UMCA preferred to emphasize Bible training rather than the conventional reading, writing, and arithmetic which formed the basis of education for the other missions, with varying other emphases.

> It is the policy of the Mission [UMCA] to use the school as auxiliary to the Church. The teachers are evangelists first and teachers after. Supervision and itineration, which are fully carried out, are more religious than for educational purposes.[3]

This preference for their own program left the Anglicans free to develop their own scheme of education. In the early years of the colonial period, this was based on evangelism. But in later years, especially with the other Protestant missions emphasizing formal school education, the UMCA changed its position to one of educating "African children for their future vocation in life," which included training in printing, carpentry, masonry, and laundry and agricultural work. The training applied to and included African teachers, interpreters, and civil servants. This program in the later colonial period was outstanding in the work of St. Michael's College, which prepared teachers for schools and candidates for the priesthood. St. Michael's College (which was located in different places from 1899) was not a coeducational institution. Women had to wait until 1945, when St. Agnes Teachers' Training College was opened. In the intervening period, the UMCA paid greater attention to women's education, through funding, for example, than did any other mission in Nyasaland. The supply of teachers for girls' schools was met by a small number of qualified European women teachers and a large number of unqualified African women trainee-teachers.[4]

The rest of the Protestant missions and churches in the country joined in search of a common program and, since the early years of the twentieth century, have been designated the Federated Missions. The members of this body[5] are remembered more for their individual contributions than for their collective efforts. Four of them deserve special consideration: the Livingstonia Mission, the Blantyre Mission, the Dutch Reformed Church Mission, and the Zambezi Industrial Mission.[6]

There were three broad categories of schools in most of these missions: (1) the vernacular or village schools catering roughly for the first two-to-three years of education and ending at the elementary or substandard level; (2) the Anglo-vernacular or middle schools located at the central mission stations and catering for standards 1–3; (3) the English schools at the main mission stations for the remainder of primary school education or standards 4–6, leading to concurrent or subsequent training in theology, commerce, teaching, bookkeeping, and medical assistant courses. To graduate at the senior level of the scale took up to ten years of schooling. In a few cases, a standard extra 6 was available in the Scottish missions. This was roughly equivalent "to the 10th grade in the contemporary American school system, although some subjects taught would be regarded as rather esoteric by the average high school sophomore of today."[7]

The Livingstonia Mission moved in stages to three parts of the country from south to north, finally setting up headquarters at Bandawe in 1881 and Khondowe (also referred to as Overtoun Institution of Livingstonia) in 1894. From these places, its educational growth was phenomenal given the fact that the country was often troubled by internal and slave wars as well as the general state of hostility which greeted the entry of colonial rule. Nyasaland was virtually in a state of war until the end of 1896.[8] But by then the Livingstonia Mission had 85 schools under its control with a school population of 11,510.[9]

Blantyre Mission fared less well. Its early history was the subject of much internal and external conflict, with the result that education started slowly. By 1897, there were 14 outstation schools (village schools) run from mission headquarters in Blantyre and 8 from the substation at Domasi some forty miles away. Unlike the operational grounds of Livingstonia Mission in the remote and sparsely populated parts of the country, Blantyre Mission operated in the Shire Highlands in the heart of the best agricultural lands for tea, coffee, cotton, tobacco, maize, and fruit of various kinds. Here the struggle for land was keen, and the opportunities for employment were more favorable than in any other part of the country. Prior to the setting up of colonial rule in 1891, and in the decades following it, this mission spread its work and influence in the Shire Highlands and beyond, into Portuguese territory in 1913 and into Tanganyikan territory in 1920. By then it had control over some 50 central village schools and 304 village schools, catering for almost 15,000 pupils, while Livingstonia Mission controlled a total of 848 schools with 45,000 pupils. Blantyre Mission employed 547 African schoolteachers and Livingstonia Mission employed 1,700.

Clearly, the scope of educational work of these two Scottish missions was unsurpassed throughout the colonial period. The educational objectives of the Livingstonia Mission could be summarized in the words of Donald Fraser, head of London Mission station (which opened in 1902 and which ranked second only to the Overtoun Institution):

> The Mission has always had a recognized national position, as through it the tribal life was led out of war into peaceable settlement; the schools have the backing of chiefs and are recognized as tribal possessions.
> The people asked for schools not because of thirst for education or evangelization, but because education increased the market value of a labourer and the presence of a teacher in a group of villagers made intercourse with the Government or with European travellers more easy and confident.[10]

The practical and utilitarian uses of education predominated for most of the colonial period. Until the post-1945 period, when, first, greater African participation in government was sought by the educated elite and, later, the call was sounded for self-government, most of those educated by Western Christian missions remained loyal to the establishment and, without always being conscious of it, served to promote the cause of the establishment as collaborators or accommodationists.

The educational objectives of the Blantyre Mission were summed up by Alexander Hetherwick, who had served the mission from 1883, in a statement to the Phelps-Stokes Committee in 1924:

> We have supplied this growing civilized community (i.e. the European settlers of Nyasaland) with trained artisans, clerks, educated native overseers of plantations, etc., who are taking no small part in the development of their country.

> We have saved the country from requiring to introduce Indian or Chinese skilled labour and in its place have trained our own Natives to do the work.[11]

The Scottish missions aimed at producing educated Africans for jobs in the government and private sectors as well as for the schools and churches controlled by the missions, but Nyasaland was too poor, too small, and too neglected to absorb the results with gainful employment. As a consequence, Nyasaland's best talents had to be exported.

Two other missions chose to handle this issue in different ways. The Dutch Reformed church directed its energies towards rural development (to keep the people in their villages rather than on settler plantations or in the towns of Nyasaland or the mines of Southern and Northern Rhodesia, the Belgian Congo, and South Africa). The Zambezi Industrial Mission emphasized African entrepreneurship as a first step towards the early assumption of African control of the country.

The Dutch Reformed Church Mission (DRCM) began its work in Nyasaland in 1889, two years before the advent of colonial rule. Like the UMCA, which preceded it by five years, the DRCM said evangelism was the main purpose of its work. There were certain obstacles, best stated in the words of a Malawian headmaster who served as principal for five years (1964–1969) at the William Murray Teacher Training College:

> The main purpose of starting mission work was evangelism. But the missionaries soon realized that education and medical work should also be introduced. Illiteracy was a handicap to the people who were to be converted to Christianity because they could not read the Bible or any religious literature for themselves. Therefore, Rev. T. C. B. Vlok opened a school at Mvera so that young as well as old men should be taught how to read and write. However, it was not easy to find many children in those early days because some parents did not have faith in the missionaries. They feared that their children might be sold as slaves, or

that they would lose their tribal customs, because the missionaries were against some of them. Therefore the attendance of those enrolled was very poor. Later a boarding house was built in order to keep children away from home interference and discouragement. It is out of the boarders that the first teachers were produced.[12]

In many ways, this statement is part of the general scenario of British colonial Africa. Even so, the DRCM was on the receiving end of a great measure of distrust, especially for its interference with age-old Chewa customs, its refusal to encourage the teaching of English, and its glorification of village industries at a time when Western education, coupled with a working knowledge of English, were factors which helped in the vertical mobility of the African population.

The emphasis on the village as the unit for development contributed to the rise of a network of village schools. From 1904 to 1914, an average of 111 such schools were started annually. At the end of that period, there were 66,700 children in attendance served by 1,400 teachers and teacher-evangelists, most of whom were Africans.

A necessary corollary to the establishment of village schools was the development of village industries (wood and iron work, bark cloth, wool, and linen weaving, basket and net making, boot, sandal, and harness making, hide tanning, making of soaps and oils, bricks and tiles) and village agriculture, and the creation of model Christian villages.

For the total success of the mission program, room was found for the training of Christian wives and mothers:

> In 1895 the first boarding school for girls was started. By 1910 there were 300 girls in these boarding schools. The prime object was to provide the church leaders with Christian wives who would spread the Gospel and improve the standard of living in the villages. To this end they were taught house craft, such as washing, ironing, cooking, making starch, soap and candles, as well as things they were traditionally taught, such as clay pot making.[13]

No mission and education program stood more for the upward mobility of the Nyasaland African than the Zambezi Industrial Mission, through its enigmatic and seemingly eccentric spokesman for African advancement, Joseph Booth.

From his arrival in Nyasaland in 1892, Booth advocated programs which were far in advance of the times, culminating in his assertion of "Africa for the Africans." He called for African partnership in agricultural and commercial business. In his African Christian Union schedule of 1897, he outlined the objectives of the union. Of the 21 clauses, clauses 12 and 13 explained the main thrust of his educational objectives:

12. To engage qualified persons to train and teach African learners any department of Commercial, Engineering, Nautical, professional or other necessary knowledge.

13. To mould and guide the labor of Africa's millions into channels that shall develop the vast God-given wealth of Africa for the uplifting and commonwealth of the people, rather than for the aggrandisement of a few already rich persons.[14]

Joseph Booth contributed towards educational developments in Nyasaland more through the influence of his teachings and his philosophies on his proteges than through his mission or schools. John Chilembwe, Elliot Kamwana, and Charles Domingo, African teachers and preachers in the early years of the twentieth century, were particularly active and vocal disciples of Booth, and became representatives of African initiatives dealt with later. They were the torchbearers of the Boothian slogan "Africa for the Africans" long before the decolonization of Africa reached the drawing boards of European chanceries.

Though the literature on Catholic churches and schools in Nyasaland does not stand comparison with Protestant counterparts, some recent publications and scholarship have gone a long way towards redressing the imbalance.[15]

The White Fathers arrived in Nyasaland in 1889, but with the establishment of a British protectorate in Nyasaland in 1891 they left for Northern Rhodesia. The first school, opened in 1890, did succeed in attracting an average attendance of 32 pupils per day in the first year.[16] The mission established by the White Fathers reopened in 1902 and in 1924 had 191 schools and a school population of 9,000 pupils. While the White Fathers limited their activities to the Central Province, the Montfort Marist Fathers started educational and church work in the Southern Province in 1901. By 1924, their operations included 10 mission schools, 32 outstation schools, and 380 village schools. The main objective in the early Catholic schools was evangelism. Of the total number of 579 Catholic schools throughout Nyasaland in 1924 with an enrollment of some 27,000 pupils, only two were comparable to the Overtoun Institution of Livingstonia Mission (1894), the Henry Henderson Institute of Blantyre Mission (1909), St. Michael's College of the UMCA (1912), and the William Murray College of the DRCM at Nkhoma (1912). These—the Mua Seminary at Dedza and the Nankunda Seminary in Zomba—provided education to likely candidates for the priesthood. At the same time, there were two Catholic training colleges for teachers, at Likuni in the central province and Nguludi in the southern province. Many years later, women teachers were encouraged and trained (Mulanje, 1934, and Bembeke, 1937), and for the first time attendance of girls at the Catholic primary schools was boosted.[17]

The official report of the Nyasaland government for 1930 expressed strong criticism at the proliferation of Catholic schools in a single district (42 out of a total of 101 mission schools), while not a single graded (i.e., qualified) teacher was posted:

> The Marist Fathers have schools scattered all over the district. This Mission undoubtedly exists chiefly with the object of spreading its own particular Gospel and education is of secondary importance. They have so many schools that their teachers are usually of a low standard and there is no doubt that most of these schools are started simply with the idea of converting the children of a village to the Roman Catholic faith regardless of what education can be given them, and also with the idea of keeping schools of other denominations out. . . .[18]

This accelerated growth of Catholic schools began in the post-1904 period. In 1904, the Protestant Missionary Federation (Federated Missions of Nyasaland) institutionalized the Protestant program for church and school, leaving the Catholic White Fathers in the central province and the Montfort Marist Fathers in the southern province to fend for themselves. They did so with such vigor and commitment that conflict became inevitable: "The proliferation of Catholic schools . . . sparked off a Protestant-Catholic confrontation of epic proportions."[19]

Allowing for the Protestant piety and bias of the Nyasaland administration, there was a measure of real substance in the complaint regarding standards and church and mission rivalries in a country with a long tradition of competing Christian missions. In one important instance, the cooperative spirit was developed. Five education conferences were held between 1900 and 1926.[20] This led to a raising of standards, a reduction in rivalries and in the direct involvement of the Nyasaland government in education.

The first of these conferences, attended by representatives of the Blantyre Mission, Livingstonia Mission, Zambezi Industrial Mission, Nyasa Industrial Mission, the South African General Mission, the Dutch Reformed Church Mission, and the Seventh-Day Adventist Mission, was held at Livingstonia in 1900 as part of that mission's twenty-fifth anniversary. It was agreed to convene again in Blantyre in 1904 for consultation and planning. At the second conference, an education code was drawn up and an education board was created. In May 1905, the board adopted a revised code, which laid the basis for the uniform program for its members until the creation of the Nyasaland Department of Education in 1926. The Education Code of 1905 provided for education at every stage from the primary village school to the Central African College and University, embracing syllabuses, textbooks, teacher training, curricula, inspection, and examinations.

In effect, these developments represented a statement of objectives which, hopefully, might be realized some time in the future as the combined resources gained strength and experience. For the present, there were real difficulties: competing missions could only cooperate to a limited degree; funds were short; a consultative machinery was lacking; government support was absent. In 1907, when the Nyasaland government was approached for support, the educational realities presented a very bleak picture in spite of the work of the different churches and missions since colonial rule was introduced in 1891:

> Education in the villages suffers very much from a dearth of good
> teachers. We have at present no adequate machinery for turning out a
> supply, and we can never have till the concentration scheme is taken up
> practically as well as theoretically. What can be done by an institution in
> the way of training teachers if it is staffed by one man who is
> schoolmaster, boarding master and ordinary class teacher all in one? A
> man cannot run a boarding school of about 250 pupils, many of whom
> are big men, supervise the work of 40 village schools, do regular
> evangelistic work, edit a paper and have much time left for the training
> of teachers.[21]

Yet responsibilities and challenges of this kind were common in the experience of Western Christian missions and churches in Nyasaland in the period 1891-1907. The Nyasaland government's involvement, beginning in 1907, did not mean the end of these responsibilities and challenges but only an easing of the harsher burdens as a central machinery was set in place to coordinate education, though not to take over the task of providing for it. The taking over of education had to await the eve of independence. Christian missions continued to dominate African education throughout the colonial period.

THE ROLE OF THE NYASALAND COLONIAL ADMINISTRATION

The British—under pressure from Scottish missionaries, who feared Portuguese influenc—reluctantly established a protectorate in Nyasaland on a shoestring budget. Both the reluctance and the stringency combined to create the conditions which led the Phelps-Stokes Committee of 1924 and the Ormsby-Gore Commission of 1925 to severely criticize the colonial administration, the former for neglecting education and the latter for allowing an exploitative and inhumane situation to develop on the European settler estates of Nyasaland.[22] The 1924 report blamed the British government for allowing Nyasaland to become its poorest African territory by failing to provide the necessary railway link to the coast. Yet this link between Lake Nyasa and the Indian Ocean at Beira was completed in 1935 without contributing to the economic development of the country, which in turn would have resulted in improved education. A recent study of the impact of railway construction on the country, coupled with recent studies on land issues, lead to the incontrovertible conclusion that both railway and land policies impoverished the country in the colonial period. Leroy Vail summarizes:

> First, the imperial government's decision to rely upon a small and undercapitalized white settler community on the Shire Highlands resulted in the treating of the African peasant community as little more than a source of labour for these settlers, accompanied by neglect of the possibility of establishing an African peasant cash-crop economy. Secondly, decisions to construct the railway that serviced Nyasaland were taken in such a way as to prevent a shift from reliance upon African peasant agriculture when the error of the first decision was fully realized in the 1920's. The railway development, which was not initially conceived of as benefiting Nyasaland, in the 1920's and 1930's functioned as an impoverishing factor that prevented the Protectorate's government from establishing a viable internal economy and ultimately forced her to pursue a policy of encouraging labour migration to the mines.[23]

As a result of the administration's lack of a positive economic policy to develop the country's potential and raise the living standard of its indigenous inhabitants, the male working population saw little opportunity for gainful employment in Nyasaland outside of the Shire Highlands. Even here, working and living conditions were hard. The result, according to G. Coleman's study, was that around 1910 about 10 percent of the male adult population was working outside the country, and the figure rose to approximately 20 percent a decade later. In the next half century, the proportion ranged between 20 percent and 25 percent. "In certain localities the level of male absence reached 75 percent and even on a District-wide level may have exceeded 60 percent."[24]

This situation pointed to a lack of Nyasaland government policy to develop natural and human resources. Education, therefore, did not feature in the administration's priorities, which included maintaining law and order, suppressing slave trade, subjugating indigenous leadership, preserving British imperial interests, and promoting British economic interests at home and abroad.

In 1924, Governor Bowring of Nyasaland, responding to the criticisms of the Phelps-Stokes Education Commission, advanced two reasons for the Nyasaland government's "neglect of native education" since 1891: lack of finance occupied first place followed by the absence of a local education code regulating and structuring the education system.[25]

Between 1905 and 1907, the Federated Missions drew and revised an education code, set up a federated board and a consultative committee and applied to the government for financial assistance. In 1908, the first government grant-in-aid for education was paid; the £1,000 was a tiny fraction of the cost to the missions. For ten years the annual grant remained unchanged, until it was doubled in 1918.[26]

The administration's paltry grant continued until the public indictment by the Phelps-Stokes Education Commission report of 1924 drew attention to the obvious and glaring inadequacies. The grant of £2,000 was shared by eleven missions providing education for 140,000 children, while African taxpayers contributed £277,000 to the country's coffers. The African taxpayers were not receiving even 1 percent of their contribution for the education of their children. The report called for greater financial support from government; the immediate appointment of a director of education, followed by a department of education, with a staff of examiners and supervisors; and the establishment of an advisory board of native education comprising government officials, European settlers, and European missionaries—only later were African members to be elected.[27]

The appointment of the first director of education was announced in November 1925, almost thirty-five years after the introduction of colonial rule. An education conference was held in 1927 and the structure of the Education Department was accepted as follows: director of education, assistant director of education, superintendent of technical training, superintendent of agricultural training, European clerk, and two African clerks.

The membership of the Advisory Board of Native Education followed the hierarchy of administrative control; there were no African members appointed though mission-educated Africans were by then serving in clerical and teaching positions inside and outside the country. The first African member of the Advisory Board, Levi Zililo Mumba, an early product of Livingstonia Mission who later became the founding president of the Nyasaland African Congress, was appointed in 1933. In 1937, he was joined by Charles Matinga, later to become the second president of the African Congress, himself an early product of Blantyre Mission.[28] The Advisory Board had asked for an African representative as early as 1927. Even when a new education ordinance was passed in 1930 and the membership of the Advisory Board, now called the Governor's Advisory Council on Education, was increased from thirteen to fifteen, there was no mention of an African representative.[29]

The Nyasaland government now assumed control over education without increasing its own financial contribution beyond a token amount. The UMCA, through the bishop of Nyasaland, found good grounds to air strong criticism of government hypocrisy in this matter:

> The main criticism of the present scheme . . . is that the Government is taking a very complete control of Education and, on paper at any rate,

dictating terms and limitations of the most drastic character while still taking it for granted that the Missions will continue to pay for the greater part of the cost. I doubt whether this has been done to the same extent before in any part of the world. Where the Government controls to anything like this extent, the Government pays. Here the familiar proverb is indeed upside down: the Government is to call the tune, but the Missions are to pay the Piper.[30]

The criticism hurt, especially when it was joined by J. H. Oldham, the influential Secretary of the International Missionary Council, who said that Africans should be represented on all boards and described the grant of £4,500 annually by government for education as far too inadequate.[31]

Despite the criticisms and the shortcomings, the Nyasaland government, saddled with an enormous railway debt, remained in the red for the rest of its life. Education for its African population received fitful infusions of support only when other government priorities and concerns were threatened. For example, the refusal of some 15,000 children of the Yao ethnic group of Muslim faith to attend Christian mission schools prompted the government to open a school for them in Liwonde, some thirty miles from Zomba, in 1928. The only other school which was financed completely by government funds until the 1940s was a police school in Zomba. In both instances, the need to promote its law and order imperatives dictated the moves.[32]

In the instance of the setting up of the Jeanes Training Center at Domasi, near Zomba, in 1928, the government was influenced by the fact that the Carnegie Corporation of New York guaranteed a grant of $5,000 for a five-year period to be matched in equal amount by the government. The center was to provide a two-year course to train selected mission teachers and their wives in rural development. The teachers would then serve as supervisors in the mission primary schools, while their wives would complement the work by promoting village upliftment through better sanitation and domestic care. Soon traditional chiefs and their wives were included in the training. Again, the investment by government was seen to be a wise and necessary one in that the chiefs would function more effectively as agents of government change and become useful instruments of "indirect" rule. By 1937, seventy-five teachers, sixty wives, and nineteen traditional chiefs passed through the doors of the Jeanes Training Center.[33] In the same year, Sir Robert Bell arrived in Nyasaland to report on the financial state of the country.

In his report, Sir Robert called for the introduction of secondary education as "a pressing requirement." Better-educated Africans, he argued, would contribute to administrative and economic developments, since even routine administrative duties were carried out by

Europeans recruited from overseas. This was an expensive procedure. He found that the less expensive services of Indians were not being utilized in the Nyasaland civil service as in the east African territories. The official policy, he noted, was that Indians were being kept out to encourage the employment of Africans. "But little effect has been given to this policy for the reason that the foundation for it in the form of a good general education for the African has not yet been laid."[34]

At the time of this investigation and report, African nationalists as well as European missionaries had reached the same conclusion: African higher education was long overdue. Indeed, the Catholic missions of Southern Rhodesia, Northern Rhodesia, and Nyasaland decided before this to build a Catholic secondary school in Zomba. This prompted the Federated Protestant Missions to follow suit. At this stage, the Nyasaland government interceded to stipulate that the proposed secondary schools would come under government control if funded even in part by the government. The missions protested this decision. Government control, they argued, would mean greater expenditure and less freedom for religious instruction. The government relented and proposed a grant of £7,000 to the Catholic and Protestant missions to build one junior secondary school each. The result was the Blantyre Secondary School (Protestant), which opened in 1941, and the Zomba Secondary School (Catholic), which opened in 1942.[35]

The Dedza Secondary School, the first nondenominational secondary school fully financed by the government, came ten years later, in 1952, sixty-one years after the introduction of colonial rule and only twelve years before the end of colonial rule. Even then, it was another six years before the first senior secondary classes (or Higher School Certificate courses leading to university admission) were introduced at Dedza in 1958.[36] Before this facility was available, students from Nyasaland were compelled to complete their preuniversity schooling outside the country.

The real accelerated growth in school education in colonial Nyasaland took place during the years 1961 to 1964 in the period immediately prior to independence, when an African majority government assumed office. In August 1961, the Malawi Congress party won a sweeping victory in the general elections; a month later the first Ministry of Education was created and the first African minister of education assumed office. The tremendous developments in the succeeding years included the introduction of a new administrative system in 1962 known as the Local Education Authority, which could be said to have vested educational responsibility in the district councils and thus virtually at the grass roots, where ordinary people were encouraged to develop the school system. The climax in the educational developments was the opening of the University of Malawi, with its three constituent colleges, in 1965, one year after the colonial era was over—although the legacy of the colonial period lingered for over a decade as the new government sought to remedy and rectify omissions. For Nyasaland, as for most of British colonial Africa, education for Africans was seriously neglected in the colonial period.[37] Government policy placed education low in the priorities. Colonies were still conceived of as appendages to the mother country and there was no hurry to provide Western education through the school system to enable the local inhabitants to assume the necessary leadership roles leading to self-advancement and self-determination.

AFRICAN INITIATIVES IN EDUCATION IN NYASALAND

In spite of official indifference to African advancement in the colonial period, neither African individuals, ethnic groups, nor secular and religious organizations were passive observers on the colonial scene. Just as Yao and Ngoni communities, for example, resisted the political inroads of colonialism for many decades, and the Tonga reached accommodation on many points dictated by local circumstances, so too did individuals and organizations look to Western education to help them move into the cash economy and industrial society as competitive and concerned agents of African aspirations. T. O. Ranger's succinct comments on African responses hold true for the story of African education:

> Africans were not completely helpless, however, during the early
> colonial period in East and Central Africa. They could not avoid the
> imposition of colonial rule, but they were not simply objects or victims
> of processes set in motion outside Africa and sustained by white
> initiative.[38]

A sampling of African initiatives in education may be gleaned from studies of the work of independent or separatist churches, the contribution of the accommodationists who remained in the conventional churches, the work of private African schools, the achievements and influence of men of the Nyasaland diaspora, the educational concerns of secular organizations, and, finally, the lobby of the Nyasaland African Congress and its successor, the Malawi Congress party.

Independent or separatist churches had a number of common features: they were African-inspired, African-led, and African-oriented; they all pursued a vigorous policy of school and church education, often extending considerable effort to approach the performance of the better-financed and older European-led institutions. In this competition, they fell short in both quantity and quality. John Chilembwe's Providence Industrial Mission (PIM), for example, had the advantage of any early start (1900), but this was counterbalanced by the schools and churches of the Montfort Marist Fathers and the

Church of Scotland Mission, which surrounded the PIM. The tendency on the part of government officials as well as European plantation owners to support European-controlled institutions contributed to the lack of relative success of the African institutions. The tragic heroism of John Chilembwe grappling on many fronts illustrates why it was impossible for such a leader to become a successful educator in the narrow sense of formal school education.[39]

But outside the ruthless field of economic competition so prevalent in the plantation economy of the Shire Highlands, independent African churches did better. Charles Domingo's Seventh-Day Baptist church (SDB) claimed that in 1911 some 8,067 children attended schools at all centers of his churches in the Mzimba district of northern Nyasaland.[40] Domingo's educational leadership in the north extended beyond the schools to such issues as the right of his adherents to choose their sabbath day and the racism of white leadership. He convened the Dwambazi Conference in 1911 to resolve these issues. Domingo realized what education could do to emancipate the minds and bodies of Africans. His statement at the conference in 1911 drew attention to the emancipated role ahead for educated Africans:

> White fellows have been here for thirty-six years, and not one of them
> sees a native as his Brother, but as his boy tho' a native is somehow
> wiser than he in managing God's work. Had these poor Europeans (tho'
> rich in Body) taught a native to use his means and faculties properly
> the counted ape would have risen up 33 years ago, and whole
> Responsibility would have been given into the hands of natives. . . .[41]

Charles Domingo was one of the first qualified teachers of Livingstonia Mission and certainly the first African to complete theological training at that mission and be licensed to practice as an evangelist. He left the mission in 1907 through frustration over the delay in his ordination to the priesthood. A generation later, other educated Africans left Livingstonia Mission to begin separate and independent churches and schools. Notable among them were two leading personalities in church and school education in northern Nyasaland, Rev. Charles Chinula and Rev. Yesaya Zerenji Mwasa. In 1933, Mwasa established an independent mission called "The Blackman's Church of God," whose educational wing was known as "The Nyasaland Blackman's Educational Society." The scheme submitted by Mwasa to promote education was deemed too ambitious and was rejected by his fellow district inhabitants and the government. There was little doubt that it was the hand of government that really destroyed the scheme. As an indicator of African initiatives in the colonial period, the document, appearing as an appendix, deserves close analysis.

Charles Chinula was more successful. His Sazu Home Mission in Mzimba district survived from 1934 for the rest of the colonial period.

His schools, though operating under poor conditions, provided education for hundreds of children for over thirty years. His position as
adviser to the M'Mbelwa Administrative Council for most of this period
was of immense value to his stature as an educator, since this council, an
important experiment in African local government, itself pursued a
progressive education policy.[42]

Chinula and Mwasa went beyond their separate institutions, and
with a fellow northerner (also a one-time ordained minister of
Livingstonia Mission), Rev. Yafet Mkandawire, formed the "Mpingo
Wa Afipa Wa Africa" or "The Church of the Black People of Africa,"
which obtained permission to open schools in northern Nyasaland.
The government gave very limited support to these schools and in
mid-1940 cut off funds largely because it could not tolerate the criticism
of Rev. Mwasa "that the Education Department is depriving him of his
rights as a leader of the community."[43]

Two other church leaders in Nyasaland deserve mention as
educators who, in their own right, through their independent schools,
earned the respect of their countrymen as well as of the government.
Rev. Hanock Msokera Phiri was the founder of the African Methodist
Episcopal Church in Nyasaland in 1924. Rev. Daniel Sharpe Malekebu
inherited the mantle of Chilembwe's Providence Industrial Mission in
1926.

Rev. Phiri opened his first school in 1925, eight months before the
first Nyasaland education department was started. Two years later,
when invited to attend the first native education conference convened
by the government, he had two schools operating, staffed by four
teachers. A detailed contemporary report indicates that these schools
were modest buildings and his own house served as a boarding house.[44]
What passed for equipment was pathetically little. But the fact that Rev.
Phiri faced these odds, overcame many of them, and inspired many to
greater heights, stands to his credit:

> ... Reverend Phiri provided an object example as the spiritual leader
> of an African-administered church with a membership in Nyasaland
> in the thousands, and as the organizer of a viable school system with
> an enrolment of several hundred children. This was no mean
> accomplishment . . . .[45]

Malekebu's role in education in Nyasaland began at about the same
time as the setting up of the Nyasaland Department of Education. His
first thrust at the PIM was in education rather than in medicine (a field
in which he was qualified) or in evangelism. He trained teachers from
neighboring missions. Attendance at his schools (80 percent) was better
than the countrywide average for 1926–1927 of 68 percent. Yet the
subsidy paid by government was a pittance (only £6 out of a total

expenditure of £541 in 1928, for example), a proportion far less than that paid to European-controlled mission schools at the time.[46]

If Phiri and Malekebu are examples of pioneers who founded private schools, there were other representatives of African initiative who were neither separatists nor independents. Serving the conventional missions and churches, they were, nonetheless, in the forefront as successful scholars, dedicated teachers, and inspiring leaders. Rev. Harry Kambwiri Matecheta, Rev. Stephen Kundecha, and Rev. Jonathan Douglas Sangaya, all products of Blantyre Mission, served with distinction as teachers in Blantyre, Zomba, and Ntcheu. Some of their counterparts in northern Nyasaland have already been discussed. Lay persons, too, Levi Mumba and James Frederick Sangala, for example, contributed actively to promoting African education as teachers, associationists, members of the African Advisory Committee on Education, civil servants, and presidents of the Nyasaland African Congress. Their biographies have yet to be written, though their varied contributions appear in scattered articles and books. Most of them were also members of native associations in Nyasaland, first formed in 1912, and later of the Nyasaland African Congress and its successor.[47]

Their individual performances were the best form of inspiration for their contemporaries and colleagues. Levi Mumba, for example, never relaxed his private and public pleas for more and better schools and higher grade education. As a founder of the first native association in Nyasaland in 1912, as the first African member of the Advisory Committee on Education in 1933, and as the first president of the Nyasaland African Congress, in 1943–1944, he used all these platforms to pursue his agitation for improved educational facilities for blacks in Nyasaland. Mumba called for the opening of government schools to counterbalance the slow pace and conservative orientation of mission schools. He proposed a program for the projected government schools in 1933 (yet the first true government school was only opened in 1952) which epitomizes the concern that Nyasaland Africans had for education:

> ... in other colonies much progress has taken place educationally ...
> already Africans are running their own private business on a large
> scale ... on account of this prosperity they have high schools both for
> literary and technical education. ... We ask for similiar facilities. ...
> Raise our social status and in so doing you will arouse the dormant
> resources of supply and demand in the different tribes. ... The main
> reason for importing skilled labour from Europe or India is that
> Africans have not the necessary education and experience to carry out
> such duties efficiently be it in the government, railways or commerce.

He concluded his memorandum of 1933 with a commonsense practical plea. Yet the plea was ignored for some twenty years:

Educate for the employer, educate for service with tribal communities, but *most of all educate the masses to stand on their own feet.* Give us this chance and I can assure you that within a period of comparatively few years the response of the Nyasaland African will be surprisingly great [emphasis added].[48]

While government delayed, rejecting such appeals, individual Africans continued to make the best use of European mission education and prepare themselves to seek employment in neighboring and not so neighboring countries. These educated individuals constituted the Nyasaland diaspora; together they earned a reputation away from home as reliable and educated clerks, teachers, priests, and trade union leaders. Soon their reputation spread to the land of their birth and inspired contemporary and succeeding generations to emulate their examples.

Among the men of the diaspora were Ernest Alexander Muwamba, a qualified teacher, who joined the Northern Rhodesia civil service in 1914 and returned home after thirty years to pursue a political career. His cousin, Clements Kadalie, the founder of the Industrial and Commercial Workers' Union, earned renown for his trade union activities in South Africa. Hanock Msokera Phiri's educational work in Nyasaland from 1924 was mentioned earlier. Before 1924, Phiri and his famous nephew, Kamuzu Banda, later the first prime minister of Malawi and later still first president, worked in various places in Rhodesia and South Africa. While Hanock Phiri returned to Nyasaland in 1924, Kamuzu Banda proceeded to the United States on the long educational journey which led to his earning a bachelor's degree from the University of Chicago and a medical degree from Meharry Medical College, Nashville, Tennessee, preparatory to further medical qualifications in Scotland.[49]

Whatever else the diaspora earned within and outside the country, African initiatives in education gained a useful ally in 1945 in Dr. H. Kamuzu Banda, now located in London as a medical practitioner and serving as overseas representative of the Nyasaland African Congress. Dr. Banda's close contact with the Africa Bureau of the Fabian Society provided him with a lobby never before available to African politicians and educators in Nyasaland. The African Congress took maximum advantage of it: in 1945 it called for a royal commission to inquire into African education; in 1946 it collected funds to send a delegation to Britain to make direct representations on this point. In June 1948, the delegation was in London. Two issues—African representation in government and educational improvements—constituted the main demands of the delegation. On the latter, the delegation made the following case:

Government should exercise a more effective control over the Mission schools; teacher training should be improved by the establishment of a Government training college; a Government secondary school combining both scholastic and vocational training should be established to provide education up to matriculation standard. Finally Congress objected to the Nyasaland Government's action in setting up a school for Euro-Africans, especially because, according to the view of Congress, this tended to create division within the African community between Euro-Africans and Indo-Africans.[50]

The persistence of African initiatives in Nyasaland was a factor in causing the first Nyasaland members to be appointed to the Legislative Council in 1949. This in turn resulted in a vote soon afterwards to authorize funds to construct the first government school, Dedza Secondary School, which opened in 1952.

CONCLUSION

Three factors provide useful insights into the patterns and progress of education for Africans in Nyasaland. The most important is Western Christian missions, both Protestant and Catholic, followed by the erstwhile efforts by Africans themselves, in spite of financial handicaps. The British colonial administration made the least important positive contribution. It placed African education low in its priorities and virtually abdicated its responsibilities to the Christian missions to do what they could to provide and promote African education.

Africans were quick to see the tremendous possibilities for advancement inherent in education; they applied themselves seriously and diligently to acquire the best education available. They went on to contribute to their country through initiative and making the most of their opportunities.

NOTES

1. The Phelps-Stokes report, *Education in East Africa*, ch. 7, 1924.
2. Ibid.
3. Ibid.
4. Monica Kishindo, "A Survey of Likoma Island from Early Times to 1935," History Seminar Paper, Chancellor College, University of Malawi, 1969–1970. On the matter of girls' education, the Phelps-Stokes report stated:

> The Universities' Mission has been more successful in attracting girls to school than any other mission in the Protectorate. This is partly due to the unusual control which the Mission has over the Native people on Likoma Island through its ownership of all the land. It is also explained by very capable women teachers. At Likoma, the schools had 1,000 girls in attendance, with two European teachers and over 25 untrained Native assistants.

Likoma Island was the headquarters of the UMCA for most of the colonial period. Today the headquarters is at Malosa, about six miles from Zomba.

See also Rev. Philip Elston, "A Note on the Universities' Mission to Central Africa: 1859–1914" in *The Early History of Malawi*, edited by B. Pachai (London: Longman, 1972), pp. 344–64.

5. United Free Church of Scotland (Livingstonia Mission), Church of Scotland Mission (Blantyre Mission), Dutch Reformed Church Mission, South African General Mission, Seventh-Day Adventist Mission, Zambezi Industrial Mission, Nyasaland Industrial Mission, and Baptist Industrial Mission.

6. Two doctoral dissertations deal with the first two, while a third deals with the educational activities of all of them: K. J. McCracken, "Livingstonia Mission and the Evolution of Malawi, 1875–1939" (Cambridge University, 1967); A. C. Ross, "The Origins and Development of the Church of Scotland Mission, Blantyre, Nyasaland, 1875–1926" (University of Edinburgh, 1968); R. J. MacDonald, "A History of African Education in Nyasaland, 1875–1945" (University of Edinburgh, 1969).

More general surveys are found in B. Pachai, *Malawi: History of the Nation* (London: Longman, 1973), ch. 2; and J. L. Pretorius, "The Story of School Education in Malawi, 1875–1941," in *Malawi: Past and Present*, edited by B. Pachai, G. W. Smith, and R. K. Tangri (Blantyre: Christian Literature Association in Malawi, 1971); and B. Pachai, "Mission Education, 1876–1945" in *Malawi in Maps*, edited by Swanzie Agnew and Michael Stubbs (New York: Africana, 1972) p. 52.

7. Roderick J. MacDonald, "Hanock Msokera Phiri and the Establishment in Nyasaland of the African Methodist Episcopal Church," *African Historical Studies* 3, no. 1 (1970): 78.

8. The disorder in the country resulting from slave raids, the Anglo-Portuguese imperial rivalry, Harry Johnston's belligerence, and the Yao, Arab, and Ngoni hostility towards the new colonial power are treated adequately in A. J. Hanna, *The Beginnings of Nyasaland and North-Eastern Rhodesia* (London: Oxford University Press, 1956); and Eric Stokes "Malawi Political Systems and the Introduction of Colonial Rule, 1891–1896," in *The Zambesian Past*, edited by

Eric Stokes and Richard Brown (Manchester: Manchester University Press, 1965), pp. 352–75.

9. *Aurora* 1, no. 1 (1897): 10.

10. K. J. McCracken, "Religion and Politics in Northern Ngoniland 1881–1904," in *The Early History of Malawi*, edited by B. Pachai, p. 236. According to John McCracken, "Livingstonia possessed 61 percent of all schools in Malawi in 1904–5, 31 percent in 1910, 16 percent in 1924 and 10.18 percent in 1934," a position of clear overall lead in that period.

11. The Phelps-Stokes report, ch. 7, "The United Free Church of Scotland Mission."

12. J. H. L. Honde, "The Formation of the Dutch Reformed Church Mission in Malawi—With Special Reference to William Murray Teacher Training College, Nkhoma (1889 to 1969)" mimeographed (Blantyre, 1969).

13. Report of the Third General Missionary Conference, Mvera, 1910, pp. 42–54, quoted in J. L. Pretorius, "An Introduction to the History of the Dutch Reformed Church Missions in Malawi 1889–1914," in *The Early History of Malawi*, edited by B. Pachai, p. 373. See also p. 372.

14. Joseph Booth, *Africa for the African*, 1897, pp. 49–51, photocopies supplied by Dr. Harry Langworthy, great grandson of Emily Booth Langworthy, daughter of Joseph Booth. Emily came to Nyasaland with her father in 1892 and later wrote the book *This Africa Was Mine*.

15. Notably the works of Rev. Matthew Schoffeleers and Ian Linden, such as J. M. Schoffeleers, "M'bona the Guardian Spirit of the Mang'anja" (B. Litt. thesis, Oxford University, 1966), and "Symbolic and Social Aspects of Spirit Workshop among the Mang'anja," (Ph.D. dissertation, Oxford University, 1968); Ian Linden, *Catholics, Peasants and Chewa Resistance in Nyasaland* (London: Heinemann, 1974).

16. Pretorius, "The Story of School Education," in *Malawi*, edited by Pachai, Smith, and Tangri, p. 71.

17. Historical survey by the Catholic Secretariat, Limbe, Malawi, 1961 (mimeographed sheets).

18. NSC 2/1/3, Report on Chikwawa district for year ending December 30, 1930, National Archives, Zomba.

19. Ian Linden, *Catholics, Peasants and Chewa Resistance in Nyasaland*, p. 146. A table of comparative growth illustrates the position:

Mission	Increase in Schools 1910–1915 (%)	European Staff Increase (%)	Staff-Student Ratio
Dutch Reformed church	150	nil	1:2,249
Catholic White Fathers	154	21	1:416
Catholic Montfort Marist Fathers	393	83	1:449

Table is from Governor Smith to Colonial office, November 27, 1916, SI 1494/19 National Archives, Zomba.

20. Roderick James MacDonald, "History of African Education in Nyasaland, 1875–1945" (Ph.D. Dissertation, University of Edinburgh, 1969), ch. 2, pp. 96–106, traces the first three conferences.

21. Pretorius, "The Story of School Education," in *Malawi*, edited by Pachai, Smith, and Tangri, p. 73.

22. Land issues in Nyasaland and Malawi are dealt with in a forthcoming publication by the author entitled *Land and Politics in Malawi c. 1875–1975* (Kingston, Ont.: Limestone Press).

23. Leroy Vail, "Railway Development and Colonial Underdevelopment: The Nyasaland Case," in *The Roots of Rural Poverty in Central and Southern Africa*, edited by Robin Palmer and Neil Parsons (Berkeley and Los Angeles: University of California Press, 1977), p. 365.

24. G. Coleman, "Some Implications of International Labour Migration from Malawi," *East African Geographical Review*, no. 13 (April 1974): 87.

25. J. C. Bowring to the Secretary of State, June 11, 1924, CO 879/121, Public Record Office, London.

26. *Annual Report* by director of education, CO 626/7, Public Records Office.

27. Native Education Conference, CO 879/21 and S1/342/27, National Archives, Zomba.

28. *Annual Report*, CO 626/7, and Pretorius, "The Story of School Education," pp. 77–78.

29. Minutes of Advisory Committee, S1/1054 A/26, National Archives, Zomba.

30. Letter from Bishop Cathrew Fisher, S2/2/28, National Archives, Zomba.

31. S1/666/28. National Archives, Zomba.

32. *Annual Report*, CO 626/7.

33. Ibid. and Pretorius, "The Story of School Education," p. 77.

34. Report of the commission appointed to inquire into the financial position and further development of Nyasaland, Colonial no. 152, 1938, p. 272.

35. CO 525/174/44070/3, 1938.

36. B. Pachai, "University Education in Malawi," *Africa Quarterly* 6, no. 4 (1967): 343–51.

37. Howard D. Chimzimu, "Development of Education in Malawi, 1875–1967," History Seminar Paper, Chancellor College, University of Malawi, 1968–1969.

38. T. O. Ranger, "African Reactions to the Imposition of Colonial Rule in East and Central Africa," in *Colonialism in Africa, 1870–1960*, edited by L. H. Gann and Peter Duignan, (Cambridge: At the University Press, 1969), vol. 1, p. 293.

39. George Shepperson and Thomas Price, *Independent African: John Chilembwe and the Origins, Setting and Significance of the Nyasaland Native Rising of 1915* (Edinburgh: Edinburgh University Press, 1959).

40. *The African Sabbath Recorder*, Langworthy Papers, no. 1, 1911, University of Zambia.

41. Ibid., April 9, 1911, Dwambazi Conference.

42. B. Pachai, "African Initiatives in the Local Administration in Colonial Malawi: The Case of M'Mbelwa African Administrative Council of Mzimba District," in *From Nyasaland to Malawi: Studies in Colonial History*, edited by Roderick J. MacDonald (Nairobi: East African Publishing House, 1975), pp. 189–214.

43. National Archives, Zomba, Misc 12/10 cited in R. J. MacDonald "Some Malawian Educational Initiatives, 1899–1939," typescript, p. 23.

44. Roderick J. MacDonald, "Hanock Msokera Phiri and the African Methodist Episcopal Church," pp. 81–84.

45. Ibid., p. 87.

46. Roderick J. MacDonald, "Rev. Dr. Daniel Sharpe Malekebu and the Re-opening of the Providence Industrial Mission, 1926–39: An Appreciation," in *From Nyasaland to Malawi*, edited by MacDonald, p. 225.

47. Jaap Van Velsen, "Some Early Pressure Groups in Malawi," in *The Zambesian Past*, edited by Stokes and Brown; Roger Tangri, "Inter-War Native Associations and the Formation of the Nyasaland African Congress," *Transafrican Journal of History* 1, no. 1 (1971), pp. 84–102.

48. MacDonald, "Some Malawian Educational Initiatives," p. 18.

49. B. Pachai, "The Malawi Diaspora and Elements of Clements Kadalie," Central Africa Historical Association, Local Series no. 24 (Salisbury: Department of History, University College of Rhodesia, 1969).

50. B. Pachai, "History of the Congress Movement in Malawi," ch. 1 of typescript submitted for publication in a volume called *The Malawi Congress Party*.

CHAPTER 7

Colonial Education and African Resistance in Namibia

CHRISTOPHER A. LEU

For Namibians, colonial education has to be placed in the context of the apartheid philosophy and policy of the Republic of South Africa. Thus, education for whites and blacks is administered separately, students are physically separated by race, and blacks are further separated by ethnically defined "nations." Depending on such "nationality," there are inter alia differences in curricula, teacher training, and salary scales, teacher-student ratios, amounts spent per student on education, attendance rates, and in laws and among administering authorities. This chapter explores how and why the current educational system developed from the time of its missionary origins in Namibia; it examines the role and political significance of the churches and points out the emergence of political consciousness among the Ovambo contract laborers whose extensive involvement in the foreign-dominated political economy led to various forms of resistance and the emergence of modern nationalist activities transcending ethnic identities. The shortcomings of colonial education, the role of the churches, the migrant (contract) labor system, and African resistance per se, together with mounting international pressures, have combined to prevent the total implementation of the South African policy of apartheid.

Education in Namibia (formerly South-West Africa) has conspicuously failed to provide opportunities for development and liberation from past deficiencies. Namibia's educational system reflects the *apartheid* philosophy and policy of the occupying power, the Republic of South Africa. In 1954, H. F. Verwoerd, then minister of native affairs and foremost architect of a separate and hence inferior system of education for the African, argued:

Equip him to meet the demands which the economic life of South
Africa will impose upon him. . . . There is no place for the native in the
European society above the level of certain forms of labor. . . . For that

reason it is of no avail for him to receive a training which has as its aim absorption in the European community. . . . Until now he has been subject to a school system which drew him away from his own community and misled him by showing him the green pastures of European society in which he is not allowed to graze.[1]

The imposition of the apartheid educational system on Namibia had two outstanding results: it assisted the occupying South Africans in their policy of fragmenting the African opposition into different so-called population groups, which was part of the openly expressed policy of "bantustanization," according to which each "bantustan" was supposed to be the homeland of a separate "nationality"; it had the effect of keeping the African population educationally inferior to the whites and thus, in the view of white South Africans, less qualified to assert their right to freedom and independence.

To the African, the aim of such an educational system is to entrench the domination of the oppressive and illegal South African regime. In the words of Sam Nujoma, president of the Namibian liberation movement, the South-West African People's Organization (SWAPO), " . . . Bantu education is simply brain-washing the African to believe that he's inferior to the White—to prepare him for a life of laboring for the white 'baas.' Many students, including myself, left school and took up correspondence studies instead."[2]

This chapter will deal with the development of the contemporary educational system from the time of its missionary origins in Namibia, the role and political significance of the churches, and the emergence of political consciousness among the contract laborers, whose extensive involvement in the growing political economy led to various forms of resistance and the emergence of modern nationalist activity.

What ties these three issue areas together is the general notion of "political education." Political education has generally been viewed as a generic concept subsuming at least two different processes: (1) "political indoctrination" in a specific ideology intended to rationalize a particular regime and make it legitimate; and (2) "civic training" in the nature and functioning of one's own polity and in how a good citizen participates in it.[3]

In Namibia, education for Africans definitely includes "political indoctrination" in the apartheid ideology of the dominant ruling elite. It excludes any notion of "civic training" in the sense of encouraging black Namibians to participate in their own political system. The shortcomings of colonial education, colored by the racist ideology and policy of separate development, have contributed significantly to the emergence of political awareness transcending ethnic identities. Colonial education and apartheid have triggered political resistance and armed struggle in Namibia.

Any thoughtful analysis of the emergence of African nationalism and armed resistance in Namibia must consider three interrelated issues: the overall impact of the biased education imparted by the local colonial administration; the role of the churches in providing an "alternative" and "more enlightened" model of missionary education; and the particular influence of the migrant (contract) labor system in enhancing African perceptions of inequality and exploitation. Their combined weight has been the catalyst for radical nationalist politics aimed at overthrowing colonialism and replacing it with a system that caters to the interests of the people of Namibia.

MISSION AND APARTHEID SCHOOLS

In Namibia, the first agents of literacy and education in the modern sense were missionaries. The Wesleyan Missionary Society, beginning in 1805, was the first to work in the southern region of the country among the Nama, Damara, and Herero. By 1842, the Lutheran Rhenish Mission extended its work throughout almost the whole of the area known now as the Police Zone. Christianity and modern education were not introduced into the northern region until 1870, by the Finnish Mission among the Ovambo, and into Okavango until 1910, when a Catholic mission started work there. Academic education was considered important for the main task of the missions, spreading the Gospel; literacy was seen as being equally significant and necessary if converts were to read the Bible and other evangelical literature. Thus, the missionaries themselves came to be the first teachers, selecting and training subsequently the best of their pupils to assist them in this task.

Very few mission schools were established prior to the annexation of Walvis Bay by Great Britain in 1878 and the advent of German rule over the whole territory in 1884. With the introduction of formal German colonization, more missionary societies started schools—particularly the Catholic church—among the Nama and Herero peoples, in 1888 and 1896, respectively.

During this early period, there was no central control of mission schools by the parent churches or the colonial administration. Each mission determined its own curriculum guided mainly by the requirements of its church or society. The vastness of the territory and its scattered population as well as intermittent conflict among the Herero and Nama limited progress in missionary educational endeavor. Nevertheless, by the end of the period of German rule, only 115 mission schools with a total enrollment of 5,490 students provided a rudimentary education, one intended mainly to assist evangelization.

The period between the inception of the Mandate for South-West Africa by the League of Nations in 1920 (under which South Africa as the mandatory power pledged to "promote to the upmost the material and moral well-being and the social progress of the inhabitants of the territory")[4] and 1960 saw both the initial expansion and the subsequent decline of missionary schooling. From the beginning of that period, mission schools retained self-control but remained subsidized by the South African state. In 1923, on the basis of a conference between state authorities and missionary societies relative to nonwhite education, educational services were expanded. Established missions increased their educational activities, while new ones such as the Seventh-Day Adventist church entered the field. Colleges for training teachers were established at the Augustineum near Okahandja by the Rhenish Mission, at Debra near Windhoek by the Catholic church, and at Onipa in Ovamboland by the Finnish Mission. The new state-enforced educational requirement enacted in 1926 split the existing mission schools into two types—those for coloreds and those for blacks,[5] foreshadowing the more rigorous application of apartheid policy requirements subsequently enacted in the 1960s.

After the assumption of power by the Afrikaner Nationalist party in 1948, the whole question of black education was reexamined in the 1950s. In 1958, the Van Zyl Commission made recommendations which were adopted by the South African government and which reinforced the determination to use education as an instrument for promoting apartheid in Namibia. Among the more important changes introduced by the new system were the replacement of missionary schools by "community schools," with the assumption that these schools would encourage the active participation of African parents; the introduction of a separate section for administering African education to be established in the South-West African Department of Education; the use of the vernacular language as the basic medium of instruction among the various ethnic groups; and the adoption of the syllabus devised by the South African Department of Bantu Education for African teacher training.[6]

These recommendations justifiably met with much opposition within the territory. All schools required registration, and it was illegal for anyone to establish, conduct, or maintain a Bantu school without registration. This obviously struck most severely at the mission schools, for registration was solely at the discretion of the minister of education. While many of the primary schools run by the missions in remote areas were either overcrowded, inadequately subsidized, or had underqualified teachers and hence rated poorly overall, there were other examples of some fine and famous schools and institutions, such as the respected and long-established Augustineum College for Africans in Windhoek. The Augustineum College had previously attracted students from all over Namibia, but this was no longer tolerated following the introduction of the policy of "separate development." That institution was finally taken over by the Department of Coloured Affairs in 1976, and those students in residence were sent to racially exclusive schools in their respective "homelands."[7]

Thus, beginning in 1960, mission schools which had since the 1920s provided at least a reasonably independent and high standard of education and produced many African leaders were converted precipitously to "community schools." While there were 211 mission schools in 1922, there were only 101 in 1966, and by 1972 that figure had been reduced to 36.[8]

With respect to the establishment of "community schools," the official emphasis was on the participation by African parents in the management of schools for their children. However, the primary objectives of such participation were to extract greater financial contributions from the African community for the costs of education and to undermine mission schools.[9] Moreover, two of the many serious criticisms by Africans of the system as it now functions are the complaints of parents and students of nepotism on the part of those identified as "puppet chiefs," particularly in Ovamboland, and the Department of Education's blacklisting of political suspects. There also is strong feeling that appointments should not be subject to departmental approval. But above all, Africans are reminded that their participation in the system gives them only administrative powers—not control of policy. The minister of education retains very wide powers to make regulations governing the control of schools, conditions of service of teachers, syllabuses, media of instruction, school funds, and so on. With the advent of quasi-self-government for some "Bantu homelands," such as Ovamboland, this has begun to change in recent years, but at the cost of an inferior education.

The South African government's dictum, extended to Namibia, that "the education of the White child prepares him for life in a dominant society, and the education of the Black child for a subordinate society"[10] is nowhere more clearly seen than in the policy of teaching African children in their mother tongue. This is required until the end of primary school, standard 7 (grade 8), and the upper level for such instruction is constantly being raised.[11] The two official languages, English and Afrikaans, are taught as subjects of instruction in the early years, after which one language—usually Afrikaans, the language of domination—becomes the language of instruction. Students taught in the vernacular in primary school are expected to complete their secondary education using Afrikaans, and to take the same matriculation examination set for white students, who start school a year earlier and are taught in Afrikaans or German from the age of six.[12] Consequently, instruction in the mother tongue is at the expense of competence in the two official languages, in which secondary and advanced education examinations are given.

In contradistinction to international educational practice, which tends to favor mother-tongue instruction for progressive reasons, the South African government has sought to impose it on the African people both at home and in Namibia as a means of inculcating "ethnic group" consciousness, perpetuating such divisions, and reinforcing the gulf between white and black. Moreover, very few Africans are taught any kind of lingua franca used in government, in industry or commerce, or in financial or professional circles because the vast majority of the African school pupils drop out of school by the time they reach standard 3 (grade 5). Therefore it is not surprising that a survey of Namibian refugees in Zambia who had attended school in the territory showed that few were able to function adequately in English without extensive remedial work.[13]

Recent figures place the problem of functional illiteracy in its proper context; they show that only 2,664 or 1.92 percent of the 138,890 blacks enrolled in 1973 were in the upper five grades, including teacher and vocational training.[14] As of March 1974, 31.3 percent of all African students enrolled in Namibia were in substandard A (grade 1) and 18.5 percent in substandard B (grade 2); thereafter the percentage of children in each grade dropped steadily, leaving only 2.1 percent in the upper five standards or secondary grades (forms 1-5); finally, those in the final year constituted only 0.06 percent of the total enrollment.[15] Thus, the attrition rate is enormous, particularly at the lower grades.

Although education is nominally free for all African students in Namibia, it is not, however, compulsory. Quite often, children drop out of school even before finishing the first year either because they are needed to help at home, or because the stipulated "contribution" cannot be afforded, or there may be political reasons involved. Leaving school for political reasons is quite clearly related to what is implicit in the laws on education and administration but never explicitly stated. That is, the main goal of the educational system is to train the vast majority of blacks for menial labor and servitude to white needs and desires, rather than for genuine education or self-development. Thus, it is not surprising that the curriculum for black students introduced in the 1950s and 1960s by the local administration remains almost identical with that devised for blacks in South Africa. This curriculum emphasizes crafts and manual training at the expense of academic subjects. Consequently, there is intense competition to get into the mission schools precisely because the students want to study subjects which will equip them to function in a modern commercial and academic world. Attraction to mission schools which offer instruction in the English language is an attempt to escape the impact of apartheid-oriented miseducation. It is therefore no surprise that the authorities have been very much opposed to the one and only existing English secondary school for Africans in Namibia, St. Mary's Anglican School at Odebo in Ovamboland, which they threatened to close in 1974.[16]

There are only seven other schools in the whole territory where secondary education can be obtained. These are called "centralized, comprehensive boarding schools," offering, among other vocations, teacher training for blacks.[17] The only agricultural school is in Ovamboland; in 1974, it had only eighteen students.[18] With the exception of the Augustineum College, which is still open to all races, each school is limited to students from the "nation" where it is located.

As one can expect, there have been numerous cases of these schools being disrupted by student strikes followed generally by mass expulsions for purely political reasons, or even for petty offenses such as "intimidation." These disruptions are obviously "a result of dissatisfaction both with the conditions and education of the schools, as well as a symptom of political unrest."[19] For example, in August 1973 alone, nearly three thousand school children went on strike.[20] The problem of the secondary school student is compounded by the fact that even after having completed all the requirements for a high school diploma there is for most no choice of jobs, and high school graduates then have to join the contract labor system.

Since there are no institutions for postsecondary education in Namibia itself, only a few of the qualified black students can go on to black universities or teacher training or technical training institutions in the Republic of South Africa. In 1966, five students pursued university studies in South Africa; in 1974, this figure had risen to only thirty-three students; the majority (seventeen) were at Fort Hare, thirteen at the University of the North, and three at the University of Zululand. Of these, twelve were enrolled in the arts faculties, five in law (compared to the relatively large number of lawyers trained elsewhere in Africa during the colonial period), four in the social sciences, and twelve in the physical sciences.[21] For these few students, there will be available scarcely any leadership opportunities when they return to Namibia. Those in the legal profession are acutely aware, for example, that they are forbidden by law to practice law on their own; they can only serve as clerks in the offices of white lawyers.

The above indicators tend to diminish the importance attached to statistics by the local government, figures which tend to bear little, if any, relationship to the education of the African population. While such figures indicate that the number of African children and young adults (many start school long after the normal age of seven) enrolled in school increased 267.4 percent between 1960 and 1973, from 37,801 to 138,890,[22] they do not, however, reveal the low quality of their education. Similarly, during the same period the number of teachers increased by 223.3 percent, from 1,068 to 3,453; but this too conceals the same fact. More important, however, are the obvious discrepancies in the relationship between student intake and the availability of trained instructors. Consequently, either the enrollment figures are highly inflated or they point to the already very high student-teacher ratio, which rose from 35.4 to 1 to 40.2 to 1 during that period. In Ovamboland, the ratio is 50 to 1[23] and the general trend of a widening student-teacher ratio for blacks suggests that the disparities in the rest of the territory will continue to widen for as long as the colonial system survives. It should also be noted that the number of schools increased between 1960 and 1973 from 257 to only 592.[24] Moreover, during the same period, the African population increased by approximately 110 percent.[25] Assuming an African population of 900,000 in 1973, only 15.4 percent of the black population was enrolled in schools, compared with 23.2 percent of all whites.

These figures on education for Africans must be compared with the favored status enjoyed by the dominant white minority. Examining the same period, 1960 to 1973, we find that in 1960 there were 63 schools of all types for whites, with 666 teachers and 16,257 pupils. By 1973, these figures had increased to 85 schools, 1,232 teachers, and 23,185 pupils. The 1960 student-teacher ratio of 24.4 to 1 had by 1973 declined to 18.8 to 1.[26] Clearly, these figures have a direct bearing upon the fact that while education for blacks is free but voluntary, for whites it is compulsory.

There is no doubt that the government has spent considerable amounts of money on primary schools for Africans. In 1973–1974, for example, the government spent R75.75, or $110, on each African student in Namibia, over half of which (R50) apparently represented the cost of books, stationery, and hostel accommodation, while the remainder covered teachers' salaries, school buildings, equipment, and administration.[27] But given the attrition rate, and with the overwhelming majority (at least 75 percent) of students leaving school in the first three years, prior to becoming fully literate (even in their mother tongue), much of the increase in African students attending primary school is vitiated. As a result, 69 percent of Africans in Namibia are estimated to be illiterate.[28] This deplorable waste obviously makes little sense from the point of view of an educational system aimed at those social and cultural goals taken for granted elsewhere. In Namibia, as in South Africa, education for blacks is subordinated to the overriding demands of apartheid and racial domination; the result of apartheid education is a waste of both talent and resources, and above all, that educational system is largely responsible for sowing the seeds of resistance and ultimately revolution. It was, after all, the South African government-appointed Eiselen Commission which pointed out in 1951 that "a Bantu child who does not complete at least standard II has benefitted so little that the money spent on his education is virtually lost."[29]

For whites in Namibia, education is not only free, as it nominally is for blacks, but also compulsory until the age of sixteen or until attainment of the Junior Certificate, or standard 8 (grade 10). Comparing the expenditure on Africans with that spent per white child in South Africa in 1973–1974 shows that there existed a range of R387 (or $542) in the Transvaal to R557 (or $780) in Natal.[30] Muriel Horrell has pointed out that the amount spent on education for whites in Namibia falls somewhere in or near this range, which is four to seven times the amount spent on black students.[31]

The level of black education is unlikely to rise until the appallingly low standard of education of teachers themselves is raised *and* the educational system itself becomes more acceptable to African students. As late as 1970, the majority of teachers, 1,187 (62 percent), were only educated to the standard 6 (grade 8) level, while 687 (36 percent) had no matriculation or professional qualifications; 27 teachers (1.4 percent) were qualified with matriculation or equivalent, and only 6 (0.3 percent) had university degrees.[32]

The low educational level of African teachers reflects not only the general inadequacies of African education but also the poor facilities for training African teachers. Moreover, poor salaries are a major factor in discouraging African graduates and matriculants from entering the teaching profession. In 1973, the majority of African teachers were on a salary scale of $99–221 per month for men and $79–185 per month for women.[33] These teachers averaged in earnings only 46 percent of salaries paid to whites with equivalent qualifications holding similar posts.[34] This situation is congruent with the requirements of the policy of apartheid, which Verwoerd made clear in 1954:

> The salaries which European teachers enjoy are in no way fit or permissible criterion for the salaries of Bantu teachers. The European teacher is in the service of the European community and his salary is determined in comparison with the income of the average parent whose children he teaches. . . . In precisely the same way the Bantu teacher serves the Bantu community and his salary must be fixed accordingly.[35]

The educational conditions of the sort described previously, when combined with the wider frustrations and indignities of life under apartheid, give rise to much dissatisfaction in the African schools. Occasionally this erupts into riots, strikes, and other militant outbursts, although less frequently, perhaps, than might be expected—a fact

which must be related to the severe competition for places in the
schools and the deprivations and penalties facing those bold enough to
rebel. Yet these disturbances occur frequently enough and are of sufficient political significance to indicate a pattern: in Namibia an enormous demand for education by Africans coexists with a widespread
rejection of the education provided by the government. Colin O'Brien
Winter, an Anglican bishop who lived in Namibia for a long time
recounts typical student rebellion, unrest, and reaction in the years just
prior to his deportation by the South African government in March
1972 for his opposition to apartheid:

> The black student body in Namibia was rapidly becoming the mouth
> piece which articulated growing black unrest and dissatisfaction. The
> white administration had the choice of entering into dialogue to resolve
> their problems, or crushing them by making an example of their
> leaders and treating them as troublemakers. It chose the latter course.
> Students were carefully watched in Namibia, paid informers abounded
> in their midst, and the state moved in with speed to smash any
> opposition before it got a grip on the black community at large. It was
> not unknown for an entire school to be closed and the greater part of
> the black students expelled for what was termed "political agitation." At
> one period, it was estimated at least 1,000 black students had been
> forcibly removed from school with all chances of furthering their
> education blocked to them. Sometimes the state would agree to have
> them back on the condition that they submitted to a flogging.[36]

Such patterns of political unrest reflect an outright rejection of
apartheid education; it also seems reasonable to assume that neither
the press, the government, nor individual accounts adequately reveal
the suppressed tensions which smolder beneath the surface in African
schools. It also can be seen that much of the unrest and political
resistance focuses immediately on the blacks in charge, whether they be
boarding school masters, school principals, or teachers. Such administrators and instructors often exercise tyranny in the schools as the price
they must themselves pay in return for rewards, status, and job security.[37] But they themselves are mere pawns to be manipulated, and
those who control them—when their hired authorities cannot cope—
are ultimately responsible for the ensuing conflict between frustrated
black youth and the colonial state, represented by draconic laws which
are implemented by the vicious triad of the police, the courts, and the
prisons.

LEGITIMIZING OPPOSITION: THE ROLE
OF THE CHURCHES

After 1884, the early missionaries were confronted almost overnight
with a dual responsibility: on the one hand, they sought to "civilize" the
African peoples they came into contact with, and on the other, they
acted as spiritual shepherds or pastors to the growing white German

garrison composed of an oligarchy of expatriate soldiers, farmers, and businessmen. Some of the pioneer missionaries who could not cope with the demands of this dual task returned to Germany.[38] Soon the German community demanded its own exclusive pastor, particularly since the building of a church was a basic priority and also because church-building required an enormous amount of energy on the part of the early ministers of the German community. Thus, gradually the ministerial and missionary activities of the German-based churches drifted organizationally and politically apart on both sides of the strict dividing line between white and black. This state of limbo remained and was not recognized officially until 1960, when the various congregations of the German community joined forces and became an exclusively separate church, the German Evangelical Lutheran Church (DELK); at the same time, the black converts of the early missionaries and their descendants got their "own" church, the Evangelical Lutheran Church of SWA (Rhenish Mission Church, ELK). The latter had become, in 1957, constitutionally independent.[39] Thus, the South-West African Lutheran Church, although developing along a different path, attained the same end result as the South African Dutch Reformed Church: a church clearly and cleanly divided along racial lines.[40]

While these ecclesiastical conflicts took place in the southern part of the territory, Lutherans of the Finnish Mission, at the specific request of the pioneer missionary, Hugo Hahn, started operating in Ovamboland, the more populous northern part. Due to the seemingly peaceful political climate there, their work progressed rapidly, with the result that the Evangelical Lutheran Ovambokavango Church (ELOK) attained its constitutional independence before the ELK (which had to deal with a smaller population and, initially, with warring ethnolinguistic groups).

Since its missionary origins, the ELOK has become the largest church in Namibia, claiming a membership of some 200,000 followers. It operates mainly among the largest ethnic group, the Ovambo, who constitute over 46 percent of the entire population and form a majority of the contract laborers in the national political economy, and it represents a major ecclesiastical and political force in the territory. Its present head, Bishop Leonard Auala, was by all accounts one of the main driving forces behind the open letter addressed to the prime minister of South Africa on June 30, 1971. This letter was cosigned by Pastor Paulus Gowaseb of the Evangelical Lutheran church of SWA, which is most active in the southern part of the territory and boasts a membership of approximately 110,000, primarily among the Damara, Herero, and Nama.[41] Its leadership has invariably attempted to form a solid united front against the increasing imposition of apartheid policy. This was demonstrated most clearly in its unanimous stand behind Moderator Gowaseb when he cosigned the controversial open letter to Mr. Vorster. The letter was based upon a referendum of Auala's church members and a consensus of opinion reached at a joint meeting of the boards of the ELK and the ELOK.[42]

The letter to the South African prime minister explained that (1) the overwhelming majority of Africans totally rejected apartheid because they were not a free and secure people in the land of their birth; (2) they did not have freedom of movement and expression; (3) they were afraid to express their opinions for fear of reprisals; (4) they were denied political participation and voting rights; (5) they were hindered in their development by the application of the job reservation policy;[43] and (6) the contract labor system destroyed normal family life.[44] This letter followed the advisory opinion handed down by the International Court of Justice, which, on June 21, 1971, ruled that South Africa's continued presence in Namibia was illegal and demanded the withdrawal of its colonial administration.[45] The decision—though not binding—legally stripped South Africa none-theless of its long-vaunted pretense to legitimate occupation under the original League of Nations mandate, which the United Nations had terminated in 1966. The letter also made references to South Africa's violation of the Human Rights Declaration of the United Nations.

The involvement of the churches in the political affairs of the territory was not new. Even before the Odendaal Commission report, which recommended dismemberment of the territory and was im-plemented by the South African government in the late 1960's, the ELOK and the ELK had protested, in two joint memoranda to the government in 1964 and 1967, the "homelands" program and the relocation of people against their will, stressing that Namibia should remain united.[46]

These predominantly black Lutheran churches have been work-ing hard to coordinate their opposition to apartheid policies, especially now that they are confronted with increasing official restrictions on their divine mission of serving their members with a view to providing them with spiritual and material sustenance. Moreover, the open letter to the prime minister also was the outcome of a joint meeting of leaders of the two churches. This and the subsequent meeting of Bishop Auala and Moderator Gowaseb with the prime minister and government officials on August 18, 1971, in which the oppressive measures of apartheid, including the use of torture by the police, were brought forcefully to the attention of the South African leadership,[47] further strengthened their resolve to work together.

The ELK and the ELOK have had support from other churches in their opposition to apartheid. The most outspoken and, as a result, the most controversial church during the 1970s has been the Anglican church, which irritated the South African government so much that its spiritual head, Bishop Colin Winter, was later expelled from Namibia. In one of his many references to the evils brought about by apartheid, the bishop told the Diocese of Damaraland:

> We as a [multiracial] church have committed the unpardonable crime of rejecting apartheid. All the power of the state is therefore brought against us. We can never accept this ideology of apartheid as solving any of the vast problems of this land. . . . Apartheid has been a barren and costly failure. As an Anglican bishop I reject apartheid on biblical grounds; on humanitarian grounds. . . .[48]

As a result of its forthrightness, the Anglican church today finds itself saddled with a series of restrictive measures imposed on its activities, measures which can only be interpreted as a deliberate policy of continuous and selective harrassment of the church.[49] Since the greater part of the church's missionary work is carried out among the Ovambo, the government obviously fears that the church's radical persuasion will spread among the most politically conscious and significant ethnic group in Namibia.[50]

The adverse effect of government persecution—for example, restricting the recruitment of more professionally trained teachers from outside to work in Namibia—is somewhat counteracted by the fact that, with its small white membership, the church is not financially dependent on the support of its white laity. State intervention has tended to inhibit the fulfillment of the tasks of other less well-disposed churches, as has been the case with the DELK. While the majority of white members appear to be apolitical in their attitude towards the state and towards the church in particular, the black members insist on political action and often look up to the church, expecting it to act as a mouthpiece of their frustrations. On both sides, however, there is a remarkable tolerance towards each other, both racially and politically.

The only other large multiracial church in Namibia is the Roman Catholic church, which is divided into two bodies, one with headquarters at Windhoek (approximately 100,000 members), and the other located further south at Keetmanshoop (approximately 20,000 members). The Catholic church has not suffered much from interference by the state authorities. Although it provided qualified support to the infamous open letter to Prime Minister Vorster, it deliberately and directly dissociated itself from the "political" questions raised therein. The Catholic church in Namibia, as elsewhere in Africa, has always sought to avoid confrontation with the state by divorcing its work from politics, an attitude consistent with the preferences of the state. Such hypocrisy serves the interests of both sides very well, albeit only temporarily.

This brief historical overview of the role of the churches in Namibia leads to several conclusions. The churches and the government appear poised, by the very nature of things, for a traumatic confrontation with each other. This is so mainly because apartheid is essentially and undeniably hostile to Christianity. As the domestic and international conflict over that disputed territory intensifies, it becomes more and more incumbent upon the churches to stand up in protest against the denial of political and human rights which emanates directly from official government policy. At the same time, these pressures make the government more likely to take harsh action against those it deems responsible for undermining its efforts to implement segregationist policies.

The churches' direct involvement in politics and their development of a particular style of protest are in part due to the fact that the seething discontent among educated blacks finds no legalized political channels for expression of any kind. Consequently, the preponderantly "nonwhite" churches have filled the political vacuum created by the government and have assumed an increasingly political role, a development which has been characterized by the present government as "subversion of the state under the cloak of religion."

Neither side really desires a confrontation—the churches fear further persecution and a severe curtailment of their activities; the state authorities are sensitive to unfavorable publicity in a delicate international situation, but in the long run neither can avoid it. Whether the leaders of the churches and their style of expressing dissent will moderate repression and contribute to freedom for all Namibians is questionable. For the principal function of the Christian churches has been, by and large, to sensitize their members to the possibility, indeed the necessity, of achieving political freedom for all if their divine mission is to be fulfilled. If one accepts that today every African political group—except those individuals handpicked by South Africa—vehemently insists on independence for a unitary state in Namibia that is territorially inviolable with equal rights for all its citizens, and if it is further acknowledged that these groups fully grasp the implications of apartheid policy for their daily existence, then the churches can rightly claim to have played a largely unrecognized, but immensely significant role in fostering the political education of their followers.

The Contract (Migrant) Labor System and the Emergence of Total Opposition to Apartheid

The majority of Namibians seem distinctly more in agreement politically than are their kith and kin in South Africa, and they have largely escaped bickering over means to achieve a commonly desired end (something which has bedeviled the political freedom movements of Zimbabwe). This is significantly due to the large proportion of the labor force involved in the economy. In 1971, 43,400 or nearly three-fourths of the 60,000 laborers were migrants allowed to enter white areas only if they had a contract binding them to a specific white employer.[51] No country in southern Africa other than Namibia has such a high proportion of migrant workers in its labor force; even in South Africa only about 30 percent of the workers are migrants. The proportion of migrant workers since then has continued to increase even further as more Africans have been moved out of white areas and forced to settle in the homelands. The logical end of this deliberate process has been to produce an almost exclusively migrant black labor force designed to serve the needs of the white-dominated political economy. This economy, which is central to the international dispute over the present status and the future of Namibia, has three significant features: (1) it is exclusively oriented towards narrowly based export industries; (2) it is entirely dominated by foreign capital and enterprises; and (3) it has a heavy dependence on manual labor.[52]

An almost equal number of contract workers are employed by government, industry, and the mines, while 25 percent work on white-owned farms. The largest employer of contract labor in Namibia is Tsumeb Corporation (largely American-owned), which in 1971 had 5,000 contract workers. The largest employer of such workers in the capital of Windhoek is the City Council.

Table 1. Occupation of Contract Workers—1971[53]

Government, Commerce and Industry	14,000	32%
Mining	12,800	30%
Farming	10,900	25%
Fishing	3,000	7%
Domestic Service	2,700	6%
Total	43,400	100%

The existing contract labor system originally evolved as a means of supplying the white economy with sufficient cheap labor. Contracts were introduced to provide a means of controlling the number of black people in the white areas. In modern times, this system has continued to minimize the number of Africans living in areas favored by the whites and cuts down on any outlay for black housing (other than compounds) and other social infrastructure. An additional advantage of the system from the authorities' point of view is that the rapid turnover of the unskilled black labor force makes it difficult for them to organize themselves politically. All this represents the practical application of the Stallard Commission's recommendations, made in the 1920s:

the Native should only be allowed to enter the urban areas which are essentially the White man's creation, when he is willing to enter and to minister to the needs of the White man and should depart therefrom when he ceases so to minister.[54]

The resistance mounted by African workers to their unpalatable situation, took the form of massive strikes in the early 1970s which virtually paralyzed the domestic economy. It has not been merely a rejection of inadequate wage levels and miserable working conditions but a position of total opposition to a political and social system the workers see as upholding the present labor system.[55] What has fueled their indignation and crystallized their attitude toward apartheid and all it stands for has been the sincerely held belief that

all people regardless of race or color, are created by God with the same human dignity and are equal before Him. This system undermines the God-given human dignity of the [Namibian] workers.[56]

CONCLUSION

In their effort to achieve independence and self-determination, Namibia's people have been politically educated by the missions and the apartheid school system, whatever the implications they attach to this subsequent to independence. The churches, the contract labor system, and African resistance per se, expressed mainly through various forms of armed action and occasional strikes by workers, together with mounting external international pressures, have combined to frustrate South African attempts to implement the wholesale policy of apartheid, including the physical dismemberment of Namibia into ethnically determined homelands organized along the model established for and being implemented within South Africa itself. Although it remains uncertain as to what kind of independence Namibia will finally have, it is nevertheless clear that the policy of apartheid which South Africa sought to impose in complete defiance of world opinion and the wishes of the overwhelming majority of Namibians has met with greater resistance than the South African government originally anticipated. Only time and the manner in which Namibia is decolonized will determine whether that disputed territory will emerge as a genuinely independent state or will drift towards neocolonialism, as so many other independent African states have.

NOTES

1. H. F. Verwoerd, *Bantu Education: Policy for the Immediate Future* (Pretoria: Information Service of the Department of Bantu Administration and Development, June 7, 1954), p. 7.

2. "Twenty Years of Struggle," interview recorded by Ole Gjerstad in Lusaka, Zambia, October 1975, and reproduced in *LSM News* (Oakland, California), nos. 11–12 (1976): 4.

3. See the introduction in James S. Coleman, ed., *Education and Political Development* (Princeton: Princeton University Press, 1965).

4. See Annexure B citing the terms confirming the Mandate by the Council of the League of Nations, in Republic of South Africa Department of Foreign Affairs, *South-West Africa Survey 1967* (Pretoria: Government Printer, 1967), p. 140 (hereafter cited as *SWA Survey 1967*).

5. Ibid., p. 110.

6. For an official version and general discussion of policy, objectives, and method of the commission recommendations, see *SWA Survey 1967*, pp. 110–119.

7. See Jo Morris, "The Black Workers in Namibia," in *The Role of Foreign Firms in Namibia*, by Roger Murray et al. (London: Africa Publications Trust, 1974), p. 171.

8. Calculated from *SWA Survey 1967*, p. 117, and *Bantu Education Journal* (August 1972).

9. See the comments of Elizabeth Landis in her comprehensive *Review of Laws Established in Namibia*, prepared for the Acting United Nations Commissioner for Namibia, 1972(?).

10. Monica Wilson and Leonard Thompson, *The Oxford History of South Africa*, vol. 2 (London: Oxford University Press, 1971), p. 224.

11. Republic of South Africa, Department of Foreign Affairs, *South-West Africa Survey 1974* (Pretoria: Government Printer, 1975), p. 63 (hereafter cited as *SWA Survey 1974*).

12. Ibid., p. 63. Education for blacks starts a year later than for whites, i.e., not until age seven. Instruction in German may be authorized where the language is widely used. In fact, Afrikaans and German predominate in the territory; English is less used.

13. See H. Lewis-Jones, *Report on the Survey of the Educational Situation and Needs of Namibians in Independent Countries* (Geneva: International University Exchange Fund, 1974), p. 7.

14. *SWA Survey 1974*, p. 62.

15. Extrapolated from the parliamentary statement submitted by the deputy minister of Bantu administration and education, in South African House of Assembly, *Debates*, March 14, 1975, cols. 497–98.

16. *Drum* (Johannesburg), March 8, 1974.

17. *SWA Survey 1974* p. 64.

18. South African House of Assembly, *Debates*, August 23, 1974, cols. 172–73.

19. Morris, "The Black Workers in Namibia," in *The Role of Foreign Firms in Namibia*, by Murray et al., p. 173.

20. Ibid.

21. *SWA Survey 1967*, p. 118, and *SWA Survey 1974*, p. 62.

22. Calculated from the 1960 figures in *SWA Survey 1967*, p. 120, and 1973 figures in *SWA Survey 1974*, p. 62.

23. Calculated from figures given in *South West Africa Yearbook 1972*, p. 179.

24. *SWA Survey 1967*, p. 120, and *SWA Survey 1974*, p. 62.

25. The 1960 figures of 428,575 Africans (excluding whites, coloreds, and basters) is taken from *SWA Survey 1967*, p. 24; I am assuming a figure of 900,000 Africans for 1973 based on a UN estimate of a total population of just over one million. The official South African figures for 1974 are 852,000 Africans and 99,000 whites. See *South Africa 1975 Official Yearbook* (Johannesburg: South African Department of Information), 1975.

26. The 1960 figures are from *SWA Survey 1967*, p. 119, while those for 1973 are from *SWA Survey 1974*, p. 62.

27. South African House of Assembly, *Debates*, September 20, 1974, col. 506.

28. Morris, "The Black Workers in Namibia," in *The Role of Foreign Firms in Namibia*, by Murray et al., p. 172, citing the Bureau of Literacy.

29. Quoted in South Africa SPRO-CAS Education Commission, *Report: Study Project of Christianity in Apartheid Society: Education Beyond Apartheid* (Johannesburg: SPRO-CAS, 1971), p. 30.

30. South African House of Assembly, *Debates*, September 6, 1974, cols. 359–60. See also the calculations in *Survey of Race Relations 1972* (Johannesburg: South African Institute of Race Relations, 1973), p. 344. In more recent years, official statistics have been presented in a way that makes this kind of comparison impossible.

31. Muriel Horrell, *South-West Africa* (Johannesburg: South African Institute of Race Relations, 1968), p. 73.

32. Cited by Morris, "The Black Workers in Namibia," in *The Role of Foreign Firms in Namibia*, by Murray et al., p. 170, based on calculations from South African Hansard, February 18, 1971, cols. 204–05. Education for blacks runs one year longer than for whites. An extra grade, standard 7A, is added after standard 7 (grade 9). Thus, a Junior Certificate standing requires three years of study beyond the upper primary level and matriculation two additional years. The extra year was initially added to help blacks overcome deficiencies in their early education. Now the government plans to discontinue the extra year so that upper primary school will consist of two years instead of the present four. There will be three years between the Junior Certificate and matriculation instead of two years. See *SWA Survey 1974*, p. 53, note 2.

33. Calculated on the basis of figures supplied by Morris, "The Black Workers in Namibia," in *The Role of Foreign Firms in Namibia*, by Murray, et al., p. 170.

34. See *Survey of Race Relations 1973* (Johannesburg: South African Institute of Race Relations, 1974).

35. Verwoerd, *Bantu Education*, p. 19.

36. Colin O'Brien Winter, *Namibia* (Grand Rapids, Mich.: William B. Erdmans Publishing, 1977), p. 73.

37. See the statement on the role of headmen and chiefs by the founder of the Namibian nationalist movement, Joivo Herman Ja Joivo, in ibid., p. 232.

38. These returning missionaries established a pattern later of immigrant ministers from Germany who under South African rule were allowed into the territory on temporary residence permits, ranging from six months to one year at a time "according to good behavior."

39. This account is heavily indebted to the report of W. B. de Villiers, *The Present State of the Church in South Africa*, included in IDOC (International Documentation Participation Project), "The Future of the Missionary Enterprise—Namibia Now!" no. 3, May 1973, pp. 81–90.

40. The South African Dutch Reformed church will not be discussed here for obvious reasons. This is the church most representative of Afrikaner religious thinking and forms the spiritual and moral bulwark of the theory and practice of apartheid.

41. See de Villiers, *The Present State of the Church.*

42. See Winter, *Namibia*, p. 112.

43. A South African law by which the most skilled and best jobs are reserved for whites only.

44. The open letter is reprinted in Winter, *Namibia*, pp. 112–14. For a general overview of the attitudes of the Christian churches in the sociopolitical development process, see Gerhard Totemeyer, *South West Africa/Namibia* (Randburg: Fokus Suid Publishers, 1977), ch. 6.

45. For this ruling and the implications of its findings for member states of the United Nations, see *Legal Consequences for States of the Continued Presence of South Africa in Namibia (South West Africa) notwithstanding Security Council Resolution 276 (1970), Advisory Opinion of 21 June 1971: I.C.J. Reports 1971.*

46. See de Villiers, *The Present State of the Church.*

47. Excerpts from this meeting, which ended inconclusively, can be found in "The Future of the Missionary Enterprise—Namibia Now!" pp. 92–98.

48. As quoted by de Villiers, *The Present State of the Church,* p. 87.

49. See, for example, the list of actions taken by the South African government against Anglican church workers in Winter, *Namibia,* pp. 16–17.

50. See de Villiers, *The Present State of the Church,* p. 87.

51. See J. Kane-Berman, *Contract Labour in South West Africa* (Johannesburg: South African Institute of Race Relations, 1972).

52. For an excellent introduction to the current political economy, see Roger Murray, "The Namibian Economy: An Analysis of the Role of Foreign Investment and the Policies of the South African Administration," in *The Role of Foreign Firms in Namibia*, by Murray et al., pp. 22–122.

53. Figures provided by J. Kane-Berman, *Contract Labour.* With the continued expansion of the mining sector during the 1970s, the number of contract workers has undoubtedly increased considerably.

54. Transvaal Province, *Report of the Local Government Commission* (Stallard), 1922.

55. For an excellent discussion devoted to the structural determinants and historical evolution of worker consciousness in Namibia, see Richard Moorsom, "Underdevelopment, Contract Labour and Worker Consciousness in Namibia," *Journal of Southern African Studies* 4, no. 1 (October 1977): 52–87. For some of the major constraints, internal and external, facing attempts by Africans to organize and to exert their labor power in the South African and Namibian political economies, see L. Douwes Dekker et. al., "Case Studies in African Labour Action in South Africa and Namibia (South West Africa)," in *The Development of an African Working Class: Studies in Class Formation and Action*, edited by Richard Sandbrook and Robin Cohen (Toronto: University of Toronto Press, 1975).

56. Report of the Contract Committee based on the mass meeting at Ondangwa, January 10, 1972, in "The Future of the Missionary Enterprise— Namibia Now!" p. 47.

CHAPTER 8

Perspectives on Colonial Education in Botswana

JACK BERMINGHAM

Even though Britain kept Botswana (formerly the Bechuanaland Protectorate) in a totally undeveloped state and severely limited educational opportunity, the territory's traditional leaders were eventually able to manipulate these deficiencies to their benefit. The quality of education was indicative of the general neglect with which Britain treated the protectorate. But it also served as an impetus and stimulated a dynamic African leadership which articulated clear goals and struggled to attain them.

The prominent feature of colonial education in the protectorate was local control. Authority was confined to primary schools until 1954 because there were no secondary institutions. This educational infrastructure combined with British indirect rule to strengthen the position of traditional authority in colonial Botswana. As a result, education became predominantly a privilege of the elite. These factors then shaped the development of African politics. Traditional chiefs became the "legitimate" nationalist leaders. Both Britain and South Africa viewed this development with approval since it was the logical extension of their convergent policies. However, education gave African leaders a clearer understanding of colonial policies, and from an early stage they sought to limit both the scope and extent of their dependence on South Africa. Moreover, these leaders unequivocally rejected South African racial policies and instead promoted a new African dynamic which stressed nonracialism. Colonial education, in part, defined this dynamic and helped to set it in motion.

Colonial education in the Bechuanaland Protectorate, including both formal education and the student experiences encountered while at school, supported the British colonial administration and was indicative of important issues that affected the protectorate. The quality of education served as an index of neglect,[1] and it contributed to the growing dependence of Bechuanaland on neighboring territories, especially South Africa. In the 1909 South Africa Act, this dependence was institutionalized as Britain mandated the conditions under which the High Commission territories—Bechuanaland, Basutoland, and Swaziland—would be transferred to the Union of South Africa.[2] Colonial education helped clarify this "Settler/Imperial Complex" and the use of Bechuanaland as a political and economic pawn. From this understanding sprang a partial framework of analysis which stimulated the rise of African nationalism in the protectorate.

These issues focus on the close relationship of colonial education to the historical development of the colony. By examining this relationship, we may clarify the function of education in Bechuanaland as it related to several unique characteristics that arose from the protectorate's particular geopolitical position.

HISTORICAL BACKGROUND

Botswana, formerly called the Bechuanaland Protectorate, was under British control from 1885 to 1966. As a colonial possession, it was a large, sparsely populated territory in southern Africa. Except for a small, disputed corner where it was bounded by Zambia, Bechuanaland was virtually surrounded by settler colonies. On the western and northern border was Southern Rhodesia; the remainder, in effect, was bordered by South Africa. This geopolitical setting limited the protectorate's opportunities, and these constraints were exacerbated by certain physical characteristics of the territory. About the same size as Texas, Bechuanaland encompassed the vast Kalahari Desert as well as the swampy delta of the Okavango River. The majority of the population was consequently spread out from the southeastern to the northeastern region, with small pockets of people clustered around other watered areas in the territory. The total population was only about 300,000 by 1957.[3] The Batswana were faced with formidable communication difficulties, which were compounded by the limited prospects for economic growth. They depended on subsistence agriculture and cattle for their livelihood, and since the success of both depended on sufficient rainfall, a shortage of water often resulted in disaster.

From 1885, when the protectorate was declared, Bechuanaland's development was shaped largely by the needs of its neighbors or the political goals of Britain. It was colonized only because of its strategic value for Britain. The British quest to restrict the Boers from German contact in Namibia (South-West Africa) and British designs on central Africa were the key elements motivating the European scramble for this African territory. As a result, the British consistently treated the protectorate as an unwanted backwater where economic exploitation was not possible. Britain asserted that the Batswana could best contribute to the prosperity of the empire by acting as a migrant labor force in South Africa or Southern Rhodesia. Indeed, those who did remain in the territory were encouraged to work for either the few mining concessions or for European farmers.[4] In no way would these jobs aid in the development of an economic infrastructure, but then that seemed to be the idea. Opportunity and prosperity in the protectorate would have dissuaded migrant laborers journeying outside the territory and would not have coincided with the desires of either the British or the settlers.

EDUCATION FOR THE PROTECTORATE

> The true educational aim is the education, not only of the young, but of the whole community, through the co-ordination of the activities of all the agencies aiming at social improvement. This involves a clear recognition of the intimate connexion between educational policy, and demands a close collaboration between the different agencies responsible for [administration].[5]

Western education in Botswana is usually regarded as having begun in 1824, when Robert Moffat of the London Missionary Society (LMS) established a mission station in Kuruman, South Africa. From Kuruman, missionary activity expanded northward, and by 1840, a few outstations and schools had been erected north of the Molopo River. At one of these posts, Kolobeng in the Bakwena area, David Livingstone helped establish a school. In 1860, the Bangwaketse capital, Kanye, had a successful primary school, and the Bamangwato had two district schools near Shoshong.

Other denominations competed for Batswana souls as mission education expanded: German Lutherans founded Hermannsburg Mission School in Ramoutsa in 1876; soon afterwards the Dutch Reformed church began missionary activities amongst the Bakgatla near Mochudi; later, the Anglicans and the Roman Catholics sent their missionaries to the protectorate, and additional schools were established. By 1901, when there were twenty African schools, the assistant commissioner in Gaborone said:

> No efforts have as yet been made to afford industrial education in any of the missionary schools in the Southern Protectorate, but it is the intention of the London Missionary Society to establish with the least possible delay an educational and industrial school at Tiger Kloof, near Vryburg, and I am informed that this new school is intended primarily for natives of the Protectorate.[6]

In fact, Tiger Kloof began in 1904 and served as the predominant secondary school for the protectorate even though it was situated over a hundred miles south of the territory's border, in South Africa. The reason offered for its location outside Bechuanaland was an ostensible breakdown in the negotiations to obtain title to land for a secondary school project within the territory.[7]

Subsequently, in 1905, the director of education for the Transvaal and the Orange Free State, E. B. Sargant, was invited by the protectorate's British administration to present an analysis of the protectorate's education system. His report, which recommended that "the Protectorate schools should be inspected at least once a year by some competent person,"[8] resulted in the appointment of a director of education for the three High Commission territories—Bechuanaland, Basutoland, and Swaziland. This post continued until 1928, when Basutoland received its own director. Finally, in 1935, both Bechuanaland and Swaziland were given full-time directors. The establishment of this position marked the beginning of an education department within the territory; this modified but did not destroy the old system of supervision of each school by local committees that usually consisted of the district commissioner, a missionary, and prominent members of the local African society.

Sargant further suggested that African education stress manual and industrial training. Apparently Tiger Kloof satisfied this directive, since the projects that had been initiated inside the territory were abandoned as Tiger Kloof went into operation. Finally, Sargant advocated the establishment of a "Board of Advice on Native Education." His report was lost, however, until 1929, so it is difficult to assess his impact. An advisory body similar to what he suggested was later constituted, but not until 1948.[9]

Initially, government financial assistance to African education was limited to small grants to mission schools in Botswana. Then in 1919, the Bechuanaland Protectorate Native Fund was created.[10] It was financed by an additional five-shilling levy above the amount of the hut tax paid by each African male. This fund accounted for the entire cost of African education until 1933, when the depression swallowed the funds and only emergency grants-in-aid prevented total abandonment of the educational system. Some reform came in 1938, when tribal treasuries were formally developed and 35 percent of the tax collected in the reserves were paid into the treasuries to defray the costs of teachers' salaries, books, equipment, and the provision and maintenance of suitable accommodations for students and teachers.[11] This financial arrangement, supplemented by occasional grants for special projects, continued until independence.

The method of funding education indicates the development of primary education in most of the territory's schools was controlled largely by tribal school committees and tribal treasuries. Local control was the distinguishing feature of the primary educational system; mission efforts were limited and government schools were confined to the sparsely populated crown lands.[12] Although local control appeared desirable, it displayed obvious problems. Education evolved in accordance with tribal estimates of needs and wants. But while the local school administration had the advantage of being closely linked with the tribal organization, it also had the difficulty of being shaped by generally conservative indigenous leaders. Consequently, this system tended to perpetuate traditional authority at the expense of "progressive" ideas.[13] It also led to further entrenchment of the traditional power structure and undercut the education system because access to educational opportunities was limited to elite families and their supporters. Those who challenged the chiefs' authority were banished, while the capable students who supported the traditional authority were promoted. Children of the royal family were given priority, for they were to be the future leaders.[14] Both the British and the Batswana chiefs hoped to effectively integrate the newly educated elites into the traditional structure while maintaining their authority.[15] This was best accomplished if those educated were from the traditional political aristocracy.

Nonetheless, there were Batswana who did not fit this pattern and who became educated elites. The best example in the 1920s was Kgalemang Motsete, a commoner from Serowe who received educational opportunities because of his father's earlier contacts with missionaries, which led to the elder Motsete's becoming a teacher and reverend. Motsete followed in his father's footsteps: he was educated at Tiger Kloof and returned to teach in Serowe, where conflict soon developed between Motsete and Chief Tshekedi Khama. Their dispute arose because Motsete argued for reforms in the Bamangwato Reserve. To Tshekedi Khama, Motsete was attempting to undermine his authority, so the chief forced Motsete out of Serowe.

Motsete left for Tiger Kloof in 1931 to take a teaching post under Rev. Governor Smith, head of the Theology Department. Motsete's popularity with his students did not save his position, for his outspokenness soon caused him trouble, as disagreements with Smith arose over political anecdotes that Motsete included in his lectures. Therefore, although admired for both his teaching and ideas by his students, he decided to resign.

Table 1. Education Expenditures (1920–21 to 1931–32)

	1920–21	1921–22	1922–23	1923–24	1924–25	1925–26	1926–27
Native Fund*	1,592	2,995	3,142	3,132	3,579	3,950	4,285
Br. Adm.†	2,198	1,102	1,488	1,825	2,618	3,388	3,830
overlap‡	2,343	2,011	1,648	1,612	1,866	2,500	2,850

	1927–28	1928–29	1929–30	1930–31	1931–32	Total
Native Fund*	4,506	5,241	5,301	5,754	7,547	51,024
Br. Adm.†	4,149	4,831	5,710	6,103	5,022	42,264†
overlap‡	2,530	2,645	2,150	1,000	1,000	24,155

Native Fund Revenue Annual Total

	1920–21	1921–22	1922–23	1923–24	1924–25	1925–26	1926–27
Revenues*	5,303	6,328	5,003	6,214	6,953	7,403	7,870

	1927–28	1928–29	1929–30	1930–31	1931–32	Total
Revenues*	7,767	8,166	10,205	10,002	7,952	89,166

* All statistics are in British pounds sterling.
† Money from these totals includes expenditures for colored and European education.
  (e.g., in 1932 it cost £13/3s/0d per European student excluding supervisors.)
‡ This category is money contributed directly to General Revenue Fund by the Native
  Fund.
Source: All figures come from the 1933 Pim report on the Bechuanaland Protectorate.
  (Cmd. 4368)

Immediately, he was approached by a group of students from Tati to open a private school in their district. Motsete seized the opportunity and hoped to create a new, "progressive" school.[16] The resident magistrate and the territorial resident commissioner in Francistown approved of the project. The only problem was to determine the location of the school. This seemingly minor obstacle soon mushroomed into a large controversy when Chief Tshekedi argued that Motsete wanted the school near the Bamangwato Reserve to subvert the chief's authority. To calm the situation, the resident commissioner asserted that the school would have to be built far from the Bamangwato border. The final result was the opening in February 1932 of the Tati Training Institution at Nyewele.

The school's philosophy was predicated on the three "W's"— worth, work, and worship. These goals were rooted in the principle of self-help, and though Motsete appreciated help from others, he felt strongly that it was essential to cultivate an attitude of self-reliance. To reinforce his position, he referred to two Kalanga proverbs that illustrated his point.

> *Mafuta o kumbila a to liga vudzi* (The cream which is always begged for does not make the hair pretty).

> *Nolzidziwa a na nungo* (One who always receives when he does hardly anything for himself can have no strength at all).[17]

Ironically, Motsete's failure to appreciate his own beliefs contributed his downfall. When he decided to move the school to Francistown for better social services, the change completely undermined the institution. With its basis in agricultural training and local support from surrounding villages, the school's success was based on the local people maintaining Motsete self-help principle and their pride in the school. Motsete destroyed their belief in him and in his principle when he moved the school against their will, and his action seemed to confirm in the minds of the local people Tshekedi's forebodings.[18] Consequently, they withdrew their support, and the school collapsed when outside funds dried up in 1940. The Tati Training Institution, however, was a noteworthy development. For the first time, the Bechuanaland Protectorate had a school within its boundaries that included more than a primary curriculum. From the school, a student could receive the Junior Certificate, and the Batswana hoped that soon there would be secondary education at the institution. But such expectations were never realized, and in fact, secondary schooling did not arrive in the protectorate until the 1950s.

Despite the collapse of the institution, there were important educational developments in the 1930s. In 1935, the protectorate was funded for a full-time director of education in the colonial administration. In addition, in 1938, the membership and powers of the tribal school committees were clearly defined by Proclamation 26, the major provisions of which delineated the basis for communal control of primary education.[19] By formalizing the committee structure, the director of education increased the power of local Europeans, and the three appointees of the district commissioner almost always included at least one missionary and often a prominent European trader. This action promoted missionary activities in primary education, and while this was not new, the proclamation did serve to entrench the missionary's position in the protectorate's system of primary education.

Clearly, the London Missionary Society (LMS) already dominated secondary education. Tiger Kloof, a LMS secondary school in Vryburg, enrolled over 150 Bechuanaland students in some years. It had been built specifically to serve the needs of the Batswana and was oriented towards both vocational and academic training. Although Tiger Kloof educated most of Botswana's prominent citizens, including President Seretse Khama, it was not the only secondary school attended by students from the protectorate. In 1947, while there were 58 Bechuanaland students in secondary school at Tiger Kloof along with 33 others enrolled in its vocational courses, there were at least 58 protectorate students in other secondary schools throughout South Africa and Southern Rhodesia.[20] While these figures illustrate the importance of Tiger Kloof, they also stress the total dependence of Bechuanaland on extraterritorial institutions. Moreover, these statistics dramatically demonstrate the paucity of educational opportunities for the Batswana.

A closer examination of some of the figures released by the Bechuanaland Department of Education from 1935 to 1945 reflect a large disparity between primary enrollments and those in secondary schools.[21] Primary education was dominated by large numbers of children in the first four years of schooling.

Table 2. Primary and Secondary Enrollment (1935–1945)

Year	Primary Students	Secondary*	University
1935	9,251	9	1
1936	11,985	11	2
1937–38	13,893	(no figures)	3
1944	18,573	200	1
1945	21,139	175	7

* There were others in vocational training.
Source: Adapted from "Education Annual Reports."

Besides this quantitative picture, there was an equally alarming qualitative one. In 1935, the annual cost per African student in Bechuanaland was about fourteen shillings, or roughly one-third the amount spent on

African students in Natal. The cost for each European student in the protectorate was £8.14. Even with this discrepancy, it was claimed that European education was of the lowest standard. This situation was further exacerbated because both groups suffered low incentive among teachers because of low salaries. An unqualified teacher for Africans made between £18 and £30 annually; a qualified teacher earned from £44 to £72 a year. The European schools offered salaries between £120 and £540 annually. Consequently, the good teachers in Bechuanaland soon went elsewhere. Maintaining a qualified staff was a chronic problem, and the turnover rate was overwhelming.

The exigencies of education and the educational crisis for Africans within Bechuanaland are further revealed by the following table:

Table 3. Primary Education (1935–1938)

Year	Primary Students	Schools	Teachers	Qualified Teachers
1935	9,251	91	172	42
1936	11,985	103	212	56
1937–38	13,893	117	236	64

Source: Adapted from "Education Annual Reports."

To be labeled a qualified teacher, a person had to have at least one year of teacher training or some primary education beyond standard 6.[22] By 1946, only 45 percent of the African teachers met these limited standards.[23]

The picture began to improve slightly by the late 1940s. St. Joseph's Mission School, a Catholic institution, developed a curriculum that included the Junior Certificate. This, coupled with Chief Tshekedi's efforts to open the Bamangwato College at Moeng, offered an inkling of hope for the future. In 1948, all eight St. Joseph's candidates who took examinations for the Junior Certificate passed. This trend picked up momentum when the British began to honor their World War II promises to help the protectorate advance in return for loyal soldiers during the war.

Thus in 1948, Britain made £100,000 available for an eight-year program of educational development in Bechuanaland. The plan provided help for the building of two central European primary schools, financed the creation of an African Teachers' Training College, and contributed to the development of agricultural and homecrafts education, including the employment of two European technical officers. The money also increased bursaries that enabled deserving students to take advantage of educational opportunities not available in the protectorate. Moreover, these funds provided for various social welfare activities, a mobile cinema unit, the development of youth movements, and the genesis of adult education. Another important development in 1948 was the beginning of the building of the Bamangwato College, for which Chief Tshekedi Khama was the driving force.[24]

Tshekedi had labored long to get a secondary school in the protectorate. He made it his personal task, and he finally raised sufficient funds through a Bamangwato self-help scheme. The basis of his funding was a "one man, one beast" philosophy. Each of the Bamangwato was requested to donate one cow for the school. These funds from the sale of the cattle, along with some British grants, finally resulted in the opening of Bamangwato College in 1949. While this was an encouraging step, the protectorate still did not offer a curriculum beyond the Junior Certificate.

The pivotal year in the protectorate's education system was 1954 because South Africa's ban on extraterritorial African students went into effect. To ameliorate this crisis situation, the Bamangwato College and St. Joseph's initiated junior matriculation instruction, and in the following year they included the matriculation class offerings. South Africa's plan had been known since 1951, yet the protectorate, under British administration, was obviously unprepared. School standards were still low, and education opportunities were limited.

Table 4. Secondary Education (1949–1954)

Year	Std. 7	Std. 8	Std. 9	Teacher Training (yr)			Extra Territorial Secondary
				1st	2nd	3rd	
1949	56	13	10	24	24	10	78
1950	83	37	12	13	18	25	72
1951	75	57	27	16	16	18	70
1952	63	46	33	22	21	16	66
1953	68	42	42	16	23	11	67
1954	87	51	31	18	19	16	56

Source: Adapted from "Education Annual Reports."

With the introduction of secondary education in 1954, more students successfully took the Junior Certificate examination, and yet between 1955 and 1957, of the twenty-seven students who sat for the matriculation examination, only two passed.

Table 5. Secondary Education and the Junior Certificate (1952–1957)

Year	Teachers	Qualified	JC Exam	Passed
1952	504	266	33	22
1953	562	289	28	20
1954	592	284	26	17
1957	765	381	65	47

Source: Adapted from "Education Annual Reports."

Education in the Bechuanaland Protectorate was an obvious failure. In an attempt to rectify the situation, in 1956 the African Advisory Council unanimously recommended that the Bamangwato College be reconstituted a territorial institution. The British administration concurred and Bamangwato was renamed Moeng College. However, there was no university training available in Bechuanaland. That had to wait until the 1970s.

Before 1954, Botswana relied on Fort Hare in South Africa for most university training, although some Batswana attended schools in England and America. After 1954, Pius XII College in Basutoland and, on occasion, Central African University in Salisbury were relied on to provide higher education. Yet there were never large numbers of Bechuanaland students at that level, and by 1962 there were only thirty-five Batswana in the country with university degrees.[25]

BOTSWANA, BRITON, BOER—AND MISSIONARY

> The educators of black humanity will do well to . . . aim at the production of good black men, and not attempt to make impossible white men out of good black men and thereby waste excellent material.[26]

Missionaries dominated education in the Bechuanaland Protectorate. More importantly, they controlled the protectorate's extraterritorial secondary schooling, such as Tiger Kloof. There Africans "tended to be more concerned with prayers and the trades than with politics," and in fact, politics was generally omitted from the curriculum.[27] There were discussions and organized debates, but they dealt with colonial policies theoretically, usually avoiding discussion of homeland political realities. The missionary, just like the traditional chief, dominated the Batswana students. Indeed these youngsters were pacified.[28] This dominance was indicative of the missionary role under colonialism.

> In civilized [European] countries, the office of the missionary is simple and well defined. In the discharge of his duty, he has to follow the example of Christ and His Apostles, preaching the Gospel of the Kingdom of God; but when the missionary has to reclaim the people, whom he is sent to instruct from a wandering life, to collect them together into villages, and to elevate them into a state of civilization, in the management of his arduous undertaking, he is left to little more than the fruit of his own observation and experience.[29]

To make his job easier, the missionary developed a hybrid religion for nineteenth- and early twentieth-century Africa. Faced with a foreign culture and race, while simultaneously aware of his government's colonial interests and his countrymen's desires, the missionary provided a colonial religion that was exclusively derived from neither the Bible nor that which was practiced in Europe. This new religion sanctioned colonization, imperialism, cultural and political domination, and pseudoscientific racism. Moreover, it gave moral legitimacy to cultural arrogance, racism, contempt, and injustice—all of which were inconsistent with Christianity. The basis for this development was the recognition that colonization and commerce were inseparable functions of the "civilizing mission." Education became an integral part of the colonial program. It produced the "good African" and as a result provided the psychological rationale and legitimacy for colonialism. In this way, missionaries brought an aura of humanitarianism to colonial administration, for they performed "noble and moral" duties by "uplifting" the "backward" Africans.

These missionaries built Tiger Kloof. Like the protectorate's administrative capital, Mafeking, its secondary school was situated outside the territory's boundaries. Worse, both were located in South Africa, where racial discrimination dominated all aspects of life. It could be speculated that once Tiger Kloof was developed, Britain would transfer its colonial authority in Bechuanaland to South Africa. In that likely event, Vryburg would then constitute a central location for most Batswana, since more lived in South Africa than in the protectorate. Vryburg was also better located for inexpensive supplies, access to Cape Town, and the authority of the missionary. Batswana chiefs found their power limited at Tiger Kloof because of the geographical separation that kept the Batswana traditional authority from interfering in the school. This arrangement was far different from their direct access to the protectorate's primary education structure, and Vryburg thus gave the missionaries some autonomy.

Yet despite this autonomy, South Africa gradually began to exercise increasing control over the school through a number of pieces of restrictive legislation. This process culminated with the establishment of the apartheid state of the Afrikaner nationalists and their promulgation in 1950 of the Group Areas Act, which closed Tiger Kloof when the act was enforced in 1955. The racism which marked the institution's environment since its inception had finally precipitated its demise.

This missionary school in the relative comforts of Vryburg bore the "white man's burden" with an autocratic system noted for its discipline and dogmatism for fifty years. Few Batswana displayed any political activism. Those who did and survived remained in South Africa, usually joining the African National Congress.

Nonetheless, some Batswana students from Tiger Kloof did show an appreciation for the uniqueness of their own territory. They understood that it was different from South Africa and Southern Rhodesia, and they actively supported Tshekedi Khama's fight against the transfer of Bechuanaland to South African control.[30] This battle against incorporation by South Africa illustrated the Batswana consciousness of the political complexities of Southern Africa, and their educational experiences clearly reflected that awareness.

There were distinct differences between what Tshekedi saw during his primary education in the protectorate under British and African control and what he faced in South Africa in secondary school. The environment as well as the instruction showed marked differences in the settler colony, and these differences soon became evident to other Batswana as more and more were educated in South Africa. While avoiding incorporation was a critical issue, it was not the only South African connection in the protectorate. Until the mid-1950s, white South Africans dominated the British colonial administrative positions in Bechuanaland,[31] and the education department most clearly exemplified this. With the South Africans came their racist cultural baggage, and their attitudes caused many clashes with the Batswana. Perhaps the best example was the animosity between Resident Commissioner Rey and Chief Tshekedi Khama in the 1930s.[32] These tensions remained throughout the colonial period. Simultaneously to the African Advisory Council debating the need to upgrade education, they asserted that South African administrators in the protectorate must change their racial attitudes or leave.[33]

By the 1950s, the Batswana had begun to sort out the "Settler/ Imperial Complex" in the protectorate. There seemed to be a policy of neglect, best illustrated by education. Money that could have been acquired through a fairer customs union was lost.[34] Those revenues could have produced a better educational system. The Batswana also saw how administrative neglect by the British froced the protectorate to become a South African dependency. Again this was particularly evident in education. By limiting opportunity, the British forced the Batswana to become a migrant labor force for South Africa. Taxes such as the extra native fund reinforced the need to work, and since there was no economic base within Bechuanaland, the Batswana were directed to the mines in South Africa. Those who were educated were also pushed to South Africa, first for the better education opportunity itself and then to market their newly acquired skills for their livelihood.[35]

For the British, the protectorate became a political pawn that could be dangled before South Africa's eyes to get concessions on various issues. However, with the rise of apartheid in South Africa came the height of African nationalism. By the 1950s, it was no longer feasible for Britain (had she so desired) to transfer Bechuanaland to South Africa.[36]

Nationalism came to Bechuanaland partially as a result of colonial education. Education yielded a growing awareness of the appreciation of freedom and a clearer understanding of degrees of oppression.[37] Nationalist fervor heightened and leaders, predominantly educated elites, began to articulate nationalist concepts. They saw their apartheid educational structure as inefficient and as a personal affront. Africans wanted education as a form of modernization, and it was believed this change could best be accomplished through political

Diagram 1. Schools for the Batswana (1954)

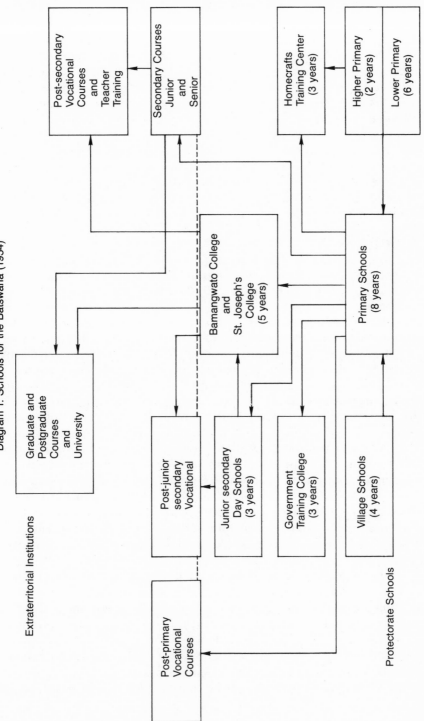

control. This desire resulted in the formation of the Joint Advisory Council and later the convocation of the Legislative Assembly. There-fore, nationalism developed as the antithesis of colonialism and a positive affirmation of freedom as well as the basis for modernization. While the general experiences of colonialism contributed to the genesis of that affirmation and modernization, perhaps the immediate stimulus came from colonial education. Certainly colonial education promoted the Batswana belief in a nonracial society rather than an exclusively black one, and Christianity and its educational influences had become a dominant factor in Batswana society.[38] Consequently, it could be argued that while colonial education in Botswana provided the seeds of destruction for colonialism, that same education caused a peaceful transfer of the political leadership but avoided any revolu-tionary changes in the system.

CONCLUSION

> As resources permit, the door of advancement through higher
> education in Africa, must be increasingly opened for those who by
> character, ability, and temperament, show themselves permitted to
> profit by such education.[39]

Most conclusions on the impact of colonial education in the Bechuanaland Protectorate are tentative because of the paucity of research material. It is clear, however, that South Africa played an important role, as the educational part of the British colonial adminis-tration was placed largely under South African influence. When Bantu education was introduced and extraterritorial Africans were not al-lowed in South African schools, the protectorate's educational system floundered because of its total dependence on South Africa. At that stage, Britain tried to shift the dependency to Southern Rhodesia,[40] but the traditional African authorities knew Bechuanaland would have to develop its own system. This was essential if the protectorate was ever going to become independent. For this independence to work smoothly, the British also had to recognize the need to develop workers sufficiently educated to enable them to create a political infrastructure. Otherwise Britain's choice was to yield to South Africa's designs on the territory.

The major rationale for South African expansion hinged on the continued undeveloped nature of the protectorate. Maintaining that Bechuanaland was even dependent on them for education, the Af-rikaners argued that a prosperous future lay only with incorporation into South Africa. In their struggle to avoid this, the Batswana found able allies in the missionaries.[41] The missionaries had humanitarian considerations, but they also knew that it was imperative for the protec-torate to remain British or become independent if the missionaries were to retain their position. After all, the missionaries had never liked the Boers, and that did not change when the LMS was expelled from Tiger Kloof.

Further, education significantly contributed to the rise of nationalism, which in turn helped facilitate Botswana independence. The Batswana educational experience yielded a keen political awareness of South Africa and led all African nationalists in the protectorate to agree that they must resist South African expansion.[42] Thus, it can be concluded that Western education helped mold independent Botswana. Parliamentary democracy was a learned concept which sprang from colonial education.[43] But we should be careful not to be dogmatic on this point; for one can argue that the *Kgotla* (a Tswana political institution that provides a forum so that each Motswana may speak before the chief and the general community) tradition offered in some ways a basis for the present governmental system. Nonetheless, there are striking similarities between the present Botswana regime and the British political system. In the final analysis, it can be argued that the present system was promoted by colonial education, and that this system encourages a close relationship between Botswana and its former imperial authority. Yet Botswana is no longer a colony; it defines its own goals and dares to seek its own aspirations, including a decrease in its dependency on South Africa. In education, Botswana has come a long way toward fulfilling that aspiration.

There is retrospective irony: the Batswana leadership that took power from the British embodied the integration of the educated elite and the traditional authority figure. Seretse Khama, as an African nationalist, demonstrated the contradiction inherent in colonial education.[44] The same education that was designed to shape him into the educated "prototype" actually produced the type of nationalist consciousness that demanded the expulsion of the colonizer, the realization of political independence, and the reduction of South African economic hegemony.

NOTES

1. Interview with G. Chiepe (minister of mineral resources), August 1977, and interview with James Haskins (minister of works and communications), July 1977.

2. See Ronald Hyam's *The Failure of South African Expansion, 1908–1948* (New York: Africana Publishing, 1972) for a discussion of this issue.

3. *Bechuanaland Department of Education Annual Report* (1957), p. 1.

4. Interview with Motsamai Mpho (opposition MP), August 1977.

5. *Education Annual Report* (1935), p. 2, quoting Colonial Memorandum no. 103 "Memorandum on the Education of African Communities."

6. Ibid., p. 3.

7. *The Financial and Economic Position of the Bechuanaland Protectorate*, Cmd. 4368 (London: HMSO, 1933), p. 78 (also known as the Pim report); interview with Rev. Albert Loch (Speaker of Parliament and former LMS missionary), August 1977. It is claimed that Chief Tshekedi Khama refused to sell land because he thought custom prohibited it. The LMS used this to legitimize their building the school outside the colony.

8. *The Financial and Economic Position of Bechuanaland*, p. 78. When this was adopted, the missionary no longer had an official function in the overall administration of the territory's education.

9. *Education Annual Report* (1948), p. 7. See also the discussions by the African Advisory Council on education in *African Advisory Council Minutes* (1948), vol. 29.

10. See section 2 of "Proclamation No. 47 for the Bechuanaland Protectorate" (1919). The initial contribution was three shillings.

11. *Education Annual Report* (1937–1938), p. 11.

12. This is an important distinction that differentiated Bechuanaland from the surrounding settler colonies. However, African participation dissipated some in the 1930s, when financial burdens required more funds from the colonial administration.

13. There are several instances of this in Chief Tshekedi Khama's disputes with Nswazwi and his followers in the 1930s, e.g., Botswana National Archives (BNA) S 78/1. Interestingly, Tshekedi himself was a member of the educated elite who had returned from Lovedale to assume the regency of the Bamangwato and as such was the perfect example of blending education (Western) and traditional society.

14. BNA S 175/11. The British wanted to make sure that the then ten-year-old Seretse Khama would be educated "properly."

15. Ballinger Papers, BC 347 Hl.6 (housed at the University of Cape Town archives), pp. 1–2. W. G. Ballinger is commenting on his 1928 visit to the protectorate.

16. BNA S 243/11-13, S 79/2, S 359/8.

17. BNA BNB 651.

18. Tshekedi called Motsete a cheat and claimed that he was treacherous. See D. M. P. Mulale's "The Life and Career of Dr. K. T. Motsete" (B.A. Thesis, University of Botswana, 1977).

19. *Education Annual Report* (1961), p. 7, quoting Proclamation 26 of 1938, "School Committees." See appendix 2.

20. *Education Annual Report* (1947), p. 20.

21. Ibid. (1935, 1936, 1937–1938, 1944, 1945). Note that the African population was about 250,000 in 1945. All statistics reflect the appropriate *Education Annual Report*.

22. Teacher training was a three-year course.

23. *Education Annual Report* (1946), p. 12.

24. See Mary Benson's *Tshekedi Khama* (London: Faber, 1960) for more information on the college and Tshekedi's role in its development.

25. Richard Stevens, *Lesotho, Botswana, and Swaziland* (New York: Praeger, 1967), p. 164.

26. Molema/Plaatje Papers A979 Ad 6.3, p. 1 (housed in the archives of the University of Witwatersrand), the observations of Solomon T. Plaatje on colonial education.

27. Interview with G. Chiepe, August 1977.

28. Interview with S. S. Molema (retired physician), August 1977.

29. John Philip, *Researches in South Africa*, vol. 2 (New York: Negro Universities' Press, 1969; originally published in 1829), p. 355.

30. Interview with Bathoen Gaseitsiwe (opposition MP and former chief of the Bangwaketse), August 1977. This is the best example of the impact of the environment around the secondary schools and to a great extent reflects more the experiences while being educated than the education itself.

31. This included positions as high as resident commissioner. In fact, the high commissioner, though not South African, was dominated by South Africa. His position was two-fold. First, he was Britain's "ambassador" to South Africa; second, he was high commissioner for the protectorates in southern Africa. This dual role made it almost impossible for him to give Bechuanaland any priority in crisis situations involving South Africa.

32. Interview with Bathoen Gaseitsiwe, August 1977.

33. *African Advisory Council Minutes* (1949), vol. 30, pp. 35–48.

34. The 1910 Customs Union Agreement gave the protectorate a small but fixed share of South Africa's collected duties. This was settled between Britain and South Africa and was not renegotiated until 1969. The later agreement gives Botswana a far greater portion.

35. Interview with Bathoen Gaseitsiwe, August 1977. The European settlers, however, were encouraged to return after completing their education outside Bechuanaland to take up administrative posts. Again, this encouraged racial animosity, for the whites had been educated in the South African system; see *Education Annual Report* (1946), p. 5. On the other hand, there were few opportunities for Africans to return and work in the protectorate unless they were part of the traditional aristocracy and supported it.

36. Interview with A. Mogwe (foreign minister), August 1977.

37. See the testimony in the *Report of the Select Committee on Racial Discrimination* by the Bechuanaland Legislative Council (1963).

38. Missionaries such as Rev. Loch are still prominent members of Botswana society, and Christian religion remains an important element in the life of the political elites. There are numerous references to God and Christianity in parliamentary debates.

39. *Educational Policy in Africa* (1925), Cmd. 2374, p. 9.

40. Interview with Rev. A. Loch, August 1977.

41. Ibid.

42. Interview with M. Mpho, August 1977.

43. Interview with Bathoen Gaseitsiwe, August 1977.

44. Seretse Khama was educated at Tiger Kloof, Lovedale, Fort Hare, and at Oxford.

CHAPTER 9

A Century of Colonial Education in Mozambique

MARIO AZEVEDO

This chapter deals with the Portuguese educational system in the former colony of Mozambique from 1876 to 1974. It is divided into two parts, factual and statistical information on education in Mozambique, and the impact of the Protuguese colonial education system on the former colony.

It discusses the nature, aims, and role of missionary and government schools; the curriculum in the primary, secondary, and university settings; racial distribution in schools; the policy of assimilation as part of the educational system and that system's political, social, and economic consequences; educational expenditures; teaching methods and discipline; and the condition of school buildings.

Out of the study, this picture emerges: the Portuguese educational effort was minimal, even during the *Estado Novo*; it was relatively accelerated in the 1960s and 1970s; and it grossly discriminated against Africans, had very little quantitative impact, and created social "classes," with the division of the population into assimilated and indigenous. It also retarded the nationalist movement in the colony. By concentrating the educational opportunities in the urban areas, particularly in the south, the Portuguese created an ethnic problem that is visible in the newly independent territory.

One of the objectives of the Portuguese government was to eliminate the prospects of an independent Mozambique. The objective succeeded to a point. But, as if by contradiction, it worked against itself and aroused the nationalist sentiment among the educated few and the masses at large.

Education is one of man's most powerful catalysts of stability, change, and progress as it preserves and interprets culture, molds the mind, influences behavior, and enlarges man's capacity for appreciating his own humanity. From an early age, most children are formally exposed to a complex educational system so that they may become productive in their society. During the colonial era in Africa, European powers realized, probably more than ever before, the power and effect education can have on the human mind. The missionary quickly understood that Africans would demand more than the simple ability to read the stories of the Bible. Intelligent administrators slowly realized that education would help modernize their colonies and maximize the advantages for the mother country, but would eventually undermine the very fabric of colonial structure and society. Once educated, Africans were bound to demand equal treatment and opportunity as a logical corollary to the ideas embodied in the Western educational system to which they were exposed. Denial of such a demand would constitute a flagrant contradiction causing inescapable embarrassment to the colonizer. Despite the Portuguese colonial policy of assimilation that may have slowed down the process toward independence, Mozambique proved to be no exception to the general social and political transformation that Africa experienced particularly in the post–World War II period.

This chapter examines historically the nature, goals, and impact of Portuguese colonial education in Mozambique. In order to make some of our conclusions more meaningful, the Portuguese colonial effort is compared with that of other colonial powers, such as France, England, and Belgium.

EDUCATION: THEORY AND PRACTICE

Very little has been written about the Portuguese educational system in the former colonies of Angola, Mozambique, Guinea-Bissau, Cape Verde Islands, and São Tomé e Principe. Studying systematically and historically the nature, structure, methods, disciplines, legacy, and impact of colonial education in Mozambique is, therefore, a difficult task. Frustrated in this respect, Walter Rodney was compelled to write about the Portuguese that "there is scarcely any education to be discussed in their colonial territories" due to the simple fact that

> for many years, the statistical data was never made available, and published towards the end of the colonial period the figures were often inflated. What is undeniable is that the African child growing up in Portuguese colonial territories stood one chance out of a hundred of getting instruction beyond Standard II or Standard III.[1]

In spite of these shortcomings, a pattern of the old colonial education is discernible.

Missionaries were in Mozambique in the seventeenth century, and consequently a handful of Africans were taught how to read and write, but mainly for religious purposes. The government, as far as we can tell from official documents, did practically nothing worth mentioning to educate the population until the nineteenth century, when the first few government schools were established. Until the late nineteenth century, according to Alan Smith, " . . . the most outstanding characteristic of the relationship between Portugal and its two African colonies of Angola and Mozambique was the indifference of the mother country." As the scramble for Africa ended, colonial interest slowly dwindled until Salazar's *Estado Novo*.[2] From time to time, however, official pronouncements called for gradual education of the Africans because "the Indigenas still find themselves in a savage or semi-savage state."[3] Africans needed to receive some education so that they could be useful in the economic activity of the colony. The official policy read:

> As integral members of the Portuguese Nation, they [Mozambicans] ought to be educated and instructed, to make them worthy of the Nation they belong to. As slaves, they could be left ignorant; but as free individuals, however, even putting aside national prestige, the mere interests of our large concessionaires demand that they be educated.[4]

The Portuguese monarchy, in a decree of August 14, 1845, created the first school system in the colony, which was expanded in 1869. Expansion came after the first effort proved "pitifully inadequate" and the minister for navy and overseas officially declared that "local difficulties, negligence, and imperfect organization annulled or paralyzed the government's attempt to establish a colonial education system."[5] Records of its impact are not clear, although we know that by 1876, Mozambique counted some 8 schools with 226 students. In 1900, the number of students had increased to 1,195; by 1909, the government had created 48 primary schools for boys and 18 for girls.[6] The Portuguese Republic expanded the program and in 1913 sent the famous *Missões civilizadoras laicas* (Lay Civilizing Missions) to the colony to expedite the feeble educational work begun by the Catholic missions. By 1929, 258 schools had been created in Mozambique, with a population of some 30,613 students. When these figures are compared to those of other east African colonies of similar population size, the Portuguese effort falls far behind expectation. Uganda, for example, had reached 157,000 students in primary and secondary education by 1922; Tanzania (1923) and Kenya (1925) registered 120,000 and 500,000 students, respectively.[7] Thus the African Education Commission that visited Mozambique in 1924 was compelled to conclude:

> Not only was the state of education backward, especially in comparision with several other areas, but observations in Portuguese Africa . . . offer practically no basis for hope of any essential improvements in colonial policy."[8]

In fact, there seems to have been a steady decline in the educational effort during the regime of the *Estado Novo* under Salazar. Almost a century from 1876, during the 1950–1951 school year, the Portuguese maintained only 63 government supported schools, taught by 164 teachers with a population of 5,055 pupils; private schools registered 931 students that year.[9] The increase represented some 55 new schools in a period of almost a hundred years, at the rate of 0.6 schools per year.

In 1956, the number of students in primary and secondary schools increased from 5,055 (1951) to 253,000; in 1957 approximately 296,000 out of 900,000 school-age Mozambican children attended school. Malawi, with a much smaller population, had 264,310 students. In 1958, some 344,000 children enrolled in private and public institutions.[10] This increase of 16 percent over the previous year is not impressive when compared to other African colonies, as shown in Table 1.

Table 1. School Enrollment in Mozambique and Some Other African Countries in 1958[11]

Countries	Mozambique	Uganda	Kenya	Tanzania	Malawi
Enrollment Total	344,000	542,633	671,291	437,315	272,042
Population	6,310,000	6,536,616	6,550,700	9,237,000	2,830,000

In 1960, the number of government schools totalled 191; Catholic missions registered 3,162 schools and the Protestant establishments 61. This gives us a total of 3,414 schools—an increase of 153 percent over 1957, at the approximate rate of 49 percent per year. Nonetheless, the increase was still slow in proportion to the Mozambican population, estimated then at six million. This was true despite the publicized education campaign launched by Sarmento Rodrigues, the governor-general of Mozambique, in the early 1960s. On August 21, 1961, Sarmento stressed the importance of education in Mozambique but admitted that the primary objective was the development of the Portuguese themselves and not the Africans, "according to the needs of the Nation's progress."[12]

In the school year 1963–1964, some 34,000 more students matriculated in 3,920 schools with 7,921 teachers. During 1964–1965, there were 426,904 primary schools, 19,761 secondary schools, and 1 university—the University of General Studies at Lourenço Marques (Maputo).[13] This was the year that FRELIMO (the Front for the Liberation of Mozambique) began its activities against the Portuguese government; in that same year compulsory education was announced for 6- to 12-year-old children living at least three miles away from school.[14] Of course, the law was never enforced. The following tables give us some idea of where the Portuguese colonies stood educationally in relation to other colonial territories in Africa. These statistics indicate that education was not a priority in the colony of Mozambique, particularly in the overall context of Africa.

Table 2. Literacy and School Enrollment in Africa (1964)[15]

Countries	Literacy Percentage	Percent School-Age Population (5-19 yrs) Enrolled in School at First and Second Levels
Algeria	20	26
Angola	3	10
Benin	5	15
Botswana	20	34
Cameroon	10	43
Central African Empire	10	19
Chad	5	12
Congo	20	49
Egypt	30	43
Ethiopia	5	4
Gabon	10	42
Gambia	8	10
Ghana	25	31
Guinea	10	13
Guinea-Bissau	--	13
Ivory Coast	20	28
Kenya	25	41
Lesotho	35	66
Liberia	10	15
Libya	30	42
Malagasy Republic	35	30
Malawi	10	40
Mali	5	6
Mauritania	5	5
Morocco	14	27
Mozambique	2	26
Namibia	30	36
Niger	5	4
Nigeria	20	30
Rhodesia	25	62
Ruwanda-Burundi	10	19
Senegal	10	15
Sierra Leone	10	12
Somalia	5	5
South Africa	45	69
Sudan	10	12
Swaziland	25	49
Tanzania	10	15
Togo	10	25
Tunisia	35	45
Uganda	25	31
Upper Volta	5	5
Zambia	10	47

Table 3 illustrates the educational problems in Mozambique. The former colony fell behind practically all Africa, including territories with smaller populations such as Burundi, Cameroon, Central African Empire, Chad, Congo, Benin, Ivory Coast, Lesotho, Malawi, Mali, Mauritania, Niger, Rhodesia, Rwanda, Senegal, Sierra Leone, Swaziland, Togo, Tunisia, Upper Volta, and Zambia. The biggest jump oc-

Table 3. Enrollment in Educational Facilities in Africa[16]

Countries	Year	Primary	Secondary	Technical	Teacher	Higher
Algeria	1964	1,270,150	40,480	34,008	1,716	5,926
Angola	1960	105,425	8,025	5,133	294	--
Benin	1964	125,231	10,083	683	354	39
Botswana	1965	66,061	1,325	102	268	--
Burundi	1964	139,015	2,304	1,419	1,781	160
Cameroon	1964	693,268	23,356	6,814	1,474	1,164
Central Africa Empire	1964	119,565	3,662	371	459	--
Chad	1964	128,031	4,173	403	241	--
Congo	1964	171,528	10,973	2,641	274	671 (1963)
Djibouti	1964	4,007	550	337	4	--
Egypt	1964	3,334,738	667,854	136,835	41,259	144,496
Ethiopia	1964	347,770	40,334	5,509	1,828	1,643
Gabon	1964	73,006	4,015	1,236	552	54
Gambia	1964	11,504	2,992	102	146	--
Ghana	1964	1,088,344	298,592	13,967	10,203	3,848
Guinea	1964	178,270 (1963)	14,133	4,721	559	1,359 (1964)
Guinea-Bissau	1961	20,428	--	--	1,520	--
Ivory Coast	1962	331,446	15,410	2,401 (1963)	2,328	1,566
Kenya	1964	1,014,719	-36,964-		4,849	2,758
Lesotho	1964	165,036	2,752	645	574	188
Liberia	1964	78,539	5,977	567	175	598
Libya	1963	158,961	21,829	2,094	2,407	1,239
Malagasy Republic	1964	633,039	50,136	4,929	2,058	2,418
Malawi	1965	331,279	10,601	839	1,397	184
Mali	1964	138,722	16,632	844	923	164
Mauritania	1964	19,103	1,380	184	107	--
Morocco	1964	1,105,182	153,431	19,052	1,276	10,136
Mozambique	1963	44,725	8,027	10,388	619	84
Namibia	1962	-71,691-		--	--	--
Niger	1964	55,146	2,079	429	502	--
Nigeria	1964	2,849,488	205,012	7,813	29,373	7,951
Rhodesia	1964	610,268	8,846	425	2,883	639
Rwanda	1963	359,542	2,268	3,370	2,016	50
Senegal	1964	206,431	21,667	5,315	--	2,545
Sierra Leone	1964	119,645	12,942	2,101	987	650
Somalia	1964	20,698	4,745	2,344	359	61
South Africa	1960	-2,632,422-		60,782	--	53,849 (1965)
Spanish Sahara	1964	2,012	332	--	--	--
Sudan	1965	492,085	92,407	6,391	1,680	7,701
Swaziland	1964	47,894	2,783	96	134	92 (1963)
Tanzania	1964	633,678	19,897	2,316	2,263	115
Togo	1965	155,880	11,381	1,681	66	30
Tunisia	1965	734,316	23,315	10,372	3,971	4,629 (1964)
Uganda	1964	525,585	12,652	3,516	3,975	1,127
Upper Volta	1964	84,370	4,538	837	1,082	--
Zaire	1964	365,237	8,981	1,118	1,463	--
Zambia	1964	1,592,225	52,309	17,334	19,248	3,136

curred in 1964, when the total student population rose to 447,457; but apparently it dropped to 113,303 in 1965.

In the school year 1971–1972, according to United Nations statistics, some 635,000 students attended school in Mozambique, 595,000 of whom were in primary schools and 40,000 in secondary and technical schools, compared to 220,000 students in Ghana's secondary and middle schools. The 1971 enrollment represented a 28 percent increase over 1958, at an average rate of 2 percent per year. At the capital, former Lourenço Marques, the rate of increase was 25 percent between 1963 and 1972.[17] When the Portuguese left Mozambique in 1975, their schools reportedly registered some 600,000 pupils out of a total population of 9 million, according to a 1975 estimate, an illiteracy rate of more than 95 percent.[18]

The Portuguese government always relied on the aid of missionaries. This is one of the reasons why there were in Mozambique, up to 1974, essentially three types of schools in terms of financial support: government schools, totally funded by the government; Catholic schools—usually primary—about 90 percent supported by the government; and foreign missionary schools, which were always self-supporting. Within the three broadly defined categories there were at least eight different types of institutions with different, specific goals: the *ensino de adaptacão* or rudimentary schools; *ensino primário comum* (elementary schools); the schools of arts and business; agricultural schools; normal or teacher training schools; secondary schools—*licéus* and *colégios*; professional-technical schools, commercial and industrial schools; Catholic seminaries; and a university, which registered 357 students in 1964.

It took approximately four years for a child to finish primary education after having passed three official examinations: the rudimentary, the elementary, and the complementary exams. Secondary school, divided into three cycles or *ciclos* differentiated by three examinations, lasted seven years. The Portuguese child began primary school at age seven and could start high school at age eleven or twelve. The majority of the Africans, who began school at a much older age—about ten—were automatically barred by the government from attending high school due to their age and lack of monetary resources. Annual tuition in the *licéus* was 2,500 escudos (about $93.00), and in the public elementary schools room, board, and tuition cost over $20.00. Both were high for an average Mozambican even in the 1960s.

What disciplines or subjects were taught in these schools? A variety—from Portuguese and German to mathematics, from biology and botany to history, from Latin and French to philosophy—was taught. The emphasis, however, was always on the Portuguese language, on the history and geography of Portugal, and on good and civilized manners—included in a special course known as *educacão moral e cívica*. History received particular attention in the Portuguese educational manuals. In 1946, official policy encouraged even the teaching of dubious historical events that aggrandized Portugal:

> It should not be concluded, however, that certain episodes which historical criticism holds to be doubtful or even unacceptable need be avoided. By . . . the color which legend has surrounded them, their narration will produce in minds which are necessarily uncultured, the light and fervor which a knowledge of rigid facts will not achieve.[19]

African languages were forbidden in schools ever since the introduction of Portuguese as the only language of instruction in 1907.

In the 1950–1951 academic year, there were 1,366 European students in Mozambique, of whom 1,040 were Portuguese; other students included 254 Asiatic (Chinese and Japanese), 429 Indo-Portuguese, 321 black Mozambicans, 488 Indians, and 1,828 of mixed parentage or *mistos*. In 1954, the racial proportion in primary schools was 5,177 Africans to 4,412 whites, almost a one-to-one ratio despite the fact that the Portuguese population was not higher than 300,000. In the colony's secondary schools, 800 white students were enrolled in the *licéus* in contrast to only 5 Africans; while 803 white students attended commercial institutions, only 73 Africans had the same opportunity. In the 1963–1964 academic year, "only 1 out of 12,500 Africans attended secondary schools in contrast to 1 out of 27 Europeans." In 1972, the Lourenço Marques school population was estimated at 1,800; "only ¼ of them were Africans."[20]

The University of General Studies at Lourenço Marques, officially opened on April 11, 1964, registered some 295 freshmen, distributed as follows: 75 in pedagogic studies, 54 in medicine, 45 in civil engineering, 56 in electrical and 20 in mechanical engineering, 2 in mining, 1 in economics, 2 in mathematics, 3 in chemicophysical sciences, 1 in biology, 1 in geology, 19 in the veterinary school, 15 in agronomy, and 1 chose to prepare himself for adjunct professorship.[21] The creation of a university in Mozambique was a great step forward. But compared to other universities and colleges in Africa, it came somewhat late, as Table 4 reveals.

While Mozambique had some African students (10–15 in 1963) in Portugal; Kenya had already reached 308, Tanganyika 211, and Uganda 268 at Makerere, in 1961; Ghana during the same period had an enrollment of more than 1,500 and 523 students in the United Kingdom, 240 in the United States, 300 in East and West Germany, 200 in the Soviet Union, and 70 in Eastern European countries.[23] The Portuguese, on the contrary, barred all education abroad to Mozambican young men for fear they might acquire ideas of freedom and

Table 4. Colleges and Universities in Africa[22]

Countries	Year of Foundation	Student Population
University of Algiers	1879	6,027 (1960)
University College, Ibadan	1948	1,100 (1960)
Kumasi College of Technology	1951	800 (1961)
University of Ruanda-Burundi	1955	30 (1960)
University of Dakar	1957	1,398 (1961)
University of East Africa (Makerere)	1950	912 (1961)
University of Lovanium (Zaire)	1954	30 (1954)
State University at Elisabethville (Zaire)	1956	104 (1957)
University of Lourenço Marques	1964	357 (1964)

independence. Hence, more than 90 percent of the Mozambican students abroad had no Portuguese passports and left the country in an aura of absolute secrecy.

In 1966, the number of university students in Mozambique rose to 540, but only 1 was "a Mozambican African." In 1970, of the 627,319 pupils, 550,701 were black, 59,941 white, 6,850 Indians, 7,793 *mistos*, and 2,034 "yellow." But at the *licéu* level, of the 4,373 students, 3,900 were white and 300 black—less than 7 percent; 43 were *mistos* and 130 Indians. How many university students were there? Approximately 1,826, but the racial composition is not provided.[24] Three years later (1973), of the 33,416 pupils matriculated in the secondary schools, 7,300 (21.8 percent) were *mistos*, 16,057 (48.1 percent) white, and 9,059 (27.1 percent) black, and ther remainder Indian and Chinese; in the primary schools blacks and *mistos* constituted the majority of the 568,355 students of the colony.[25] Secondary schools had a slight increase, 416 students, over the year before (1972), when secondary schools registered 33,000 students.[26]

The Portuguese considered education in their colonies to be the best instrument for propaganda of their aims and the perfect forum for the molding of Africans into loyal and completely submissive subjects of the mother country. The Organic Law of the Overseas Provinces of 1963 clearly states that the purpose of education was to instill the "national sense of our civilizing task and the development of the relations of those activities with similar acitivies in the Metropolis."[27] Even the Catholic missions to which most of the primary education was entrusted were viewed by the government as "instruments of civilization and national influence . . . to be protected and helped by the state."[28] This inseparability of church and state was not new. Portuguese missionaries always had their God and king in mind, as they often admitted, hoping that "in gaining souls for Christ they were also gaining . . . vassals of the King our Lord."[29] This harmony on the ultimate goal was never destroyed despite certain disagreements between the church and the state as new circumstances arose.

The education of the African was directly derived from Portuguese interests and goals in the metropolis. Accordingly, the role of the history teacher in the colonies was to make the students "understand the civilizing mission of the Portuguese activities during the age of discoveries, showing how the Portuguese (governors, missionaries, and navigators), were the greatest carriers of Western Civilization." Such an approach would "awaken in the student the great civic virtues, the awe and the love for Portugal." Exams, although made up in the colonies, had to be in conformity with those given in continental Portugal, with no or little concern for particular local needs or situations. The Portuguese expected that education "would in time create an African people speaking only Portuguese, embracing Christianity, and as intensely nationalist Portuguese as the metropolitan citizens themselves."[30]

The methods used to implement these educational goals were certainly antiquated and unacceptable in an age of African independence. Teachers mercilessly beat children, insulted them, made them work in their fields, compelled them to spend hours kneeling on brick floors, pulled their ears, kicked them, and in some instances made them bleed. When one visited a Mozambican school in the 1960s, one invariably found two devices of punishment: a stick or whip and a palmatória—a wooden device shaped like an arm and a hand. The hand part had several holes so that when it struck the child's hand, it sucked some of the flesh, causing severe pain. Rarely was there a difference of punishment between boys and girls.

The buildings where these activities took place were usually nonconducive to learning. Most of the primary schools were constructed of mud and wood, exposed to heat and cold; students sat on the floor or on pieces of wood because the government did not allocate enough money for furnishings. The miserable condition of the buildings, however, seems to contradict the 1929 decree, which specifically stipulated (insofar as private schools were concerned) that "no private school for the education of Natives may function except in a stone or brick building of sufficient capacity for the accommodation of a number of pupils, and of which the hygienic conditions are certified by the competent office of health."[31] Neither the private nor the public schools complied with this provision announced by José Cabral, governor-general of Mozambique (1926–1938).

The expenditures on education for Mozambique measure fairly well the level of governmental concern for the educational advancement of the colony. In 1950, the allocation of money for education constituted 1.3 percent of the colony's budget. In 1961, notwithstanding the fact that Africans contributed some $6 million to the colony's budget, only $1.05 million was given in support of missionary schools; in 1962, the school budget rose to 4.0 percent.[32] In 1967, out of a total budget of 4,521,200,00 escudos—approximately $150,706,670 (at 30 escudos/dollar)—the school subsidy amounted to 253,100,000 escudos ($8,436,666)—about 5.59 percent—distributed as follows: 19 million escudos ($633,333) for the University of Lourenço Marques; 69,500,000 ($2,316,666) for the Catholic mission; and 164,600,000 escudos ($5,486,666) for the government-supported establishment (mostly for Caucasians, *mistos*, and the assimilated). This compares unfavorably to some 678,400,000 escudos ($22,613,333) allocated for defense for that year—approximately 15 percent of "total ordinary expenditures."[33]

Likewise, the Portuguese educational expenditure in the colony falls far below that of the British and the French even in their poorest colonies, such as Chad, as illustrated in the following table.

Table 5. Educational Expenditures in Some African Territories[34]

Territories	1960–1961 (in British pounds)	Percentage of Territorial Budget	1961–1962 (in British pounds)	Percentage of Territorial Budget
Bechuanaland	138,000	5.6	321,000	11.1
Chad	2,000,000 (dollars)	12.5	--	--
Ghana	16,281,000	13.2	17,264,000	13.4
Ivory Coast	8,850,000 (dollars)	10.0	15,720,000 (dollars)	14.0
Kenya	6,489,000	14.9	66,526,000	16.9
Malawi	1,194,000	17.2	1,153,000	14.5
Mozambique	--	4.0 (1962–1963)	9,000,000 (dollars)	5.6
Nigeria	15,550,000	42.0	14,216,000	38.8
Senegal	8,000,000 (dollars)	16.0	--	--
Sierra Leone	1,668,000	13.6	--	--
Swaziland	497,000	16.0	401,000	17.6
Tanganyika	5,051,000	16.5	--	--
Zambia	2,634,000	14.1	3,866,000	19.1

These figures reveal that Mozambique was spending three to five times less money than most African colonial governments. Of course, the figures should not be taken as absolute truths. Yet, they point to the basic trend in the Portuguese overseas territories: the low priority given African education. In considering the colonial budgets, one has to keep in mind the poverty or wealth of the colony, its population, its local taxes, the official colonial policy, and the length of the colonial presence. When all these variables are weighed carefully, one would expect much more from Mozambique in educational opportunities. But the facts do not meet logical expectations.

THE IMPACT OF
COLONIAL EDUCATION

The implications of the Portuguese educational system briefly outlined here are far-reaching. Despite the seeming growth of the number of schools within the colony in the course of years, particularly in the 1960s, the actual impact of the system on literacy in Mozambique was negligible. At no point in time in that territory did the Portuguese educate 5 percent of the inhabitants. Following is a table of literacy for Africa in 1970.

Literacy in Africa as a whole was not very impressive in 1970.[36] But the Portuguese colonies of Mozambique and Angola showed among the lowest literacy percentages that year. Besides, more than 90 percent of the educated few finished only their elementary schooling. High school had always been the privilege of a few. University education in Mozambique was unheard of until 1964. Mozambique was at least a half century behind most of the African colonies in terms of university education. But even after 1964, the senior year had to be spent in a Portuguese university. Furthermore, in Mozambique, the university was created primarily for the Portuguese population. A discussion of its establishment in Mozambique had been going on since the early 1950s. A seminar on the "overseas provinces" took place on May 10, 1951, at the University of Coimbra. The keynote speaker for that gathering of intellectuals was Almerindo Lessa, who argued for a university in Mozambique not for the education of Africans, but to offset the educational dependence on South African institutions and on materials written in English that were flooding Mozambique.[37]

The enrollment figures announced by the Portuguese government are often misleading, particularly for secondary school and university education, since most of the students have always been Portuguese, foreign whites, and Indians. Furthermore, the type of education administered was totally foreign to local needs and cultures of the Mozambican people. A Mozambican child ended up knowing much more about continental Portugal than about his own motherland. He could recite the railway lines running from Lisbon to other Portuguese cities and knew about Dom Afonso Henriques, but would likely be unaware of the Beira-Malawi railway system and the ancient kingdom of Mwene Mutapa. Naturally, this state of affairs was in line with the Portuguese policy of assimilation, which tended to mold Africans into Portuguese citizens. Ricardo Patée put it this way:

> The fundamental theory behind the whole thing, with the later modifications of 1951, is that the empire is a whole, that it is a family and that the purpose is to assimilate, within the pattern of common Portuguese nationhood and way of life, these diverse peoples.[38]

Table 6. Estimated Literacy in Africa (1970)[35]

Countries	Population	Literacy Percentage
Algeria	12,600,000	15
Angola (Port.)	5,400,000	3
Benin	2,600,000	10
Botswana	600,000	20
Burundi	3,400,000	10
Cameroon	5,600,000	10–15
Central African Empire	1,500,000	15
Chad	3,500,000	5–10
Congo (Braz.)	900,000	20–25
Equatorial Guinea	300,000	not available
Ethiopia	23,900,000	5
Gabon	500,000	12
Gambia	400,000	10
Ghana	8,400,000	25
Guinea	3,800,000	5–10
Ivory Coast	4,100,000	20
Kenya	10,200,000	20–25
Lesotho	900,000	40
Liberia	1,100,000	9
Libya	1,800,000	27
Malagasy Republic	6,500,000	35
Malawi	4,200,000	15
Mali	4,900,000	2
Mauritania	1,100,000	1–5
Mauritius	800,000	61
Morocco	14,600,000	14
Mozambique	7,200,000	2
Namibia	600,000	27
Niger	3,700,000	1–5
Nigeria	45,500,000	25
Rhodesia	4,700,000	20
Rwanda	3,400,000	10
Senegal	3,800,000	5–10
Sierra Leone	2,500,000	10
Somalia	2,700,000	5
South Africa	19,000,000	35
Sudan	14,800,000	10–15
Swaziland	400,000	36
Tanzania	12,500,000	15–20
Togo	1,800,000	5–10
Tunisia	4,700,000	30
Uganda	8,100,000	20
Upper Volta	5,200,000	5–10
Zaire	17,000,000	58
Zambia	4,100,000	15–20

The French, whose policy was essentially assimilationist, revised several times their curriculum in Africa to conform to local circumstances. They not only stressed African geography in Senegal, but the teaching of French culture slowed down before educators "began to gather data about African cultures and the abilities of African children upon which to base the new curricula in some areas."[39]

A one-sided assimilation often resulted in a psychological problem sometimes referred to as "de-culturation." The educated African found himself in a true dilemma, well expressed by Kane in *Ambiguous Adventure*; the educated Mozambican was caught in a labyrinth—should he become Portuguese, assimilated, or continue as an African or Mozambican in culture and identity. In the final analysis he was neither Portuguese nor African. Repeatedly, of course, the Portuguese denied that it was their intention to mutilate African culture. Adriano Moreira, once minister of overseas colonies, wrote in 1962:

> Because our way of thinking throughout history has rejected racism, we
> also regard with due respect all the cultural forms of the various ethnic
> groupings. . . . For this same reason our policy of assimilation should
> have been understood, on the political plane, in terms of the creation of
> a will to live together, not the mutilation of the originality of the various
> groups that have come together under the protection of the same
> sovereignty.[40]

But how could that be if one was not allowed to speak in one's mother tongue or to study a Mozambican language in school? Certainly such policies were not conducive to rapid educational advancement. Thomas J. Jones noted: "The disregard of the Native language is a hindrance even to the acquisition of the European language. Much more does it limit the sympathetic and real exchange of ideas and influences, which are necessary to mutual confidence between Africans and Europeans."[41]

The educational system in Mozambique created a social problem as well. The educated few were considered to be civilized while the illiterate were labelled uncivilized or *indígenas,* who could be used for forced labor by whites and educated Africans at any time with or without pay. The official census book of 1958 gave the following definitions:

> A civilized population is the number of whites, yellow and mixed-blood
> individuals and also those of the negro race that satisfy the following
> conditions: 1. Speak Portuguese; 2. Do not practice ways—and
> customs—proper to the natives; 3. Have a profession, are engaged in
> commerce and industry, or own property for their living. Those who do
> not satisfy these conditions are uncivilized.[42]

Accordingly, primary schools were segregated. Some were designed for the assimilated few and the Portuguese, financed by the government and better maintained. Others were for the *indígenas.* The official reason given again was that the *indígenas,* as savages, could not be civilized as fast as the Europeans or the sons of the assimilated, that this segregation was not based on color but on the "different degrees of civilization that teaching must be geared to if it is to be effective."[43] As a result of the system, the Portuguese created a superiority complex in some individuals an an inferiority complex in the majority of the Mozambican people. The consequences were tragic: exploitation of Mozambicans by Mozambicans. The application of the term white *(muzungu)* to educated Africans illustrates the assimilation problem within the colony.

The educational system distorted the minds of African teachers, who came to believe that they would gain respect from their students and guarantee discipline in the classroom if they inflicted severe corporal punishment upon the students. Today the distrust between assimilated and nonassimilated, the uneasy harmony and cooperation between *mistos* and the rest of the population, is also a residue of the preferential educational treatment afforded the former during the colonial era.

How does one explain the slow and late emergence of the nationalist movement in the Portuguese colonies? That political parties were forbidden in the "provinces" and that Mozambicans lacked education were important. There is also the impact of the assimilationist policy on Mozambican leaders. The traditionally assimilated population of Mozambique was rather small (only 1.4 percent of the population in 1970).[44] However, in the other colonies, the élite assumed leadership in the independence movement much earlier. In Mozambique as well as in Angola, the educated few, mostly assimilated, persisted in the belief that the Portuguese would eventually mean their theory of complete integration and equality before the law for whites and blacks. In the words of Paul Whitaker, the colonial system in the Portuguese territories

> . . . inhibited the formation of an educated elite or even a minimally
> educated mass following to push towards a "democratic" decolonization.
> The "Portuguese" Africans were virtually unchanged by the War
> [World War II], while others were gaining new experience and
> self-respect in the British and French administrations and overseas
> fighting units.[45]

When they finally realized they had been deceived, practically all Africa was independent.[46]

Portuguese preference for urban areas and the southern part of the colony also played a negative role in the nature of the leadership of Mozambique. More than 70 percent of the ministerial and other important positions were occupied by people from the south, especially from Lourenço Marques (Maputo), Gaza, and Inhambane. More schools were located here than elsewhere in Mozambique. By 1924, two-thirds of the schools and missions had been built in the south despite the fact that only one-tenth (some 350,000 people) of the population of the colony lived in this region.[47]

Looking at the majors pursued at the University of Lourenço Marques, one notices that natural sciences, at which the Portuguese were least competent because of inadequate equipment of their laboratories, were heavily emphasized to the neglect of the social sciences. Mozambique certainly needed scientists and engineers, but she could not totally ignore an equal need for historians, geographers, sociologists, social workers, psychologists, and others. The Portuguese rationale for favoring natural sciences was that creating natural scientists spared the colony politically minded individuals and agitators, who were most likely to emerge from the ranks of graduates in social sciences.

As a rule, Mozambicans were educated to occupy secondary positions in government or the private sector as secretaries, interpreters, assistants, and teachers, to facilitate the economic exploitation of the colony, or to help Christianize the Africans. This was the official policy, as Marcello Caetano, the ousted premier, once declared: "The natives of Africa must be directed by Europeans, but are indispensable as auxiliaries. The Africans did not yield any meaningful contributions to the evolution of mankind. . . . Therefore, the Africans must be seen as productive elements organized or to be organized in an economy directed by Whites."[48]

In this respect the Portuguese colonial aims differed from those of the other colonial powers. The British thought education must "raise the standard alike of character and efficiency of the bulk of the people but provision must also be made for the training of those who are required to fill posts in the administrative and technical services, as well as those who as chiefs will occupy positions of exceptional trust and responsibility."[49] They further believed this opportunity had to be extended to all Africans who showed ability. While the French stressed the need to form an elite with guaranteed jobs, the Belgians emphasized that primary education should be made available to as many Africans as possible. They were not interested, however, in forming *évolués*. This partly explains why Zaire has the second highest literacy rate among black African states, Mauritius having the highest.

Yet, all colonial powers were interested in safeguarding their supremacy on the African continent. Thus the education of the African had to be inferior or limited. This is how L. H. Gann and Peter Duignan differentiated the nature of the educational systems of colonial powers in Africa:

> The French aimed at creating a small Gallicized elite; they emphasized intellectual achievement and urban values. The Portuguese . . . shared

the preference of the French for teaching in the metropolitan tongue, but otherwise set their sights much lower and differed from the French in always using religious instruction as an integral part of instruction. The British . . . allowed each of their dependencies to formulate its own policy. Their theory of education stressed the values of rural life and local rule.[50]

For the British, this was in tune with the acclaimed theory of indirect rule, although paradoxically they "produced a larger number of partially Europeanized Africans, imbued to some extent with metropolitan values, than the supposedly assimilationist-minded French."[51]

The Portuguese considered Mozambicans and all Africans to be indolent and lazy. By 1941, it was hoped that education would eventually instill in them a national conscience, love for work, and moral uplift defined as "the abandonment of indolence and the preparation of future rural and industrial workers who will produce enough to meet their social obligations."[52] In other words, the Portuguese wanted to provide both education and instruction to a few privileged Africans, since they believed in the superiority of their culture and in the inability of the African to acquire good manners and proper behavior from his parents. Hence, there was the need to teach him specific courses in religion and moral behavior. If the Portuguese ever had a consistent philosophy of education, it could be summarized as follows: education for the Africans in Mozambique had to be limited to a very few individuals who would facilitate the economic exploitation of the colony. Their education had to be inferior to that of their colonizers—equality in this respect was understandably undesirable.

It was a romantic rather than a political education; it stressed the glories of and the love for Portugal. The principles of nineteenth-century liberalism and democracy were systematically put aside to stifle any aspiration for self-determination in the colony. It was assimilationist, geared to making the African a carbon copy, however blurred and incomplete, of a Portuguese citizen.

The process was supposed to be gradual and not accelerated because, so it was justified, the African was still in a state of primitivism. This task could be done better by missionaries, who would impart good conduct and love for Portugal. In addition, the educational system was designed to guarantee the maintenance of Portuguese supremacy over the Mozambicans forever. But the few educated Mozambicans and FRELIMO shattered these hopes and finally the colonial apparatus crumbled with the signing of the Lusaka Agreement in September 1974. In this sense, Portugal, and for that matter, the European powers through their unwarranted treatment of Africans and their educational programs, "sowed the seeds of the ultimate destruction of the colonial system."[53]

The Portuguese did educate some Mozambicans, particularly during the 1960s. Indeed, their effort in education can be seen as partly responsible for the successful independence of Mozambique in 1975 because not all FRELIMO leaders were foreign-educated nor was the battle won exclusively by FRELIMO militants. Others inside and outside Mozambique, assimilated and nonassimilated, educated in Portuguese schools contributed to the final victory. What made the difference, perhaps, was the "wisdom" of allowing missionaries, particularly the foreign White Fathers, the Swiss Protestant missionaries, the Spanish Burgos, the Italian Capucins, and others, to take charge of the educational system. Despite the adverse impact of Christianity on African culture resulting from missionary work, the fact remains that a great, if not the greatest, number of nationalist leaders were mission-educated. In Mozambique and elsewhere, the Christian-educated African successfully argued

> . . . not only that he was equal to his colonial master, but that the
> secular and religious premises of the latter's culture demanded that he
> recognize not only the fundamental equality of the African as a man,
> but also that he recognize individual achievement when he saw it.[54]

Eduardo Mondlane, Filipe Magaia, Urias Simango, and Samora Machel, known Mozambican nationalists, were all products of missionary schools. In 1969, the majority of the Central Committee members of FRELIMO were Catholic-educated and so were almost all of the students who left Mozambique to study abroad during the 1960s.[55] Robert Strayer points out that nationalists have constantly accused missionaries of having " . . . acted hand in glove with the administration to subvert African political movements, especially during the interwar period."[56] In Mozambique the criticism holds true for most Portuguese priests—Secular, Franciscan, Jesuit, and Lazarist. The White Fathers, on the contrary, increasingly sided with the liberation forces, and in 1971 decided to leave the colony rather than submit themselves to the status of tools of Portuguese repression. Their subsequent campaign in Europe on behalf of the Africans in Mozambique, particularly by Father Jean-Pierre Pickard and the late Father Caesar Bertuli, exposed Portuguese atrocities in the colonies abroad. Even among the Portuguese clergy there were exceptions. Within the church hierarchy, the late bishop of Beira, Dom Sebastião Soares de Resende, like a voice in the wilderness, was constantly reminding his fellow Portuguese that independence was inevitable. He favored a gradual process toward that goal in Mozambique, in contrast to the former archbishop of Lourenço Marques, Dom Custódio Alvim Pereira, who opposed the liberation forces even after the Portuguese military coup of 1974. (The Vatican had to rescue him by recalling him permanently to Rome.)

Portugal is the poorest country in Europe today, and about 40 percent of its own people cannot read and write. Under such circumstances, the backwardness of its colonies can be appreciated if not excused. It can also be argued that since Portugal was in Africa longer than any other European power, the educational advancement in her colonies should have reflected that reality. But it did not. Had the Portuguese organized their educational system better, made it relevant to local needs, followed their policies with determination, and spent much more money on education, Mozambique would have been much better off educationally today. We know, however, as Thomas Jones said in 1925:

> Educational legislation in the Province of Mozambique is disorganized, scrappy, self-contradictory and full of gaps. So abundant are the laws, however, that, one may say, with the French savant, "the land of forty thousand laws is the land of no law."[57]

Available historical evidence warrants the conclusion that education for Africans in the colony of Mozambique was always one of the lowest priorities of the Portuguese government in Lisbon and Lourenço Marques, the former capital. When Vasco da Gama set foot on the island of Mozambique in 1498, his mind was set on trade and adventure and definitely not on African education. The captains and governors entrusted with the administration of the colony throughout the centuries were interested in defending their forts, in fostering Portuguese colonial aims, and in getting some wealth for themselves, but not in opening the minds of Africans to the world of literacy. Charles Boxer was not far from the truth when he noted that until the early nineteenth century " . . . the Portuguese colonial empire was [at first] a commercial and maritime organization cast in a military and clerical mould" where the "cross and sword; God and Mammon; Christians and spices" were intertwined, and later a backward empire whose primary purpose was to provide a steady flow of slaves.[58] Mouzinho the Albuquerque, for example, one of the most celebrated governors in the colony (1890–1892), concerned with collecting taxes and exploiting the colony's natural resources, did practically nothing for the education of the Mozambicans.[59]

The policy of assimilation, based on the sound principle that all men are born equal and that through education they can be radically changed, should have produced more educated Africans within the colony. Unfortunately, it contained the implication that Portuguese culture was superior to the African in every respect—a culture that had no right to exist but to be completely dismantled. For centuries the policy brought comfort to the Portuguese. But in the final analysis, it proved detrimental and untenable. It left Mozambique with one of the lowest literacy rates in Africa in a century of rapid educational development throughout the world. The present situation in Mozambique is certainly a major challenge for the leaders of this emerging nation; it is up to them to speed up the campaign to wipe out illiteracy in the shortest possible time.

NOTES

1. Walter Rodney, *How Europe Underdeveloped Africa* (Washington, D. C.: Howard University Press, 1974), p. 244.

2. Alan K. Smith, "António Salazar and the Reversal of Portuguese Colonial Policy," *Journal of African History* 15, no. 4 (1974): 654–55.

3. *Circular da Secretaria Geral da Província às Câmaras Municipais de 5 de fevereiro de 1881* (Lourenço Marques, 1881).

4. Ibid.

5. James Duffy, *Portugal in Africa* (Baltimore: Penguin African Library, 1963), p. 128.

6. Ibid.

7. Thomas J. Jones, *Education in East Africa* (New York: Phelps-Stokes Fund, 1925), pp. 115, 153, 179.

8. Duffy, *Portugal in Africa*, p. 129.

9. Boleo Oliveira, *Moçambique* (Lisboa: Agência Geral do Ultramar, 1951), p. 281–82.

10. *Tempo*, June 25, 1955, p. 24.

11. Adapted from Donald Burns, *African Education: An Introductory Survey in Commonwealth Countries* (London: Oxford University Press, 1965), pp. 40, 73, 446, and Helen Kitchen, *The Educated African* (New York: Praeger, 1962), pp. 128, 145, 160, 215, 235. The author's assumption here is that between 1958 and 1962 the population of these five countries increased at approximately the same rate, that is from 1.5 to 2.15 percent per year.

12. M. Sarmento Rodrigues, *Presenca de Moçambique na vida da Nacão* (Lisboa: Agência Geral do Ultramar, 1964), p. 108.

13. C. F. Spence, *Moçambique* (Cape Town: Howard Timmons, 1963), p. 35.

14. Allison Herrick et. al., *Area Handbook for Mozambique* (Washington, D.C.: USGPO, 1969), pp. 91–2.

15. L. G. Cowan, *The Dilemmas of African Independence* (New York: Walter, 1976), pp. 112–113.

16. Ibid., pp. 114–115. See also *Boletim Geral do Ultramar*, 1966, p. 232, and *Boletim Geral do Ultramar*, 1967, pp. 68–150, for discrepancy in statistics for 1964 and 1965.

17. Colin Legum, *Africa Contemporary Record*, 1971–1972, p. B457.

18. Robin Wright, *Mozambique: Six Months after Independence*, RBW–16 (New York: Alicia Patterson Foundation, January 1976), p. 3. See also Robin Wright, *Janet Mondlane of the Mozambique Institute: American "Godmother" to an African Revolution*, RBW–3 (New York: Alicia Patterson Foundation, 1975), p. 8.

19. In Marvin Harris, *Portugal's African Wards: A First Hand Report on Labor and Education in Mozambique* (New York: Columbia University Press, 1960), p. 17.

20. Boleo, *Moçambique*, p. 283.

21. *Annário da Província de Moçambique* (Lourenço Marques: Oficinas Graficas da Minerva Central, 1966), p. 70.

22. Adapted from Kitchen, *The Educated African*, p. 245.

23. Ibid.

24. *Annuário da Província de Moçambique*, 1966, p. 70.

25. *Educacão* (Lisboa: Associacão Portuguesa das Empresas do Ultramar, 1970), p. 15. All sources were silent on racial proportions in schools in countries included in the study, except for Mozambique.

26. *Southern Africa* 6 (June-July 1973): 70.

27. Herrick et al., *Area Handbook*, p. 91.

28. Boleo, *Moçambique*, p. 463.

29. Charles R. Boxer, "S. R. Welch and His History of the Portuguese in Africa, 1495–1806," *Journal of African History* 1, no. 1 (1960): 63.

30. *Anuário da Província de Moçambique*, 1940 (A Title II, Art. 24a) p. 27.

31. *Anuário da Província de Moçambique*, 1930, pp. 64, 144.

32. Eduardo Mondlane, *The Struggle for Mozambique* (Baltimore: Penguin Books, 1968), p. 68.

33. Herrick et al., *Area Handbook*, p. 284.

34. Adapted from Burns, *African Education*, p. 195, and Kitchen, *The Educated African*, pp. 442, 447, 463.

35. Department of State, *Africa: This New Dialogue* (Washington, D.C.: USGPO, 1970), pp. 36–37.

36. The problem of illiteracy will apparently worsen in the Third World as the population increases. The World Bank estimates that in 1974 the rate of illiteracy was 74 percent and that by 1985 illiteracy in the "poorest countries . . . is expected to jump from 470 to over 865 million people" (Ursula Wolff, "Who Needs Literacy," *Africa Report* (July-August 1975): 53.

37. Almerindo Lessa, *Semana do Ultramar* (Lisboa: Agência Geral do Ultramar, 1951), pp. 69–71.

38. Recardo Patee, *Portugal and the Portuguese Stand* (Milwaukee: Bruce Publishing, 1962), p. 261. For a diversified African response to the policy of assimilation in Senegal, consult G. Wesley Johnson, Jr., "The Senegalese Urban Elite, 1900–1945," in *Africa and the West: Intellectual Responses to European Culture*, edited by Philip Curtin (Madison: University of Wisconsin Press, 1972), pp. 139–88.

39. Priscilla Blakemore, "Assimilation and Association in French Educational Policy and Practice: Senegal, 1903–1945," in *Essays in the History of African Education*, edited by Vincent Battle and Charles Lyons (New York: Teachers College Press, 1970), p. 100.

40. Adriano Moreira, *Portugal's Stand in Africa* (New York: University Publishers, 1962), pp. 111–12.

41. Jones, *Education in East Africa*, pp. 19–20.

42. *Moçambique, Recenseamento geral da populacão civilizada* (Lourenço Marques: Imprensa Nacional de Moçambique, 1958), p. ix.

43. *Anuário do Ensino, Colónia de Moçambique* (Lourenço Marques: Oficinas Graficas da Minerva Central, 1930), p. 3.

44. Basil Davidson, in *The Liberation of Guine* (Baltimore: Penguin African Library, 1969), estimated the assimilated population in the whole Portuguese African empire at "little more than one half of the total African population."

45. Paul Whitaker, "The Revolutions of Portuguese Africa," *Journal of Modern African Studies* 8, no. 1 (1970): 16.

46. Of course, this is not intended to portray the image that there was peace at all times in Mozambique and that the Africans did not offer resistance to the Portuguese colonial presence. From 1505 to 1917 the Portuguese faced uprisings in several areas of the colony. For details read Manuel S. Alberto and Francisco A. Toscan, *A Guerra em Moçambique* (Lisboa: Editora Ulisseia, 1942), pp. 9–16, and Allen Isaacman, "The Tradition of Resistance in Mozambique," *African Today* 22, no. 3 (July-September 1975): 37–51.

47. Jones, *Education in East Africa*, p. 305.

48. *The Guardian*, July 18, 1973.

49. David G. Scanlon, *Traditions of African Education* (New York: Teachers College, Columbia University, 1964), p. 94. For further detail on British colonial education see Burns, *African Education.*

50. L. H. Gann and Peter Duignan, *Burden of Empire* (Stanford: Hoover Institution Press, 1967), p. 279.

51. Ibid. For a comparative study of the shortcomings of both the assimilationist and indirect rule colonial policies, see Remi Clignet, "Inadequacies of the Notion of Assimilation in African Education," *Journal of Modern African Studies* 8, no. 3 (1970): 425–44.

52. Harris, *Portugal's African Wards*, p. 15.

53. Laing Gray Cowan; James O'Connel; and David Scanlon, eds., *Education and Nation-Building in Africa* (New York: Praeger, 1966), p. 17.

54. Michael Crowder, *West Africa under Colonial Rule* (Evanston: Northwestern University Press, 1968), p. 368.

55. Mondlane, *The Struggle for Mozambique*, p. 71. This is how the author came to the United States after twenty years of Catholic mission and seminary training.

56. Robert Strayer, "Mission History in Africa: New Perspectives on an Encounter," *African Studies Review* 19, no. 1 (April 1976): 11. The article gives an important picture of the complexity of missionary education in Africa.

57. Jones, *Education in East Africa*, p. 296.

58. Charles R. Boxer, *Four Centuries of Portuguese Expansion, 1415–1825* (Berkeley and Los Angeles: University of California Press, 1969), pp. 63, 91.

59. Read his memoirs in *Mouzinho de Albuquerque, Governador de Lourenço Marques* (Lourenço Marques: Imprensa Nacional de Moçambique, 1956).

CHAPTER 10

Revolutionary Development and Educational Decolonization in Mozambique

AGRIPPAH T. MUGOMBA

Postcolonial education in Mozambique is geared towards realizing specific objectives which include the following: to redesign and operationalize an educational model that places education, both academic and vocational, within the context of a revolutionary society and culture in which particular emphasis is attached to the development of a new identity and personality (both individual and national) completely purged of colonial imagery, values, and aspirations; to use education as an instrument for decolonizing both the colonial minds of Mozambicans and the inherited political, economic, and social institutions; and to make education contribute directly and positively to the overall political, economic, social, cultural, and spiritual development of Mozambique. Revolutionary education is thus viewed as a vital requirement in Mozambique's continuing struggle to realize its cherished "dream the size of freedom."

When Mozambique became independent, only 10–15 percent of the indigenous population was literate; only 14 percent had attended part of the six-year primary education program; 0.9 percent had secondary or vocational training; and a mere 0.1 percent had ever had the opportunity to attend a university.[1] This is the legacy colonial education left behind in Mozambique. Since regaining independence in June 1975, the new government has attached great importance to education, both formal and informal. The main areas of emphasis are adult education, formal academic training, the teaching of the history and culture of Mozambique, and political education, to enable Mozambicans to participate effectively in the tasks of nation-building and revolution. In addition to introducing a system of state schools and making education free and compulsory for all citizens of all ages, the government has been, methodically, overhauling the entire curriculum for primary and secondary schools, and the role of the university has been sharply redefined. The ruling party, FRELIMO, is deeply committed to the view that education, and in particular its political dimension, is of strategic importance for the success of the Mozambican revolution.

The principal focus of postcolonial educational theory and practice in Mozambique is (1) to uproot the old ideas of racism, sexism, tribalism, exploitation, and individualism; (2) to acquire a new vision of the individual, the country, the people, and the world; and (3) to link literacy and education directly to the ideals and philosophy of a *socialist revolution*. Such a monumental task is difficult to accomplish without instilling a revolutionary mentality of unparalleled dimensions among Mozambicans. Along with this reorientation, there is a genuine and determined attempt to place women firmly in the center of the struggle to overcome the consequences of colonial exploitation characterized by massive illiteracy, poverty, and underdevelopment. This is a radical break with a colonial heritage which placed women on the margins of a male-dominated society. This chapter picks up where Chapter 9 left off; it examines and analyzes the postcolonial educational policy and goals designed to prevent Mozambique from being ensnared by the model of neocolonial development, social change, and system transformation.

EDUCATION FOR DECOLONIZING INSTITUTIONS AND INDIVIDUALS

Mozambique differs from the postindependence, neocolonial practices of most African states by setting education in a new ideological context in which knowledge is seen as a tool for serving the masses rather than for personal enrichment. Under colonialism, the few who were taught were encouraged to view education as a means of personal advancement and acquiring wealth. FRELIMO has described the nature, function, and objectives of colonial education as follows:

> All the programmes came from Portugal, all the books, all the administrators, all the qualified teachers, all the exams. Mozambique existed as a far-flung European island, cut off from its own history and geographical perspective and as effectively isolated from the rest of its African continent as if the miles that separated Mozambique from Portugal in fact separated Mozambique from Africa.
>
> This so-called education had religion as the dominant factor with literacy and Portuguese so as to be able to read the bible and some maths so as to calculate better the compulsory quota of cotton production or to be more lucrative boss-boya in South African mines. Our children grew up with a deformed picture of the world composed of those destined to govern and those destined to serve, where the educated work with their heads and despise the uneducated who perform with their hands the lowest form of work, physical labour. Instead of being the agent of change of his society and environment, man was the subservient recipient of divine will.[2]

In the new Mozambique, education is not an ideal, nor is it just a pragmatic solution to a social problem. It is an important basic political principle. President Samora Machel has stated that "he who has studied should be the match that comes to light the flame that is the people." The implications go far beyond the conventional meaning of education as such:

> The new revolutionary education in Mozambique is aimed at forming a new Mozambican African personality, a New Man, free from all complexes of superiority and inferiority, free from superstitious beliefs, self-reliant and ready to make his scientific knowledge the basis of the new society based on unity and equality. In sum, education for us is the principal instrument for our liberation, for our real political, economic, social and cultural independence.[3]

Educational policy operates at three levels in Mozambique: (1) the "Pilot Centers" established in the former liberated zones, which during the war of liberation served as the laboratories for testing the policies now being applied throughout the country; (2) the old primary and secondary schools, which are now being dismantled and reorganized to suit revolutionary objectives; and (3) the Eduardo Mondlane National University, which in the colonial era was the center for the development of the "elitist" scourge, now being uprooted systematically. To these should be added the nationwide literacy campaign conducted by the National Service for Adult Education, a department run by the Ministry of Education and Culture. The principal agents for political mobilization in the overall educational effort are the Dynamizing Groups (involving party cadres, students, teachers, and other workers) which feed into an administrative structure with representatives of these same Dynamizing Groups, plus the local communities, headed by FRELIMO-appointed school directors.[4]

The schools as new institutions of people's power are symbolized by the Pilot Centers, located deep in the forests of the former liberated zones. These party residential schools operate on a type of half-work, half-study pattern, with self-reliance established both as a principle and a necessity during the ten-year war of national liberation. Cultural activities, political study, sports, production, and a rich interaction with the surrounding peasant communal villages are all integral parts of the life of these schools. The schools are also model democratic centers, with students, teachers, and employees collectively participating in decision-making. Even classrooms are divided into smaller units or study groups. Student leaders organize schoolwide cultural activities, production, and hygiene, and send representatives to a management committee which works with the director (or headmaster). This is the model which is being applied throughout Mozambique (see diagram below).[5]

Diagram 1. Structure of Primary and Secondary Schools

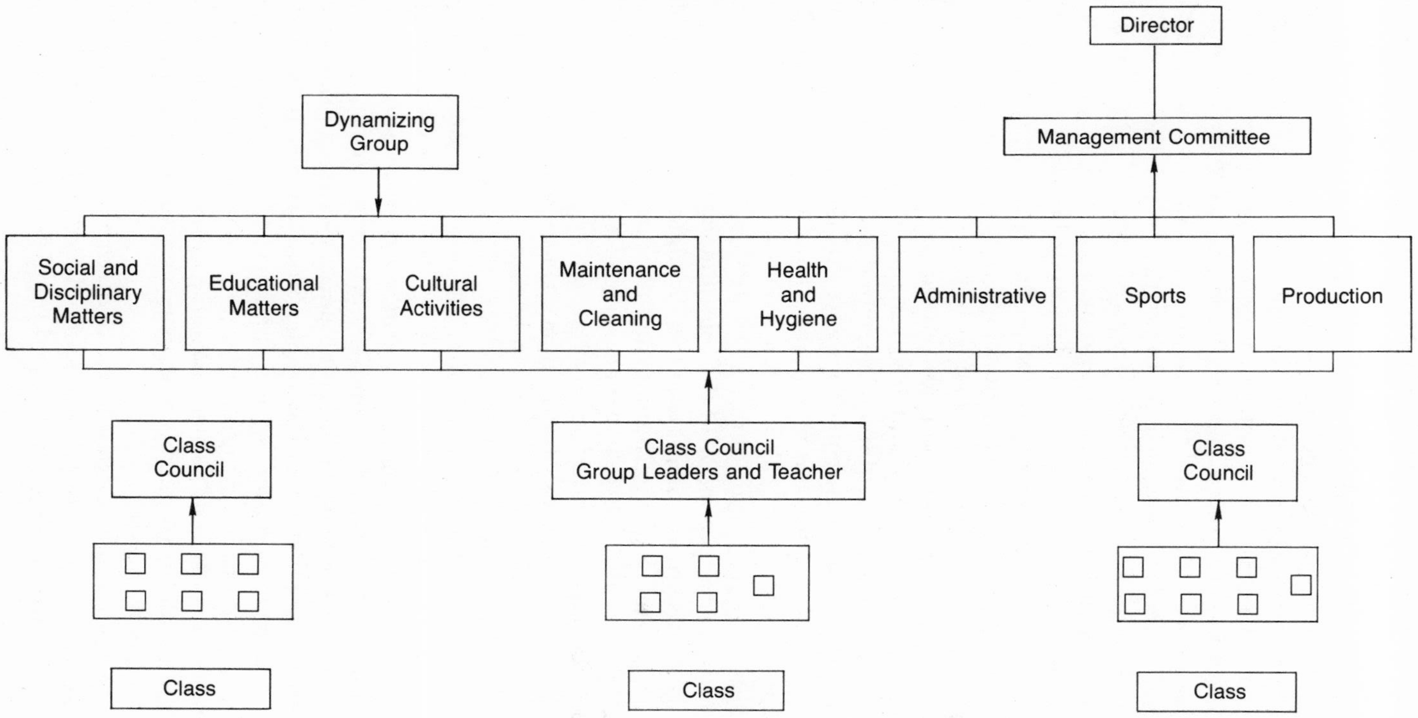

A primary task in the reorganization and reorientation of the school system has been the setting up of national seminars where teachers from FRELIMO schools exchange ideas and experiences with those from the inherited colonial system, for the principal purpose of helping teachers who were trained in the colonial tradition achieve the difficult but necessary transition to the educational policies of a new and revolutionary society. Teachers from the colonial educational system that is being destroyed are thus given the opportunity to attempt to grasp, for the first time perhaps, the ways in which the colonial school system alienated students from African history and culture and shaped the small handful of educated Mozambicans to function as a handy intermediary between the colonialists and the peasant masses. Only through such a "cleansing" process can those teachers contribute to the fleshing out of genuine educational alternatives.

A number of significant changes have been introduced since June 1975. School vacation periods are now used for retraining programs throughout the country and for bringing together new groups of teachers into programs of intensive self-education. Through collective discussions, the teachers come to realize that curriculum development in the new Mozambique is much more than the simple substitution of Mozambique for Portugal. It is not a question of, say, understanding the history or geography of the new state without reference to Europe but, rather, an appreciation of the role of man as the principal agent of change in his environment, who has the ability to transform Mozambique's natural resources (human and other) into the material base for a prosperous and self-reliant new society. This is the essence of the vigorous campaign underway to create a new personality that present and future generations of Mozambicans can take pride in.

This process of reexamination has led to another major change. Barely six months after independence, all colonial textbooks were prohibited from further circulation. Though obviously creating a serious crisis, especially acute because of lack of advance preparation (both technically and psychologically), the idea was to force teachers to begin working on their own texts and lessons rather than merely limping along with the old ones, which both portrayed and glorified a foreign culture and a totally alien way of life. Since that sharp break with the past, groups representing subject areas in each school work to prepare lessons; vacations bring together larger groups to lay the groundwork for new textbooks; and a small task force within the Ministry of Education and Culture simultaneously generates such interim texts as are most urgently needed.

Another important development occurred in June 1976. The government introduced new primary school readers throughout the country. These are simple texts oriented towards rural society and having themes pointing to Mozambican realities: the land, rivers, trees, and the labor of Mozambicans as the basis of national reconstruction and the development of a new culture.[6]

The timing of school vacations has also been deliberately made to fit seasonal cycles. Long holidays now coincide with the warmest months in the year. During these intervals, student brigades work on school improvement and community projects, for example, technical students work with the Central Registry Office, primary school pupils tend school gardens or mend furniture, while graphics students may be involved in making toys for child care centers (these being widespread as a means of freeing women and men to participate fully in the tasks of national reconstruction and development).

The Eduardo Mondlane National University has also been brought into line with these fundamental changes. The "July Activities" performed each year take professors, students, and support staff to the northern provinces (obviously to study what had been going on long before independence) and to rural development projects throughout the countryside, where they help the peasants in harvesting crops and constructing houses in communal villages. The value of this exercise was realized during the liberation struggle. It is a means for combating isolationist academic tendencies and the development of elitist attitudes that do not fit in with the realities of an independent Mozambique. There is a deliberate attempt to destroy the barriers between the intellectual minority and the illiterate majority and between teachers and students, part of a dysfunctional model which colonial education worked hard to maintain. By seeking to eliminate some of the most obvious contributory factors to class consciousness, Mozambique is moving towards creating an egalitarian society (quite apart from the practical contribution made by the students to national self-reliance). The government realizes that education was at the center of colonial structures, and it is using education to free the people from the complexes which the colonial educational system helped to create and develop. The specific purposes of the "July Activities" are (1) activating the internal transformation of the university from a colonial-capitalist institution to one which serves all the people of the country; (2) allowing workers, students, and teachers to see some of the realities of the rural areas; (3) allowing the academic community to engage in some aspect of national reconstruction; (4) combating elitism and other obscurantist tendencies; (5) putting specialist knowledge to the test of practice; and (6) increasing knowledge of Mozambique's history, economy, and culture which was suppressed under colonialism.

In essence, the idea is to help foster a revolutionary consciousness on the part of those people most likely, because they are literate, to fall into the temptation of regarding themselves as a distinct intelligentsia superior to all others within society and therefore entitled to living a very different life-style from the masses. That is the central basis of this reeducation program, which is a complete negation of the values colonial education endowed to those Mozambicans who managed to acquire any education, however little. And this ties in very closely with another purpose of revolutionary education in Mozambique, that is, to teach students at all levels to identify correctly the principal enemy in the postindependence era, namely the "national bourgeois establishment" still seeking to maintain links with the colonial past. The old educational system is thus being transformed into a weapon to destroy the vestiges of privilege and a tool to serve the people as a whole and to establish genuine popular democracy.

EDUCATION AND SOCIAL TRANSFORMATION: DETRIBALIZATION AND WOMEN'S LIBERATION

Education in a revolutionary society means a lot more than the formalized transmission of knowledge from teacher to student (and vice versa) patterned on the traditional classroom model. Here education takes on a *political* dimension; it seeks to intensify the process of mental decolonization of society as a whole, as part of the postindependence struggle to eliminate the social contradictions promoted and magnified by colonialism. Countries recently liberated from colonial shackles and attempting to stage a genuine revolution must link education to a social transformation that involves as one of its most important objectives the ideological reorientation of elites, the detribalization of the masses (as well as the elites themselves), and, perhaps most significant of all, the liberation of women from classical colonialism and male chauvinist domination.

One of the cardinal principles of FRELIMO policies is to strictly forbid the selection of individuals for party and governmental positions on the basis of race, sex, color, or some other erroneous criteria; in particular, the party takes a resolute and vigilant stand against attempts to promote secular or parochial interests based on ethnicity and regionalism. The struggle to combat "tribalism" and "regionalism" is being waged relentlessly as part of the mobilization effort to create a national consciousness among all Mozambicans. That, of course, does not mean that individuals and ethnic groups will not try to advance sectarian interests. But it does mean that once these activities are uncovered by party vigilante brigades, they are dealt with in a ruthless manner. Prominent individuals have been dismissed summarily from the party (including expulsions from the Central Committee and the People's Forces for the Liberation of Mozambique). Thus, the patterns of interactions among the various ethnic groups, particularly at the countryside level, are carefully manipulated by the party so that they contribute to a rapid breakdown of the traditional barriers between communities, in the belief and hope that a spirit of national unity will be forged in the process. The development of communal villages and production cooperatives is a key element in this well-planned strategy of "detribalizing" Mozambicans. The new village structures, because they are built around a revolutionary base stressing production, education, vigilance, and unity, aim at breaking down the ethnic divisions previously enforced by colonialism.

It is still too early to expect FRELIMO to have achieved considerable success in altering centuries-old patterns between the modern "urban" and the traditional "rural" societies. There have been no large-scale physical efforts designed to shift populations in an attempt to break down the existing barriers. The only relocation being carried out thus far is the resettlement of refugees and other displaced persons as part of the tasks of national reconstruction after the war of national liberation. While great strides have been made in the former liberated zones to "modernize" traditional society, on a countrywide basis the relationships between modern and traditional societies remain very much as they were before. The aspirations, tastes, and interests of the two societies are still poles apart, and it is unrealistic to expect the situation to change radically within the next decade, much as the Mozambican government might want to achieve this revolutionary feat. Even in the older socialist countries around the world (e.g., China), there are still marked differences between modern and traditional societies. The government is making every effort to alter or reorient the life-style of the urban society to reflect the dominant pattern of life in Mozambique, which withstood colonial intervention and remained rural and "traditional." The national leadership is pursuing its socialist principles and values, by arresting the strong, externally oriented materialistic ethics and consumerism of the modern society and slowly "modernizing" the traditional society. Hopefully, the two sectors will develop a more stable relationship. Experiences elsewhere in Africa have demonstrated decisively how important it is to change the unbalanced, unidirectional, and exploitative relationships between the urban and rural sectors if there is to be true national integration and genuine revolution.

By far the most significant development in this direction in Mozambique is FRELIMO's campaign to liberate women from the yoke of colonial and traditional oppression.[7] The fundamental commitment to the emancipation of women stems from the central role women played during the anticolonial war in the party, the guerrilla army, and the liberated areas. Indeed, one of the four public figures whose names are household words in Mozambique and whose portraits are found everywhere throughout the country is Josina Machel, President Machel's first wife, who died during the war, on April 7, 1971. The other three figures are Machel himself; Eduardo Mondlane, the father of modern Mozambican nationalism and founding leader of FRELIMO; and Marcelino dos Santos, vice-president of FRELIMO and the last surviving member of the first Central Committee, elected in 1962. April 7 is now recognized in Mozambique as a public holiday dedicated both to the memory of Josina Machel and other women who laid down their lives during the war and to the continuing role of women in general in the Mozambican revolution. The Organization of Mozambican Women (OMM), formed in March 1972, is the principal movement seeking to incorporate women in the reconstruction of the society envisioned in the new Mozambique.[8]

Since one of the aims of the government is to transform the rural subsistence economy into organized, planned, and collectivized agriculture, Mozambican women, by participating in this process, will play a direct role in transforming the society and their place in that society. The role of women in establishing bridges between the traditional and urban sectors of the society and in the political economy of Mozambique is reflected in official interpretations of the position of women in both spheres of activity. According to President Machel, the Mozambican woman is confronted by

> the most elevated degree of oppression, backwardness and exploitation in our society. . . . Reduced to the role of being an object of pleasure, producer of children and subsistence for the family, unpaid worker at the service of the "head" of the household, the man, she possesses a great revolutionary potential that the Mozambican revolution cannot do without.[9]

The government recognizes that urban women face a different and complex set of social and economic problems. As the pivotal center of Portuguese colonialism and bourgeois values, the cities and towns are still where, in FRELIMO's view, the class struggle is the sharpest and where a woman feels most violently her double exploitation deriving from sexism as well as economic deprivation and political disenfranchisement. In this context, the president has observed that the urban environment is

> the sector of Mozambican society where the ideological and cultural domination of capitalism and colonialism is most felt. [The Mozambican woman] in the city is daily subjected to the model of life and the logic of consumption mounted by the propaganda machine of the dominating class. The necessities of capitalist growth forced the system to integrate increasing numbers of women in production, counting on a salary discrimination because of sex. At the same time, it gave the woman a capacity to buy, to consume, facilitating the penetration of bourgeois values, as a model to copy . . . assimilated like varnish.[10]

The plight of urban women is thus of particular concern to the Mozambique government. As a worker, the urban woman must sell her labor at the lowest wages, and she is often reduced to selling her body as well in order to supplement her meager earnings. If she is a homemaker, she must, like the rural woman, exist almost solely to serve her husband. The urban setting especially is seen as the center of ever sharpening social and economic contradictions directly linked to colonialism. There, the contrasts between misery and luxury, inferiority and superiority, helped foster the growth of class consciousness. Thus it is in the city or town that women—as factory workers, single mothers, homemakers, civil servants, "domestics," etc.—become "marginalized" and alienated, and it is there that the "class nature" of the women's situation becomes obvious. Recognizing this, the OMM, with the active support of the party, is committed to the struggle against the sexual division of labor and discrimination in production opportunities and its benefits, and for a greater role for women in making decisions for the society as a whole. In the new Mozambique, then, it is necessary that the emancipation of women be integrated into the larger context of national reconstruction. Women must be given equal opportunities to learn new techniques and theoretical knowledge, must have access to modern technology, and, above all, must participate in political structures, management, and administration. The emancipation of women is central to the strategy of integrating traditional and urban societies; in a broader context, it is vital for women to engage in erecting the material and ideological base for the construction of a socialist society in Mozambique.

CONCLUSION

Postindependence educational policy in Mozambique has a decisive role in promoting national consciousness and socialist development; it has the even more critical function of resurrecting and rehabilitating, in the postcolonial era, the tradition, culture, and values which colonial education sought to banish, suppress, or subordinate in the name of "European civilization." In Mozambique and in other recently liberated African states, such as Angola and Guinea-Bissau, education is finally being recognized and treated not as a privilege but a right to be enjoyed by society as a whole; above all, it is now being recognized for what it should have properly been, an instrument for promoting national development as part of the total process of a revolutionary transformation of the inherited colonial state and its institutions and supporting structures and personnel. Postindependence educational policies that deviate from such a natural path can only serve to strengthen neocolonial development, which is a complete negation of the aims of the struggle against classical colonialism.

Whether Mozambique and other like-minded African states will succeed or fail in this venture will depend to a very large extent on the actual nature of the interplay between a number of interdependent variables, as well as the peculiar circumstances facing each postcolonial state. Only time will tell whether or not the revolutionary-oriented leaderships in these countries will be affected appreciably by the often moderating or mellowing influences of both financial constraints and domestic and external opposition to their exemplary policies. Success or failure may also depend on the long-term survival of the infant regimes now in control of those countries, which must constantly guard against either real or contrived challenges from vested interests, both internal and external. Finally, elite perceptions of the cost-benefit relationship, again over time, may have a profound effect on this gigantic vision of new, egalitarian societies finally emerging in Africa.

NOTES

1. See "Spotlight on Mozambique," *Africa* 46 (June 1975): 113, and Chris Searle, "'Escola Nova': The New Secondary School in Mozambique," *Issue: A Quarterly Journal of Africanist Opinion* 8 (Spring 1978): 32.

2. Cited in Judith Marshall, "Education in the New Mozambique," *This Magazine* (Toronto) (November-December 1976): 24. See also Elisio Martins, *Colonialism and Imperialism in Mozambique: The Beginning of the End* (Akademisk Forlag, n.d.), pp. 85–108.

3. Marshall, "Education in the New Mozambique," p. 24. Searle has noted, similarly, that

> post-independence education here in Mozambique is not a question of
> extending what was here before, creating new elites to replace the old
> ones, or bureaucratically contriving to say that liberation comes simply
> with more people being educated to live submissive or exploited lives.
> Education in the new Mozambique carries with it the mighty concept of
> the creation of the New Man—not a few "new supermen" to control
> and manipulate the mass of the People, but nine million New Men and
> Women who will pull themselves and their country from the
> backwardness of colonial inheritance to the creation of a just and
> dynamic socialist society. Searle, "'Escola Nova,'" p. 32.

4. See Appendix III on the constitutional functions of the Ministry of Education and Culture.

5. See diagram on the new administrative structure of schools devised by the Ministry of Education and Culture in mid-1976. See also Chris Searle, "Classrooms of Freewill," *New Internationalist* (August 1977): 9–10; Ruth Minter, "People's Republic of Mozambique—One Year," *Southern Africa* 9 (June-July 1976): 7–8; and Carole Collins, "Education for the People," *Southern Africa* 10 (June-July 1977): 21–23.

6. Education, culture, and development are so closely linked together in Mozambique that even pieces of wraparound cloth worn especially by women as part of traditional dress depict the changes taking place throughout the country. It is equally significant that the present minister of education and culture (Graca Simbine) is not only a woman but also the First Lady of Mozambique. On the role of culture in the overall development process, see Barbara Barnes, "Creating a National Culture: An Overview," and Russel Hamilton, "Cultural Change and Literary Expression in Mozambique," in *Issue* 8 (Spring 1978): 35–38; 39–42.

7. See also Stephanie Urdang, "'Precondition for Victory': Women's Liberation in Mozambique and Guinea-Bissau," *Issue* 8 (Spring 1978): 25–31.

8. See Appendix IV on the postindependence roles of the OMM.

9. Mimi Edmunds, "Conference of the Organization of Mozambican Women: Guaranteeing the Continuity of the Revolution." *Southern Africa* 10 (March 1977): 3–4.

10. Ibid., p. 4. See also Collins, "Education for the People," pp. 14–15.

PART IV

Conclusion

CHAPTER 11

The Political Economy of Colonial Education in Southern Africa: Summaries and Conclusions

DAVID CHANAIWA

The authors of the essays contained in this volume have attempted to provide a genuinely scholarly investigation, comparison, and analysis of colonial education; the anthology makes an invaluable contribution to our understanding of the history, economics, sociology, politics, and legacy of European colonialism in southern Africa in particular and Africa in general. So far, scholars have tended to concentrate on apartheid, the pass system, Bantustans, and their effects upon the African. But as the authors revealed, education probably was the most pervasive instrument of colonial control, social change, and Westernization. Education was the means by which the Europeans justified their colonial culture of domination, racism, and materialism. The Europeans transmitted their technology, religion, customs, and values through education. Thus, education is an appropriate barometer of the effects of European colonialism upon African individuals and groups.

On the whole, the authors set out to investigate the goals, curricula, administrations, and effects of colonial education in southern Africa. They also compared the British (imperial and settler), the Boer, and Portuguese colonial educational systems, as well as missionary, government, and African-run schools. They explored different forms of colonial education: formal and informal, academic and experiential, secular and religious, oral, written, and visual. Finally, they sought to establish the cause-and-effect relationship between colonial education and African traditions, leadership, nationalism, aesthetics, and the new socioeconomic formations of postindependence southern Africa.

The conclusion emerges from this collection of case studies that colonial education of the British, Boers, or Portuguese, and in missionary, government, or African-run schools, was largely a function of the socioeconomic formations of the particular settler-type colonialism in southern Africa. Thus, colonial education among the Africans of southern Africa, as opposed to either west or east Africa, presents a complex picture that cannot be understood without reference to the expediences of the settler colonialism which determined and controlled it. The chapters by Hunt Davis, Marable, Chanaiwa, Nyaggah, and Azevedo clearly demonstrate this point.

Characteristically, settler colonialism in southern Africa was born out of racioeconomic conflict. European settlers conquered and dispossessed the Africans of their lands, livestock, and civil rights. They relegated the African populations to the status of "permanent reservoirs of labor" for white farms, factories, mines, hotels, schools, houses, yards, and cemeteries. The exigencies of maintaining alien minority rule, exploitation, and privileges against an overwhelming indigenous African majority necessitated a particular type of colonial education that would reflect and reinforce settler colonialism.

On the one hand, the socioeconomic realities demanded that some Africans be educated to occupy secondary positions in government, missions, industries, farming, transport, and communications. As teachers, ministers, secretaries, clerks, interpreters, messengers, drivers, nurses, orderlies, foremen, and soldiers, Africans were indispensable auxiliaries in the administration and economic exploitation of the colonies. Therefore, the political and economic principles required that the settlers provide at least elementary and technical education for the simple reason that the colonies would not develop economically and could not be managed politically if the vast African majority remained traditionalist. As demonstrated by Hunt Davis, Azevedo, Leu, and Nyaggah, the ideal of colonial education was to produce efficient but subservient semiskilled laborers and capitalist-oriented consumers.

On the other hand, the economic principle had to be reconciled with the racist principle. Ideologically, colonialism in southern Africa was based on the raciocultural principle of white supremacy. The notorious Boer policy of apartheid, the Portuguese policy of assimilation, the English policies of the Cape franchise in South Africa, and partnership in Zimbabwe, Malawi, and Zambia were all derived from the presumed raciocultural superiority of the white race. Furthermore, being tiny alien white minorities in the midst of overwhelming and fast-growing African populations, the settlers were particularly fearful of what they perceived as the Black Peril—meaning racial integration, "miscegenation," and cultural absorption. Consequently, all regional structures, institutions, and values were based on the racist principle.

As demonstrated by Hunt Davis, Azevedo, Chanaiwa, and Pachai, another ideal of colonial education was to produce the "good African," by a caste educational system that indoctrinated the African to accept white superiority and supremacy, to submitting to and serving the whites as well as despising himself, his fellow Africans, and his heritage. In addition to its overall purpose of perpetrating white supremacy, colonial education sought to depersonalize the African. The educated African was supposed to be a selfdeprecating, blackskinned European and a docile tool of settler colonialism whose highest ambition was to live like the settler in whose image he had been molded.

In missionary, government, and even African-run schools like Ohlange, the student was removed from his parents and peers whom he was taught to despise. At boarding school, he was taught the settlers' history and culture and instilled with their capitalist individualism, materialism, and ethics. Thus, removed from his village, people, and values, and living on imported ideas, the culturally "born-again" African became alienated from himself and his heritage. Often, this alienation created a serious identity crises.

In addition to the economic and racist principles, there was the political principle. Politically, the settlers wanted an educational curriculum that would be revolutionary in creating efficient workers and dependent consumers out of the Africans, but conservative in matters of politics and civil rights. The settlers did not want to compete for jobs and promotions with the educated Africans. While they saw the need for African doctors, engineers, teachers, ministers, and administrators to relieve the problem of manpower among white minorities, they did not want these educated Africans to question colonial rule and morality, to qualify as voters, and to provide leadership for the African masses.

As demonstrated by Nyaggah, Azevedo, and Leu, the settlers maintained a policy of calculated neglect of African education, accompanied by strict governmental control of admissions, examinations, curricula, and placement. In all the colonies, African education officially was separate from and unequal to white education, and was deliberately and disproportionately underfinanced, understaffed and underdeveloped. In each colony there were national education for whites and special (Bantu) education for Africans. The deliberate educational differentiation and impoverishment of the Africans were, in turn, used as evidential justification for job reservation, disenfranchisement, and racial discrimination. African education was never free or compulsory, unlike white education.

Under apartheid, educated Africans were arbitrarily denied the vote on the basis of color. On the other hand, under the English policies of the Cape franchise and partnership, educational and property qualifications continually were raised for the sole purpose of minimizing the African vote. And under assimilation in the Portuguese colonies, qualified Africans had to be resident in Portugal to vote. Economically, African civil servants (teachers, doctors, ministers, etc.) were placed on lower salary and promotion scales for fear that they would compete with and supervise whites as well as qualify for the franchise in large numbers. As revealed by Hunt Davis, Azevedo, and Chanaiwa, there was settler political control of the curricula under which African education consisted of religion, industrial arts, social sciences, humanities, and classical languages. Professions such as law, medicine, and engineering generally were prohibited in African schools. Many Africans then ended up as teachers and ministers because for a long time these were the only careers open to educated Africans.

From their analyses of the structural organization and administration of colonial education, the authors have demonstrated an historical progression from the generally laissez-faire missionary control of the late nineteenth and early twentieth centuries to the tight governmental control of the post–World War II period. As revealed by Chanaiwa, Leu, Bermingham, and Nyaggah, up to World War II African education primarily was the responsibility of missionaries, with settler political control of the curricula and financial subsidies of teachers' salaries.

The earliest institutions of higher education for Africans, such as Marianhill in Natal (Catholic), St. Matthew's in the Cape and St. Peter's in the Transvaal (both Anglican), Hilltown in the Cape and Kilmerton in the Transvaal (both Methodist), Tiger Kloof in the Cape (London Missionary Society), and Adams College in Natal (American Board of Missions), were operated by missionaries. As demonstrated by Marable, Bermingham, Hunt Davis, and Chanaiwa, the earliest African teachers and ministers were all mission-educated, "Christian ladies and gentlemen."

The settler/missionary alliance on African education stemmed from the convergence of their interests. Both shared the ideology of racism, cultural imperialism, white supremacy, and capitalist materialism fashionable among Europeans. Settler capitalists, soldiers, and administrators patronized missionary churches and schools because of the driving psychological need to justify and legitimize white supremacy and privilege in the name of the "white man's burden." Because of his commitment to cultural imperialism and the desire to attach a significance to his labors among the so-called heathens, the missionary unscrupulously glamorized the "ignominious backwardness" and "inherent inferiority" of the Africans. Consequently, the missionary sanctified the colonial machinery as humanitarianism and as a "civilizing mission." He anointed settler industrialists, farmers, merchants, soldiers, administrators, and housewives as superior custodians of civilization, values, morals, and ethics. Hence, colonialism was no longer simply an economic process of capitalist exploitation of African resources and labor, but a noble and moral act of sacrifice for the rest of humanity. The missionary, therefore, was the best agent to produce the efficient, lawabiding, subservient African laborers and consumers, through a "good Christian education."

The missionaries also benefitted from their partnership with the settlers; many were themselves settler farmers and investors, pursuing easy economic fortunes under the protection and privilege of white supremacy. Because of colonialism, the missionaries were able to overcome African resistance and to easily convert and educate the Africans. Conquered and dominated Africans, their gods and spirits vincible and powerless, their political, social, and economic structures shattered, were easier to acculturate. White supremacy guaranteed free movement and security for missionaries and their converts against eviction by traditionalist African rulers as well as against persecution of Christian converts by traditionalist Africans. African customs such as polygamy, bride dowry, clitoridectomy, and divination, deemed repugnant to European tastes, were annihilated by settler colonial decrees, and the so-called witch-doctors were executed or "driven into hiding." Under white supremacy, English, Portuguese, or Afrikaans automatically became the official lingua franca, thus facilitating conversion, education, and acculturation. The presence of white settlers rendered moral support, companionship, and an abundant and constant supply of European manufactures (clothes, shoes, utensils, tools, tea, etc.) to overhaul African societies and educate Africans to European tastes, values, and habits. Settler colonialism brought railways, telegraphs, roads, and the postal service, which facilitated missionary living, movement, and, thus, diffusion of the white man's culture over larger areas. In short, a very large part of the missionary's so-called civilizing mission was accomplished through a "let's get-them" missionary/settler partnership against the Africans.

As demonstrated by Hunt Davis, Marable, Pachai, Bermingham, Chanaiwa, and Leu, African education was perceived as a constituent of Christianity, and, thus, a missionary responsibility. At missionary boarding schools, Africans were given religious, academic, industrial, and civic education. They were indoctrinated into supposedly civilized and universal but actually Western notions of ownership, work ethic, kinship, courtesy, temperance, diet, marriage, and friendship. They also were indoctrinated into colonialist-oriented notions of elitism, class distinctions, and "proper manners." In this way, mission education was primarily a brainwashing process which perpetrated the colonialist myth of white superiority and African inferiority. It essentially represented a capitalist, middle-class, Christian ideology which legitimized settler colonialism and promoted African humility, obedience, and usefulness to white supremacy.

The settlers reciprocated by acknowledging the missionaries as experts in African traditions and by consulting them on matters pertaining to African "interests." Comparatively, southern Africa had many more missionaries and missionaries' sons in politics and African administrations than both west and east Africa. Among the most outstanding examples were the famous Sir Theophilus Shepstone, plus the Revs. John Moffat and John Mackenzie in South Africa and Reginald Todd in the then Southern Rhodesia. As professional reformers, politicians, and administrators, the missionaries perceived themselves as the real spokespersons of the African masses. Given their guardianship principle and mentality, they relegated Africans to the legal category of inarticulate, incompetent, if not mentally retarded, wards and treated African civilization as abnormal and African cultural resistance as backward and sick. They also adopted the settlers' ethnocentric view that southern Africa was "the white man's country," in which education was being offered to the Africans as the white man's act of magnanimity.

However, as demonstrated by Chanaiwa, Hunt Davis, Marable, and Azevedo, the same missionaries also taught Africans universalism, nonracialism, nonviolence, individualism, and capitalist free enterprise that exposed the flagrant contradictions between the myths and realities of the "white man's burden." The missionary's Christianity established the universalist equality and brotherhood of mankind; his doctrine of a capitalist, materialistic, and middle-class work ethic presumed fair play, nonracialism, and social mobility which were denied in the settler society. The missionary's underlying educational principles of cultural assimilation and economic prosperity ran head-on with the settlers' self-interests of white supremacy and exclusive privilege.

Consequently, mission education became the nemesis of settler colonialism in southern Africa because it essentially was education for frustration. By exposing the Africans to the idealistic universalism, nonracialism, and individualism of Western society, which the colonized African in turn took too seriously, the missionaries unwittingly were sowing the seeds for the eventual destruction of white supremacy by the educated African elites. As Azevedo, Hunt Davis, and Marable have revealed, the inherent contradiction between Christianity and education on the one hand and settler colonialism on the other constituted an inescapable embarrassment to the colonizers.

The denial of racial equality and economic opportunity as logical corollaries of the Western Christianity and education to which the African elites had been exposed did not lend itself to the expected African subordination and docility. By colonial standards, the educated elites waged a progressively militant revolt which was antithetical to white supremacy. A good example was John Dube's Ohlange Institute based on African economic self-determination. Then, shortly before and during the interwar period, the educated elites formed the first national, nonethnic political movements, such as the African National Congresses of South Africa (1912) and Southern Rhodesia (1934), based on the Christian ideals of nonracialism, nonviolence, and economic opportunity.

Ultimately, the forceful wind of change caused by post–World War II African nationalism and demands for decolonization scared the settlers and forced them to revise their educational policies. As demonstrated by Nyaggah, Leu, Bermingham, and Azevedo, the settlers had come to realize the subversive potential of mission education and of the educated elites. They decided to eradicate Christian idealism in African education, to institute secular political indoctrination of their own, and, hopefully, nip African nationalism in the bud. The classic example was the South African Bantu Education Act of 1953, which was partially adopted by the post–Unilateral Declaration of Independence (UDI) Smith regime of the then Southern Rhodesia in 1966. Under the Bantu Education Act, African education was strictly separated from European education, placed under complete settler political control, and balkanized into ethnic structures and curricula. Up to secondary school, Africans are now being taught in the vernacular languages, such as Zulu, Xhosa, Sotho, and Tsonga, instead of the official English and Afrikaans languages.

Thus, the settlers have sought to isolate Africans from each other and from the outside world through a carefully engineered colonial educational system. Besides, since the African languages of South Africa have not kept pace with modern knowledge and terminology, especially in science and technology, African students are evidentially and psychologically reminded of their cultural deficiencies and supposedly inherent racial inferiority. Then, by the time the African student completes secondary school, he/she is already educationally unequipped to compete with the white students, who have had all their instruction in English and Afrikaans under the best facilities and staff.

Whether under missionary or settler control, however, African education was perceived as one of the major instruments (together with the passes, hut tax, and *Corvee*) of colonial control of the indigenous

Africans for the purposes of perpetuating the socioeconomic formations of the settler society. As evidenced by the numerous separatist
churches established by frustrated educated elites, the missionaries
themselves had no intention of practicing racial equality nor of Af-
ricanizing the top administrations of their churches and schools. They,
too, were Christianizing and educating for frustration. Like overprotective parents, they misconstrued demands for racial equality and
expressions of self-respect by the mission-educated teachers and ministers as acts of insubordination and rebellion.

But, as demonstrated by Marable, Mugomba, Azevedo, and
Chanaiwa, colonial education has left an enduring legacy upon individuals and groups of Africans in southern Africa. Because of the
combined cultural assault from Western Christianity and education,
African societies, villages, and families were split into Christians and
"heathens," the school and the "bush," and into the urbanites and
"country" people. Politically, Africans found themselves with two types
of leadership: the traditionalist leadership of kings, chiefs, headmen,
parents, and medical practitioners, and the Western-oriented leadership of teachers, ministers, doctors, and politicians. Christianity and
education also led to new socioeconomic class formations within the
African societies, typified by the *assimilados* and *indigenas* in Angola and
Mozambique.

The "choice" was between acceptance of Christianity and, thus,
Western education on the one hand, and remaining traditionalist and
illiterate on the other. In practice, however, the more the African
acquired colonial education, the more he was able to enjoy the
socioeconomic opportunities accruing from colonialism and vice versa.
Having acquired an extensive knowledge of the colonial socioeconomic
system, including its individualistic, materialistic work ethic, the educated elites also were more enterprising and efficient than the
traditionalists. Many of the mission-educated elites went into private
business and agriculture. Consequently, in the major urban areas like
Johannesburg, Salisbury, and Luanda, there was a colonial African
upper class of professionals and businessmen, a middle class of
teachers, nurses, policemen, small businessmen, and junior civil servants, and a lower class of wage earners and peasants. In contrast, there
still was the traditionalist aristocracy of chiefs, subchiefs, and headmen,
and a commoner class of subsistence-level farmers in the rural areas.
The urban and rural worlds historically have been linked together by
the overall socioeconomic infrastructure of settler colonialism, by kinship ties, and especially by the largely migrant urban workers.

More important, Christianity and colonial education have had
profoundly disorganizing and divisive effects on the African value
system and moral fibre. To appreciate these effects, it is necessary to

take into account the formal mission or governmental education discussed in this book, as well as the massive informal education by advertisement in newspapers, radio, television, movies, display windows, and billboards, and examples from life-styles of the African and settler bourgeoisie. Informal education impressed upon every African the contrast between the "superior" clothes, cars, trains, airplanes, canned foods, tea, and alcohol of the white world and the "inferior" African world of "heathenism" and "superstition." Teachers, ministers, and the media told Africans their traditional technologies and economic systems of shifting cultivation and nomadic pastoralism were backward, irrational, inefficient, and precarious; European industrial goods were in fact always superior to African handcrafts; and capitalist production, consumption, and values were always superior, progressive, beneficial, and universal. The overall message was that all people share a universal desire for the Western model of material possession and high standard of living; African communalism, kinship, and reciprocity were viewed as elements of ignorance and retardation due to lack of educational exposure to the superior technological alternatives offered by the Western industrial civilization.

Consequently, African traditions became peripheral and subordinate to the dominant Western values derived from capitalism and individualism, and from the idea of "progress" measured primarily by the levels of material consumption. Africans were enticed into abstaining from polygamous marriages, traditional rituals, beer parties, *lobola*, diviners, and practitioners. This led to the emergence of individuals and groups whose beliefs, values, and life-styles were quite alien and antithetical to African traditions. Some from the boarding schools and urban townships have considered going back to their rural villages and kinfolk a temporary relapse into "primitivity," and have learned to despise traditional forms of dress, cosmetics, entertainment, and etiquette. Simultaneously, those Africans who have not acquired formal education, hence good jobs and material possessions, due to either traditionalism or lack of money and schools, are made to feel inferior and worthless.

Between these two extremes, the Westernized elites and the traditionalists, are the vast majority of the partially transformed Africans who have roots in both the African and settler cultures, languages, and value systems. The continuity of African traditions was due to the resilience of African value systems, to the shortcomings of the colonial educational systems, which have been pointed out by the authors, and to the racioeconomic principles of the settlers, which mitigated against total cultural assimilation of the Africans. This continuity then was reinforced by post–World War II African nationalism and negritude, both of which advocated a return to the basic African value systems.

However, as Chanaiwa, Marable, and Mugomba have amply demonstrated, modern African leadership and nationalism stemmed from an ideological and cultural environment created by Western Christianity, education, and capitalism. Mugomba shows that the average modern African nationalist leader was miseducated by the colonizers. Chanaiwa demonstrates how most nationalist leaders ended up living in three worlds: the utopian world of universalism, nonracialism, nonviolence, and materialism which they sought to establish here on earth; the practical world of settler colonialism which they misunderstood; and the traditionalist African world which they despised and from which they attempted to escape.

Viewed from the modern African scene of anticolonialism, political independence, and racial and cultural pride, the ideas and activities of the colonial-educated elites appear extremely neocolonialist. The personalities were essentially Christian intellectuals, preachers, teachers, lawyers, businessmen, and administrators—educated in either mission or government schools. They perceived settler colonialism as a matter of providence; admired whites for their technology, religion, power, and wealth; and aimed at advancing Africans through Christianity, education, and economic self-help. They accepted the supposed cultural inferiority of the black race. They also shared the puritanism and utopianism of missionaries and philanthropists, as well as the political liberalism of some settlers.

Their responses to settler colonialism were constrained by their dichotomous status—they were rejected by the settler class and alienated from their African masses and culture. First, they acquiesced to colonial expansion and conquest because they erroneously associated settler capitalism with the spread of Christianity, education, and economic prosperity. Some, like Dube, attempted to register their protests against racist, colonialist restrictions by vindication of the black potential. They sought to establish African economic self-determination and even self-sufficiency through vocational education under which they inculcated Western bourgeois attitudes, work ethic, and consumptive principles.

Politically, these elites were awfully naive and accommodationist. They failed to understand the underlying principles of settler colonialism in general. They lost a power base when they despised African traditionalism and discouraged African historical and racial consciousness. In the face of their own powerlessness and the settlers' intransigence, they adopted utopianism, which made then natural allies of their equally powerless but privileged missionary mentors and white liberals. The possibility of conspiracy, as opposed to commitment to color-blind humanism, by some missionary and settler liberals to alienate the African elites from the masses and, thus, arrest the emergence of African nationalism, cannot be overlooked.

In spite of their limitations, the educated elites made an essential contribution to the overall continuum of African nationalism and the liberation struggle in southern Africa. They were the forerunners of modern African cross-ethnic unity, leadership, and Pan-Africanism. They were the first leaders to undermine the ethnic, collaborationist potential of the chiefs. Furthermore, the bitter experiences of both the elites and the masses partially account for the post–World War II revolutionary flavor in southern Africa. Comparatively, modern African nationalists have abandoned the reformist, capitalist approaches of the previous elites for a militant struggle against Western colonialism, racism, and values that have demeaned and shackled the African.

For the educators and intellectuals, the real historical significance of the educated elites lies in their literary legacy. Their sound educational training, their commitment to high intellectual standards, coupled with their personal and eyewitness experiences, enabled them to combine in their voluminous writings anecdotes of their authentic experiences and the actual machinations of settler colonialism.

The educated elites had the political and moral support of the African masses, especially the partially transformed urban proletariats. Formal and informal education had established the dominance of Western socioeconomic formations among the Africans. Thus, the capitalistic self-determination and education exemplified by John Dube's Ohlange Institute found support among the masses, who saw in the self-confidence, self-help, individualism, courage, and success of the educated elites the embodiment of their own dreams and expectations. Until they had learned from bitter experiences and frustrations, the masses generally went along with the utopian ideals of universalism, nonracialism, and nonviolence because of missionary indoctrination and their own conviction that the utopianism was a viable antithesis to the racioeconomic world of white supremacy. The failure of utopianism partially accounts for the militant demands and armed struggle in southern Africa, which began in earnest in the 1960s.

It is probably due as much, if not more, to Christianity and colonial education as to the sense of security deriving from their numerical majority that African nationalist movements and postindependence governments have never advocated exclusively black nation-states, associations, or privileges. On the other hand, the progression from accommodation and nonviolence to militancy and violence was characterized by a corresponding decrease in religiosity, materialism, and elitism. Thus, contrary to conventional Eurocentric analyses, missionary Christianity and education did not "produce" modern African nationalism and leadership. The goals, structures, and curricula of missionary churches and schools were set up to create an African population that was economically efficient and consumptive and politically acquiescent to white supremacy. Therefore, modern African nationalism developed in spite of Christianity and colonial education.

The utopianism of the mission-educated elites and the Christianized masses was equally antithetical to missionaries and settlers, hence the proliferation of separatist churches. Giving the missionaries credit for African nationalism is similar to crediting overprotective parents with the subsequent success of their rebellious child because they oppressed him enough to force him to demand independence and assume responsibility for his own welfare. The African liberation struggle was a rebellion against settler colonialism, Christianity, and colonial education; this is demonstrated by the fact that Africans of the late nineteenth and early twentieth centuries were more receptive to missionary leadership and indoctrination than Africans of the post–World War II period were. There also is an important generation gap in ideology between the traditional nationalist leadership born out of mission schools and the youth born out of the revolutionary armed struggle of the 1960s onwards.

As Mugomba demonstrates in his study of postindependence Mozambique, there is need for a cultural reeducation and an emancipation of the leaders and the masses out of their colonial heritage of capitalism, individualism, and materialism. It is important to appreciate the need to reeducate the masses because they too were deeply affected by Christianity and colonial education, especially the informal education of materialism. Failure to Africanize colonial culture, institutions, and values will, Mugomba points out, only facilitate neocolonialism in southern Africa.

It is too early to comment on the postindependence educational systems of southern Africa: part of the region is still actively preoccupied with the military liberation struggle and the political transfer of power from the white settler minority regimes to African majorities. Based upon the history of postindependence educational systems in other parts of Africa, in Asia and Latin America, it is safe to point out that African leaders in southern Africa will soon face complex tasks of having to Africanize the educational system of the colonial era, in order to meet the sociopolitical demands and economic realities of the new age. The worst that could happen in southern Africa has already become common practice among some states in Africa, Asia, and Latin America. The Western-educated and urbanized elites use education as a mechanism of cultural domination, political oppression, and economic exploitation of the masses.

This can happen easily if African leaders presume the intrinsic superiority of Western technology, materialism, culture, and values; if they continue to hunger for Western manufactures and amenities and, thus, despise the vast rural sectors where these Western products are lacking. Among the neocolonialist states in Africa, Asia, and Latin America, the nationalist leaders largely have inherited the colonial educational strategies which were responsible for the underdevelopment of these countries. Their major orientation is still towards Western models of education and Western standards of educational achievement. Their major goals still are to eradicate illiteracy and to produce Western-type teachers, administrators, technicians, and professionals. Most of their universities are so highly developed imitations of Western models that they become irrelevant to the socioeconomic needs and activities of their predominantly rural populations. In short, their educational goals and practices do not take into account the obvious and invidious dichotomy between the industrialized and nonindustrialized nations and between national and international realities.

The result has been internal, indigenous colonialism, under which the Western-oriented, urban-centered, governmental and managerial class dominates and exploits the rural villagers, who lack Western education and, thus, political power to make themselves felt. The ruling elites have become self-appointed successor-missionaries and have adopted a gap approach to educational planning under which the ideas, technology, and values they acquired through colonial education are to be filtered down to the supposedly backward rural masses. The elites then apply colonial education ostensibly to hasten African transformation from rural poverty, ignorance, and disease to modern industrialization, urbanization, and prosperity. Being admirers of Western culture and products, the elites have perpetuated a colonial-type "civilizing mission" with only a slight shift in content from the racist "white man's burden" to Western education, technology, materialism, and values.

In reality, the Western-oriented social class has not only exercised cultural domination over the traditionalist masses, but also accentuated the economic disparity between rural villages and the urban centers. The elites have distributed educational and other resources unequally for their own benefit. Through their political control of capital, raw materials, means of production, labor, and communications, they have distributed educational funds, facilities, supplies, and personnel in favor of urban education and higher education. The result has been two dichotomous educational structures, if not ideologies, under which primary education is considered adequate for the rural populations and urban proletariats, while secondary and, especially, higher education primarily serve the children of the urban, Western-oriented elites. The elites then fill vacancies in public institutions with their own children and, thus, deny rural children the opportunities and benefits that should derive from political independence as well as from government and commercial services. Hence, despite the heartless parody of socialist ideals, it has become increasingly difficult for village students to qualify for secondary schools, technical schools, or universities. Educational neglect, accompanied by the undue emphasis upon Western educational achievements in job placements and promotions, has led to rural underdevelopment. Rural areas have become colonies of urban centers, and the disadvantaged villagers have become the "hewers of wood and drawers of water" for their urban masters.

Therefore, there will be a need in postindependence southern Africa to decolonize education by reorienting the curriculum from its colonial, Western framework to one that is pointedly African. Along with other national institutions, the educational system ought to be brought into the political arena and its policies and programs closely harmonized with other organs of the state that are concerned with the achievement of public interests. Education should be one of the most important means of creating a highly centralized, cross-ethnic nation-state based upon the acceptance of common nationality, ideology, and destiny. It should equip both urban and rural children with the knowledge and techniques for achieving personal success as well as exercising effective citizenship within the postindependence society. It should not be manipulated to produce rural underdevelopment and continued poverty. The national leaders should seriously and sincerely face the inevitable inequities that will accrue to the disadvantaged, illiterate rural children under a Western-type, urban-centered educational system. An educational system that sustains internal colonialism will deprive southern Africa of one of its greatest resources—rural manpower.

Furthermore, there is need for an educational system that is deeply embedded in the cultural life of the community and is one aspect of a rich African civilization. In reality, rural villages are reservoirs of traditional African culture and values which existed before European colonization and should not be ignored, despised, or exploited. The educational curriculum should make African languages, history, geography, and arts basic subjects instead of mere electives. The first step is for the national leaders to fully examine the premises on which the colonial educational system of the country was organized when the country was a constituent territory of Britain, Portugal, or South Africa. Then, they should undertake extensive revision of the system to bring its postindependence objectives into harmony with the other goals of the new nation-state, as defined by national, and not class, interests.

Education will play a crucial role in the postindependence reconstruction of southern Africa. If planned properly it can produce African graduates who will be quite different from the typical products of colonial education discussed in this book. Reliance on Western models and the presence of internal class distinctions can cause the educational system to undermine the process of cultural consciousness and Africanization that is crucial for true African independence and majority rule.

The educational system should not be alien and irrelevant to the vast majority of the citizens, for the benefit of a small ruling elite. Nor should it educate graduates for frustration, unemployment, or underemployment; it should restrict overseas studies by inducing countries that offer scholarships to contribute instead to the establishment of local educational fellowships, programs, and facilities. The restriction will eliminate the students' human and financial problems abroad, and brain drainage, while assuring full development of the African personality. At home, the students, teachers, and intellectuals should be made to feel like research pioneers revealing the richness of the traditional African heritage that was contemptuously ignored under colonial education. They should be actively involved in the creation of truly independent, African-oriented nation-states.

Appendixes

Submission of an Application to Government, for adoption and sanction of the Scheme entitled: "The Nyasaland Black Man's Educational Society".

Sir,

1.   I have the honour to submit the above scheme before Government for consideration, adoption and sanction.

2.   The definition and scope of the aforesaid scheme is neither denominational nor particular to a single tribe in Nyasaland but is national and coextensive with the Black Man as a race within and outside Nyasaland—so that those whose interests, whatever locality are arrested and are inclined to may comply with and adopt it without misgivings of that sort—on the understanding that the scheme is for *the Common Summum Bonum*.

3.   The aim and purpose of the aforesaid N.B.E. Society is to improve or develop the impoverished condition of the Black Man—religiously, morally, economically, physically and intellectually by starting a purely native controlled High School or College; and as a means thereof to raise a considerable sum of money.

4.   *A provisional or verbal consent is already got from Nyasalanders* working in both Southern and Northern Rhodesia as well as from most Tonga Chiefs, headmen and people generally, though actual collection has never been attempted.

5.   *The purpose of the money in prospect is for:*
    1. Establishment of a Black Man's High School or College.
    2. Training of Teachers.
    3. School Buildings, Dormitories, Hospitals, Clothings and Foodstuff for patients and school boarders.

6.   *Method of collecting the money under review:*
    1. There shall be formed a fund collecting sub-committee in every area concerned made up of (a) Chairman, (b) Treasurer, (c) Secretary under the supervision of the local area Chief.

Appendix II

Bechuanaland Protectorate
Proclamation 26 (1938)
"School Committees"

(a) "The Committee shall consist of the District Commissioner, the Chief, a Secretary, and six members, three of whom shall be appointed by the District Commissioner and three by the Chief or African Authority in consultation with the Tribe."

(b) "The Committee shall be responsible for the upkeep and equipment of all schools within its jurisdiction."

(c) "The Committee shall be responsible generally for dealing with matters affecting the schools and for securing teachers for the schools under its jurisdiction and for entering into contracts with such teachers, provided that the approval of the Director of Education as to the suitability and terms of contracts have first been obtained."

(d) "The Committee shall meet at least twice in every calendar year and one of the meetings shall be held in August each year, at which meeting estimates for the coming financial year shall be discussed."

(e) "In purely professional matters the teachers shall be responsible to the Director of Education and to him only, but it shall be within the power of the Committee to make recommendations to the Director of Education as regards professional matters."

Appendix III

Functions of the Mozambican Ministry of Education and Culture

Translated from Republica Popular de Moçambique, *Programa Geral de Actividades do Conselho de Ministros: Tarefas e Funcoes que Competem a Cada Ministerio*. Maputo: Imprensa Nacional de Moçambique, 1975, pp. 24–27.

The triumph of the Revolution depends fundamentally on the creation and development of a new man and a new mentality.

It is the function of the Ministry of Education and Culture to create the conditions for instruction, education and culture to be really at the service of the popular masses, fighting energetically and systematically the burden of inheritance left behind by colonialism: illiteracy, ignorance and obscurantism.

It is the main task of this Ministry to spread political, technical and scientific knowledge so that by freeing the creative initiative of everyone and giving value to the talents of each one, the nature and the human potential for the development of the Mozambican Society may be mobilized.

The Ministry of Education and Culture promotes the cultivation of all the cultural manifestations of the Mozambican people, giving them a revolutionary content and propagating them at the national and international levels for the projection of the Mozambican personality.

The Ministry of Education and Culture creates the conditions for stimulating the practice of physical education and sports at the level of the popular masses throughout the country. The Ministry of Education and Culture functions

In the Domain of Education

1. To orient and control the educational system including:
    (a) the development and execution of school programmes at all levels
    (b) establishment of the rules that may secure the uniform functioning of the schools
    (c) production of books, texts and manuals for teaching

   (d) organizing and dynamizing all campaign programmes of adult education
   (e) orienting production of teaching material, ensuring its relationship to the Mozambican society and environment
   (f) preparing new teachers and promoting the constant and progressive improvement of all teaching staff from the scientific, educational, cultural and political points of view
   (g) building schools of professional training and reformulating the orientation of the ones already in existance in the light of the demands of national development and the Revolution and in co-operation with other Ministries
   (h) organizing intensive courses of professional and specific training
   (i) organizing courses, conferences, colloquia and scientific levels and the updating of knowledge
   (j) contacting friendly countries regarding the training and specialization of technicians
   (k) building art schools
   (l) building centers of physical and sports culture
2. To promote the work of scientific and technological research, in accordance with the needs of the economic development of the country
3. To implement the nationalization and socialization of education

IN THE DOMAIN OF CULTURE

4. To collect data concerning the action already taken by FRELIMO in this domain which will serve as a reference point for future action
5. To promote and stimulate artistic activity (literary, visual, theatrical and musical):
   (a) to promote the gathering of national artistic heritage, namely traditional literature, oral narratives of historical events, music of popular tradition and material of popular theatre
   (b) to promote the exchange of experiences among sculptors and poets, plastic artists, musicians and actors, orienting them so that their production may be popular and revolutionary in its inspiration, content and form
   (c) to search for talents among the people and encourage and spread their works
   (d) to publish works on the various fields of artistic production
   (e) to organize public libraries, exhibitions and museums, namely of the history of societies and natural history

(f) to encourage the use of traditional musical instruments

(g) to control the importation and exportation of works of sculpture, paintings and drawings

6. To promote cultural interchange among the various areas of the country and with friendly peoples and countries

7. To create the conditions for external marketing of artistic production to be solely in the hands of the State

In the Domain of Sports

8. To promote the practising of sport by the masses throughout the country

9. To reformulate the tasks of the Council of Physical Education and Sports within the perspective of popularizing the activities of physical and sports culture

10. To organize and supervise the preparation of national sports delegations

11. To promote sport interchange with other peoples and countries

The Ministry of Education and Culture supervises in the following services and organisms:

Directorate of Educational Services

Inspectorate of Educational Services

Extramural Service

National Service of Adult Education

Physical Education and Sports

Institute of Scientific Research

Directorate of Cultural Services

Eduardo Mondlane National University

Institute of Professional Orientation

Historical Archives

Museums

National Library

Resolutions from the 2nd Conference of the Organization of Mozambican Women, Maputo, November 1976

SOME OF THE PROBLEMS CONFRONTING WOMEN TODAY

INTRODUCTION

The present predicament of Mozambican women reveals a lower level of development compared with men in cultural, sociopolitical and economic terms. This stems from discrimination in education in traditional society, aggravated by racial, social and sexual discrimination imposed by Portuguese colonialism. It is in this context that we can understand why illiteracy, religious mystification, tribalism, regionalism and racism, and inferiority complexes are all more deeply rooted in women.

ILLITERACY

Women's secondary status in traditional society was reinforced by their inability to acquire new knowledge and skills under colonialism, especially literacy.

Illiteracy affects the vast majority of the Mozambican people. It has a particularly high incidence among women who were doubly exploited in traditional and colonial society, which instilled in women a feeling of inferiority and dependence and conditioned them merely to please men and run a household.

Colonial education only reached a small number of Mozambicans because of racial discrimination and class differentials. Unbridled exploitation made it impossible for the people to afford education, school materials and other related expenses. That only left the missions, which nurtured a spirit of conformism and passivity through teaching mystifying ideas. This only added to the feelings of inferiority stemming from traditional society.

The difficulties produced by illiteracy are evident in various everyday situations.

1. During the armed struggle we needed training to help us handle certain problems—for instance, how to assess distance—so instruction had to be given in schools.

2. Those who cannot read or write cannot understand or put into effect the written directives of state and party organs. This also applies to other instructions such as books on politics, circulars from party headquarters, principles of hygiene, use of medicines, medical prescriptions, use of fertilizer and so on.
3. The illiterate person cannot exchange correspondence.
4. Ignorance about weights and measures and the value of money makes it easier for people to be cheated in shops.
5. A husband might deceive his wife about the level of his earnings.

In Mozambique, the problem is made worse for those who have not been to school because that means that they cannot speak Portuguese either, which is the official language of communication. This limits women's access to information. These difficulties were evident even during the course of the Second Conference: because of illiteracy, a large proportion of the delegates could not follow the reading and discussion of the reports.

Divisions among Women

"Assimilation," the colonial policy whereby some western-educated Mozambicans were granted Portuguese status, divides the people and weakens them politically, as do tribalism and racism. All these things affect solidarity among women.

Within the OMM there are women who refuse to work under a comrade from another province or race. How many cases do we know of children who despise their parents because they are black or ignorant? How many cases do we know of parents who act like servants to their own children because the latter are "mulatto"* or "assimilado"? Racial prejudices still give rise to erroneous ideas about who is Mozambican and who is not. The criterion is still always race. This is particularly a problem in the cities. Lack of political awareness—resulting from a failure to take part in study and political work among the people—leads to the perpetuation of these errors with all their serious consequences.

Many women suffer from a lack of self-confidence, making them ineffective, and suspicious of each other. They are further divided by class and social status. Single and divorced women are also socially isolated and stigmatized, whereas men in the same position are not.

The process of rendering women inferior originates in traditional education. It is reinforced by "initiation rites" and other such traditional practices which lead to passive acceptance and lack of initiative. The woman becomes an object of appropriation and pleasure, bartered by her family and subjugated to her husband's will. On top of this

---

*Mulatto or "mestizo": being of ethnically mixed parentage (mestizos were considered of slightly higher status than blacks).

age-old process, women also suffered the humiliation of colonial society which robbed them of their husbands and children and exploited them at work. Colonialism very often left prostitution as the only means of a livelihood. . . . By discriminating against the illiterate woman, it made her feel more inferior because she neither understood nor belonged to the (alienating) way of life in the urban areas.

This feeling of inferiority holds women back from participating in meetings and even in family discussions—in front of their husbands and children, women feel unable to express their own opinions. Their inhibitions and lack of initiative in turn produce an inability to take on responsible jobs or to break away from this conditioning. Furthermore, the "assimilated" woman humiliates her "non-assimilated" sister by adopting showy manners and idiosyncracies, talking in incomprehensible terms and setting herself apart from the rest.

Another form of superiority is "veteranism" which is reflected in the need to be forever reasserting the fact that one has been involved in the struggle for a long time. Women who do this think that in this way they will increase their own social standing.

If the situation is not objectively analyzed, women run the risk of coming to regard not only men but also other women as their enemies. Married women and women who are generally frustrated tend to regard single women—that is single mothers, divorced women and spinsters—as emancipated. Women whose feelings of inferiority and dependence in relation to men are deeply embedded are incapable of conceiving of life without men.

PROBLEMS IN THE TOWNS

The special problems of women in the towns are seen not just from their personal dependence on men, but also as a result of colonialism. Abortion, prostitution, divorce, alcoholism, abandoned children, unemployment—all call for practical measures of education and organization. But they also must be seen in the context of the fight against cultural imperialism, and the undermining of Mozambican society. Through the imposition of western bourgeois values, individualism and promiscuity are mistaken for emancipation.

The aim of the revolution is the ending of all forms of exploitation and oppression. For the revolution to succeed, we must completely eradicate the exploitation and oppression suffered by all Mozambican people; women also had to bear the special victimization of their sex. The city, the bourgeois fortress and the focal point for the sharpening of the class struggle, is where women feel this double oppression and exploitation most acutely.

As workers, they are obliged to sell their labour for miserable wages, and to sell their bodies to their exploiters—only to find themselves rejected and discriminated against by their own class. As house-wives, they are cut off from the essential problems of social life and reduced to serving their husbands, who are themselves exploited and oppressed. Finally, women of the petty-bourgeoisie (sic) and the bourgeoisie assimilate bourgeois cultural and moral ideas and become vehicles for, and agents of, conservative and reactionary ideology. In the city, traditional social values are broken down, only to be replaced by the vices, alienation and decadence characteristic of the colonial bourgeoisie. It is also in the city that the people are least organized. This leaves them more susceptible to vices, and at the same time makes it more difficult to work out a plan of action to combat them.

The assimilation of bourgeois values brought about by colonialism (particularly in the cities) led women to consider a bourgeois life style as the ideal situation to aim for. This leads them to believe that to be emancipated is to be free as an individual, regardless of the norms of social conduct. This liberalism denies the importance of putting FRE-LIMO's political line into practice in daily life. It denies the importance of collective living and extols individualism.

PROBLEMS IN THE RURAL AREAS

Traditional practices still exist which endanger women's physical and psychological health, and deny them control over their own lives. A proper analysis must be made of these customs, so that women may understand them and so resist more effectively.

In the rural areas, the Mozambican peasant woman knew of colonial exploitation through the pillaging of the lands and the shops. She knew colonialism as a repressive system which, through the administrative machine, took her husband and children away for the degradation and misery of forced labour.

Quite apart from this exploitative and oppressive system to which all the people were subjected, the Mozambican peasant woman is subjected to a second form of oppression which stems from the traditional feudal ideology. That ideology conceives of the woman's role as serving men—as an object of pleasure, as a procreator and as an unpaid worker.

The ideological values of the traditional feudal society are inculcated in a woman from the moment she is born by a whole educational system within the family. That education is different for a boy than for a girl. It inculcates in her the spirit of submission to the man, and in him the spirit of authority. The woman's societal position is consecrated in ceremonies and institutions like "the initiation rites" and the system of marriage; that is, Lobolo,* premature and forced marriages and

---

*Lobolo: bride price.

polygamy. And the educational effect of ceremonies and institutions, practised in traditional feudal society for centuries, brought the woman to assume an inferior and passive position. Because the capacity to revolt and to have a critical mind were destroyed, the woman later became the disseminator and defender of retrograde and reactionary values.

Initiation rites: Initiation rites inculcate into women submissiveness and total dependence on men. Women are conditioned to submit and gradually come to take their inferiority for granted. They are brought up with the sole aim of serving men—as objects of pleasure, sources and producers of labour. The treatment of women is the same throughout the country: the form may vary, but the final objective is always the same. To make the young girl submissive and resigned to physical suffering, terrible treatment is inflicted.

Lobolo: This practice exists throughout the country. Its rationale is that it is compensation for the transfer of labour power from one family to another. This puts women into a situation of total dependence on men, who because they have paid for them, can use and disown them like mere objects. Despite work already carried out, this practice still persists. Experience has shown that women are still not aware of their oppressed condition or of the real implications of "lobolo." Many still defend it on the grounds that without the payment of a "lobolo" they have not been taken as legitimate and honest women.

Polygamy: In our patriarchal society, the man is the owner of all material goods produced within the family. Polygamy is a system whereby the man possesses a number of wives. As head and proprietor of the family, he acquires more wives to augment the labour force at his service. In addition to this, society's contempt for the single woman leads her to marry a man even if he is already married. It should also be pointed out that in the majority of cases it is the wife herself who procures other wives for her husband, with the object of increasing the labour force to help her in family production.

PROGRAMME FOR ACTION

The strategy in the present phase of the Mozambican revolutionary struggle was laid down by the 8th Central Committee Meeting of FRELIMO, held in February 1976. It was reiterated by our Comrade President in his opening speech to the 2nd Conference. It is:

The development of the material and ideological basis for the construction of a Socialist society.

Production must be the principal work in building socialism. The principal activity must be that of class struggle.

The OMM took part in the working out of this programme. Its objective was defined as being: to find ways to achieve woman's emancipation from all forms of exploitation through her integration into the principal task. To do this OMM should:

1. See to it that every woman becomes involved in production (either in the factory or in the agricultural cooperative), in the organization and planning of work and social life. Women must also become involved in the development of the new man and the new society.

2. Organize the fight against old ideas which are a huge obstacle to the full involvement of the woman as a citizen in public and social life. Such ideas inhibit her participation in economic life as a producer and in family life as a truly revolutionary companion and educator.

3. Fully review the present structures so as to ensure that the OMM's new structures effectively reflect the worker-peasant class as the vanguard leading Mozambican society in the construction of socialism.

WOMEN IN THE COMMUNAL VILLAGE AND AGRICULTURAL COOPERATIVE

Agriculture is the basis of our economy and of the economic development of our country. It is also the sector in which the majority of women are involved. Their participation up to now has been limited to the carrying out of projects and activities developed and led by men. The reorganization of agriculture on a collective basis through communal villages and cooperatives opens new perspectives for the development of the countryside and the life of the peasant. It also opens up greater possibilities for woman's involvement in that process, on an equal footing with men. This will accelerate her emancipation.

THE CONFERENCE RECOMMENDS THE INVOLVEMENT OF WOMEN IN SETTING UP COMMUNAL VILLAGES AND PRODUCTION COOPERATIVES

Throughout all of this, the OMM's main concern is to establish a woman's belief in her own abilities. Job discrimination must be rejected at the outset . . . by making woman value herself, and learn to do those jobs which are traditionally man's preserve.

WOMEN IN THE FACTORY

The 2nd Conference feels that the woman worker is relegated to doing the routine jobs which demand least mental exertion. They are usually non-mechanized, manual jobs. Discriminated against by her fellow workmates, inhibited by feelings of inferiority from actively participating in the political struggle within the firm, the woman has not developed a class consciousness.

Freed for work by creches and canteens, women must be trained in all aspects of production, and be proportionally represented on production councils. Similar recommendations for political work, collective organization and involvement of women in production are made for those in the service and industrial sectors, and for housewives.

THE IDEOLOGICAL CAMPAIGN

EDUCATION

Recommendations are made on schooling, and on political, scientific and vocational training for women as an essential part of the programme to raise their political consciousness. The media should be used to promote these aims and project a new image of women, participating in all areas of rebuilding society.

Women and men must also be made conscious of their own roles in the educational process.

Discrimination against women starts soon after birth. It is obvious in the different treatment given to a male child. A girl is, from earliest infancy, trained to carry out domestic tasks and serve men. That includes even her younger brothers.

The boys, on the other hand, are trained to assume responsibilities and also to be always waited on by women—their mother, their sisters and, therefore later, their wife.

This process of indoctrination is carried out by the actual parents. It has a logical continuation in school life. The boys always have more demands made of them. The girls always follow. They never lead.

It is a matter of urgency that the OMM:

- Make the mother aware of her responsibility in the development of new attitudes and outlook amongst the family. The OMM must show women that they themselves contribute to the oppression from which they suffer because of the education they give their own male children.
- Encourage the idea that school, above the age of 7 years, is as much for girls as for boys.
- Recommend that the Party's political courses include the problem of the emancipation of women. This will help all cadres to understand and carry on the fight for women's liberation. It should be a matter of priority to all revolutionaries of both sexes.

EXTERNAL RELATIONS

During the armed struggle for national liberation, FRELIMO always attached great importance to international solidarity and cooperation. It was in this spirit that the OMM developed relations with other women's organizations. However, because of deficiencies in the politics, organizations and structures of the OMM, the true value of these contacts with women in other countries was never realized.

The OMM should work to renew its relations with other women's organizations, especially those whose objectives and activities identify with ours, that is, those who are involved in a revolutionary process and the construction of socialism and with whom FRELIMO and the People's Republic of Mozambique have good relations.

These relations are designed to:
- Get to know the experiences of female vanguard revolutionaries in the class struggle and building of socialism.
- Give an idea of our struggle and experience as a contribution to women in their fight for liberation.
- Reinforce relations with all liberation movements throughout Africa and the world, in line with the spirit of proletarian internationalism.

The struggle continues!
Maputo, 17 November 1976

Selected Bibliography

African Committee on Linguistics. *Symposium on Multilingualism, Braz-zaville, 1962*. Draft agenda and papers, second meeting of the International African Committee on Linguistics, Brazzaville, July 16–23, 1962.

African Education Commission. *Education in Africa: A Study of West, South and Equatorial Africa by the African Education Commission, under the Auspices of the Phelps-Stokes Fund and Foreign Mission Societies of North America and Europe; Report Prepared by Jesse Jones, Chairman*. New York: Phelps-Stokes Fund, 1972.

———. *Education in East Africa, 1923–1924*. New York: Phelps-Stokes Fund; London: Edinburgh House Press, 1925.

"African Education Problems in Rhodesia." *South African Outlook* 77 (1947).

Almeida, Antonio de. "Formacao colonial: O ensino colonial em Portugal." *Boletim Geral Colonial* 169 (1939).

———. "Fomento do artesanato em Angola." *Trabalho* 12 (October–December 1965): 67–100.

Alston, M. C. "A Pioneer School in Southern Rhodesia." *United Empire* 22 (1931): 16–18.

Alves, C. "O ensino da lingua portuguesa aos indigenas nas unidades militares da colonia." *Boletim da Sociedade de Estudes de Mocambique* 6 (1932): 353–80.

Andre, Lourenco. "Cartas." *Portugal em Africa* 5 (1898): 351–54.

Antonio (Bishop). "Padroado de Portugal em Africa." *Boletim da Sociedade de Geographia de Lisboa* 14 (1895): 565–738.

Antunez, Jose Maria. "Lettres." *Annales Apostoliques* 1 (1886): 113–15.

Ashlay, Sir Eric. *African Universities and Western Tradition*. New York: Alfred A. Knopf, 1964.

Atkinson, N. D. *Teaching Rhodesians: A History Educational Policy in Rhodesia*. London: Longman, 1972.

Aucamp, Anna Jacoba. "Bilingual Education and Nationalism with Special Reference to South Africa." Ph.D. dissertation, Teachers College, Columbia University, 1926.

Barr, F. C. "Native Education in Rhodesia." *Month* 35 (June 1966): 352–59.

Barradas, J. P. Paixao. "Colonizacao missionaria do sul de Angola." *Revista Gabinete dos Estudios Ultramarinos* 2 (1951): 22–29.

Barros Gomes, Henrique de. *Missoes em Africa.* Lisbon: Imprensa Nacional de Moçambique, 1893.

Basutoland. Commission Appointed by His Majesty's Secretary of State for Dominion Affairs to Enquire into and Make Recommendations upon Education in Basutoland. *Report.* Pretoria, 1946.

Battle, Vincent M. and Charles H. Lyons, eds. *Essays in the History of African Education.* New York: Teachers College Press, 1970.

Benson, Lavinia. "Some Problems and Policies in African Education in the Federation of Rhodesia and Nyasaland." M.A. thesis, University of Wellington, 1956.

Berman, Edward H. *African Reactions to Missionary Education.* New York: Teachers College Press, 1975.

Bevan, L. E. W. "The Education of Natives in the Pastoral Pursuits." *NADA* 2 (1924): 13–16.

Biesheuul, Simon. *African Intelligence.* Johannesburg: South African Institute of Race Relations, 1943.

Binns, A. L. "Education of Africans in East and Central Africa." *Colonial Review* 7 (December 1952): 232–35.

Birley, Sir Robert. *African Education: Talk Given to Cape Western Region.* Johannesburg: South African Institute of Race Relations, 1956.

Birmingham, David. "UK African Studies Symposium on African Studies, London, September 1969." *Journal of Modern African Studies* 8 (April 1970): 138–40.

Boavida, Antonio Jose. *Annales das missoes portuguesas.* Lisbon: Typographia Nacional, 1889.

Boehmer, Anton Christophe. *Die Fisiologiese Perk Van Subnormale Leerlinge T.C.V. Sekere Skolastiese en Psigofisiese Bekwaahede.* Pretoria: Universitief Van Pretoria, 1952.

Boemke, Mathias Julius Felix. "The Rural School Problem in the Province of the Cape of Good Hope, South Africa." Ph.D. dissertation, Teachers College, Columbia University, 1919.

Botelho, Sebastiao Xavier. *Memoria estatistica sobre os dominos portugueses na Africa Oriental.* Lisbon: Jose Baptista Morando, 1835.

Brian, J. B. *Catholic Beginnings in Natal and Beyond.* Durban: T. W. Griggs, 1975.

"Britain and Rhodesian Students." *Africa* 31 (March 1971): 24–26.

Brookes, Edgar Harry. *Native Education in South Africa.* Pretoria: Van Schaik, 1930.

Brownlee, Margaret. *The Lives and Work of South African Missionaries: A Bibliography.* Cape Town: University of Cape Town, School of Librarianship, 1952.

Brueker, K. Robert. "Curriculum Implications from the Changing Culture and Civilization of the South African Native, with Particular Reference to Natal and Zululand." Ph.D. dissertation, Teachers College, Columbia University, 1933.

Cabral, R. C. Ribeiro. "Maneira de educar os indigenas." *Mensario Administrativo* 18 (July-August 1953): 57–59.

Cannon, J., Jr. "Cecil Rhodes and Religious Education." *Methodist Quarterly Review* (Ocotber 1924): 634–37.

Cape Town, University of. School of Librarianship. *A Bibliography of African Education in the Federation of Rhodesia and Nyasaland, 1890–1958.* Cape Town: University of Cape Town, 1958.

Carruthers-Smith, E. E. "African Education in Bulawayo from 1892." *NADA* 48 (1971): 81–93.

Chalmers, John A. *Tiyo Soga: A Page of South African Missionary Work.* London: Hodder and Stoughton, 1877.

Charles, S. J. "Southern Rhodesia." *Practical Education and School Crafts* 61 (July 1964): 201–03.

Chirenje, J. Mutero. "The Afro-American Factor in Southern African Ethiopianism, 1890–1906," in *Profiles of Self-Determination: African Responses to European Colonialism, 1652 to the Present,* edited by David Chanaiwa. Northridge: California State University, Northridge, Foundation, 1976.

Clark, E. *Quebec and South Africa: A Study on Cultural Adjustment: A Lecture.* London: Published for the Institute of Education by Oxford University Press, 1934.

Clatworthy, Frederick James. *The Formulation of British Colonial Education Policy 1923–1938.* Ann Arbor: University of Michigan, School of Education, 1971.

Conference on the Development of Higher Education in Africa. "Development of Higher Education, Tananarve." *Report.* (September 1962) Paris: UNESCO.

Cook, Peter A. W. "The Education of a South African Tribe (The Bomvanal)." Ph.D. dissertation, Columbia University, 1934.

Cooper, J. D. Omer. *The Zulu Aftermath: A Nineteenth Century Revolution in Bantu Africa.* Evanston: Northwestern University Press, 1966.

Cousins, H. T. *From Kafir Kraal to Pulpit.* London: S. W. Partridge, 1899.

Cowan, Laing Gray; James O'Connel; and David Scanlon, eds., *Education and Nation-Building in Africa.* New York: Praeger, 1966.

Currie, Sir J., et al. "Indirect Rule in Africa and its Bearing on Educational Development." *Overseas Education* 4 (1933): 82–84.

Damant, D. G. "Ecumenical Co-operation in African Education: Basutoland." *Religion in Africa* 27 (Summer 1960): 126–27.

Davidson, Basil. "African Education in Bantu Central and Southern Africa." *Presence Africaine* 6 (1956): 106–12.

Davidson, H. Frances. *South and Central Africa: A Record of Fifteen Years of Missionary Labors among Primitive Peoples.* Elgin, Ill.: Brethren Publishing House, 1915.

Davie, T. B. *Education and Race Relations in South Africa.* Johannesburg: South African Institute of Race Relations, 1955.

Davies, Horton, ed. *South African Missions, 1800–1950:* An Anthology Compiled by Horton Davies and R. H. W. Shepard. London and New York: Thomas Nelson, 1954.

Davis, Richard Hunt, Jr. *Bantu Education and the Education of Africans in South Africa.* Athens: Ohio University Center for International Studies, 1972.

Delgado, Ralph. "Historia da instrucao em Angola." *Revista do Ensino* 2 (1951): 19–28.

De Oliveira, Jose. *A Missao Civilisadora do Estado em Angola.* Ferreira Diniz: Centro Tipografico Colonial, 1926.

Drake, Howard. *A Bibliography of African Education South of the Sahara.* Aberdeen: University Press, 1942.

———. "A Bibliography of Publications on Colonial Education." *Overseas Education* 18 (1948).

Duffy, James. *Portugal in Africa.* Baltimore: Penguin African Library, 1963.

———. "Portuguese Africa: Some Crucial Problems and the Role of Education in Their Solution." *Journal of Negro Education* 30 (Summer 1961): 294–301.

Duminy, P. A., ed. *African Pupils and Teaching Them.* Pretoria: Van Schaik, 1968.

———. *Trends and Challenges in the Education of the South African Bantu.* New York: Alfred A. Knopf, 1967.

Du Plessis, Johannes. *A History of Christian Missions in South Africa.* Cape Town: C. Struik, 1965.

Ellenberger, Victor. *A Century of Mission Work in Basutoland, 1833–1933.* Marija: Sesuto Book Depot, 1938.

Evalds, Victoria K. "The Bantu Education System: A Bibliographic Essay." *Current Bibliographies on African Affairs* 3 (1977–1978): 219–42.

Fletcher, Basil Alais. *The Background of Educational Development in the Federation.* Salisbury: University College of Rhodesia and Nyasaland, 1959.

———. "Educational Enterprise in Africa." *School and Society* 88 (May 23, 1959): 242–43.

Fortune, George. *African Languages in Schools: Select Papers from the 1962 and 1963 Conferences on Teaching African Languages in Schools.* Salisbury: University College of Rhodesia and Nyasaland, 1964.

Good, Jane. *The Crimes of Bantu Education in South Africa.* Dar es Salaam: All-African Convention and Unity Movement, 1966.

Good, Kenneth. "Education for the Colonised." *New Society* (November 1, 1973): 268–70.

Good, R. "Intelligence and Attainment in Rhodesia." *Overseas Education* 28 (April 1956): 17–27.

Great Britain, Colonial Office, Advisory Committee on Education in the Colonies. *Mass Education in African Society.* London: HMSO, 1943.

Grimston, Brian. *Survey of Native Educational Development in Southern Rhodesia.* St. Albans, 1938.

Grossert, John W. *Art Education and Zulu Crafts: A Critical Review of the Development of Arts and Crafts Education in Bantu Schools in Natal with Particular Reference to the Period 1948–1962.* Pietermaritzburg: Shuter and Shooter, 1968.

Gustav, Bernhard August Aerdener. *Recent Developments in the South African Mission Field.* Cape Town: N. G. Kerk, 1958.

Hammond, H. E. D. "African Education." *NADA* 35 (1958): 12–15.

Harris, Marvin. *Portugal's African Wards: A First Hand Report on Labor and Education in Mocambique.* New York: Columbia University Press, 1960.

Hassaiug, Schioldberg. *The Christian Missions and the British Expansion in Southern Rhodesia 1888–1923.* Ann Arbor: University Microfilms, 1960.

Hendrikz, E. A. "A Cross-Cultural Investigation of the Number Concepts and Level of Number Development in Five-Year-Old Urban Shona and European Children in Southern Rhodesia." Master's thesis, University of London, 1965.

Hirschmann, David, and Brian Rose. *Education for Development in Southern Africa.* Johannesburg: South African Institute of International Affairs for the Foundation of Foreign Affairs, 1974.

Hoernle Memorial Lectures for 1945, 1946, 1947. Johannesburg: South African Institute of Race Relations, 1948.

Hollick, John Elmar. "The Influence of Apartheid on Education Policies in South Africa." M.A. thesis, UCLA, 1970.

Honey, John Raymond De Simons. *Tom Brown in South Africa: Inaugural Lecture Delivered at Rhodes University on May 10th, 1972.* Grahamstown: Rhodes University, 1972.

Horrell, Muriel. *African Education: Some Origins and Development to 1953.* Johannesburg: South African Institute of Race Relations, 1963.

––––––. *A Decade of Bantu Education.* Johannesburg: South African Institute of Race Relations, 1964.

Hunter, Archibald Peter. *The Re-Orientation of Educational Policy in South Africa since 1948.* Ann Arbor: University Microfilms, n.d.

Hurewitz, Nathan. *The Economics of Bantu Education in South Africa.* Johannesburg: South African Institute of Race Relations, 1964.

Innes, Duncan. *Our Country, Our Responsibility.* London: Africa Bureau, 1969.

Inter-Territorial Conference. *Village Education in Africa: Report of the Inter-Territorial "Jeanes" Conference, Salisbury, Southern Rhodesia, May 27th–June 6th, 1935.* Lovedale, S.A.: Lovedale Press, 1936.

Irvine, S. H. "Education for Citizenship." *NADA* 38 (1961): 74–83.

––––––. *Selection for Secondary Education in Southern Africa.* Salisbury: University College of Rhodesia and Nyasaland, Faculty of Education, 1965.

Jabavu, Davidson Don Tengo. *Bantu Literature: Classification and Reviews.* Lovedale, S.A.: Lovedale Press, 1921.

––––––. *The Black Problem: Papers and Addresses on Various Native Problems.* Lovedale, S.A.: Lovedale Press, 1920.

Jackson, H. M. G. "Native Education in Southern Rhodesia." *African Observer* 2 (1934): 28–30.

Jones, Neville, "Training in Community Service in Southern Rhodesia." *Overseas Education* 2 (1931): 32–35.

Jowitt, H. "The Protectorate of Southern Africa." *Yearbook of Education* (1954): 144–54.

Junod, H. A. "Native Language and Native Education." *Journal of African Society* 5 (1905): 1–14.

Kalso, Milton Lloyd. "A Study of Selected Aspects of Three Elementary School Programs in the United States with Implications for Rhodesia." Ed.D. dissertation, University of Oregon, 1969.

Karis, Thomas, and Gwendolen M. Carter, eds., *From Protest to Challenge: A Documentary History of African Politics in South Africa 1882–1964.* Stanford: Hoover Institution Press, 1972. Vol. 1, *Protest and Hope,* by Sheridan Johns, III.

Kazembe, Phillip Thomas. "Shona in the Schools." *Teacher in New Africa* 4 (June 1967): 16–18.

Keyston, J. E. "Report on Regional Organisation of Research in the Rhodesias and Nyasaland." *Nature* 164 (November 26, 1949): 911–13.

Kgware, W. M. *In Search of an Educational System: A Critical Appraisal of the Past and Present Administration of Bantu Education.* University College of the North, Department of Practical Education, 1961.

Kingwill, D. G. *The Development of Science in the Federation of Rhodesia and Nyasaland.* Salisbury: Government Printer, 1957.

Kitchen, Helen, ed. *The Educated African: A Country by Country Survey.* New York: Praeger, 1971.

Kumalo, Cleopas. "Ideological and Instrumental Factors in the Debate on African Education in Kenya and South Africa." Ph.D. dissertation, Boston University, 1959.

Kunene, Daniel P. *The Beginning of South African Vernacular Literature: A Historical Study.* Los Angeles: African Studies Center, UCLA, 1967.

———. *The Works of Thomas Mofolo: Summaries and Critiques.* Occasional paper no. 2. Los Angeles: African Studies Center, UCLA, 1967.

Kuper, Leo. *Passive Resistance in South Africa.* New Haven: Yale University Press, 1960.

Lacey, C. "Christian Racism in Rhodesia." *Christian Century* 89 (March 15, 1972): 301–06.

Latourette, K. S. *History of the Expansion of Christianity.* London: Eyre and Spottiswoode, 1947.

Laws, R. "National Education in Nyasa." *Journal of African Society* 25 (1929): 347–67.

Leone, Andrew. *The Development of Bantu Education in South Africa, 1952–1954.* Ann Arbor: University Microfilms, 1965.

Leoy, Goldie. *European Education in South Africa, 1922–1946: A Select Bibliography.* Cape Town: University of Cape Town, 1946.

LeRoy, A. E. "The Educated Native: Fact vs. Theory." Paper read before the South African General Missionary Conference, 1906.

Lewis, Cecil. *Historical Records of the Church of the Province of South Africa.* London: Society for Promoting Christian Knowledge, 1965.

Lewis, Leonard John. *Equipping Africa: Educational Development in British Colonial Africa.* London: Edinburgh House Press, 1968.

Lewis, Thomas H. "The Problem of the Semi-Educated African." *Oversea Education* 13 (January 1942): 265–73.

Linden, Ian. *Catholics, Peasants and Chewa Resistance in Nyasaland, 1889–1939.* London: Heinemann, 1974.

Lloyd, B. W. "School Library Facilities for Africans in Southern Rhodesia." *Oversea Education* 32 (April 1960): 36–41.

Loram, Charles T. *Adaptation of the Penn School Methods to Education in South Africa.* New York: Phelps-Stokes Fund, 1927.

———. "The Education of the South African Native." Ph.D. dissertation, Teachers College, Columbia University, 1915.

Lugard, Frederick. *Dual Mandate in British Tropical Africa.* London: Blackwood, 1926.

MacDonald, Roderick James. "History of African Education in Nyasaland, 1875–1945." Ph.D. dissertation, University of Edinburgh, 1969.

————, ed. *From Nyasaland to Malawi: Studies in Colonial History.* Nairobi: East African Publishing House, 1975.

Makanya, Violet Sibusisiwe. "The Problems of the Zulu Girl." *Native Teachers' Journal* (Natal) 10, no. 3 (April 1931): 116–20.

Makulu, Henry F. *Education, Development and Nation-Building in Independent Africa.* London: SCM Press, 1971.

Malan, Johannes R. "The Reorganization of Rural Education in the Cape Province of the Union of South Africa." Ph.D. dissertation, Columbia University, 1924.

Malherbe, Ernst Gideon. *Education for Leadership in Africa.* Durban: Natal Technical College, 1960.

————. *Education in South Africa (1652–1922).* Cape Town and Johannesburg: Juta, 1925.

————. *The New Education in a Changing Empire.* Pretoria: Van Schaik, 1963.

Mans, Peter W. "A Comparative and Critical Study of Developments in Differentiation and Examinations in European Secondary Education in Natal and Rhodesia with Special Reference to Existing Practices in Selecting Groups of Schools in Pietermaritzburg and Bulawayo." M.A. thesis, University of Natal, 1971.

Marable, Manning. "A Black School in South Africa." *Negro History Bulletin* 37, no. 4 (June-July 1974): 258–61.

————. "John Langalibalele Dube, Booker T. Washington and the Ideology of Conservative Black Nationalism," in *Profiles of Self-Determination: African Responses to European Colonialism, 1652 to the Present*, edited by David Chanaiwa. Northridge: California State University, Northridge, Foundation, 1976.

Marais, J. M. *European Education in South Africa, 1946–1955: A Select Bibliography.* Cape Town, 1956.

Martin, Christopher. "Educational Need in Rhodesia." *Race Today* 3 (January 1971): 19–20.

Martins, E. de Azmbuja. *Accao educativa as populacoes indigenas de Moçambique consequente da instrucao militar do soldado indigena.* Lisboa: Agência Geral das Colonias, 1938.

Martires, Bartolomeu dos. "Descricao dos establecimentos religiosos da ciudade de Moçambique extraida de um manuscrito do Bispo de Sao Tome e Prelado de Moçambique em 1882." In *Alamanaque Civil-ecclesiastico Historico Administrativo da Provincia de Moçambique para o anno de 1959.* Lourenço Marques, 1958.

Mason, Reginald James. *British Education in Africa.* London: Oxford University Press, 1959.

Matthews, T. H. "Parent Involvement in the European Schools in Rhodesia." Bachelor's dissertation, University of Rhodesia, 1972.

Mayhew, A. I. *Education in the Colonial Empire.* London: Longmans, Green, 1938.

McHarg, James. "Influences Contributing to the Education and Culture of the Native People in Southern Rhodesia from 1900 to 1951." Ph.D. dissertation, Duke University, 1962.

McKerron, Margaretha Emma. *A History of Education in South Africa, 1652–1932.* Pretoria: Van Schaik, 1934.

Meacham, F. T. "Boost Native Education." *Christian Century* 73 (May 23, 1956): 653–54.

Mendonca, R. Zuzarte de. "Escolas tecnicas profissionais em Angola." *Angola* 18 (1950).

Menezes, Victor Hugo de. "A Instrucao do indigena." *Mensario Administrativo* 14 (April-May 1949): 21–22.

Merwe, Hendrick W. van der, and David Welsh. *Student Perspectives in South Africa.* Cape Town: Philip Publisher, in association with the Abe Bailey Institute of Interracial Studies, 1972.

Metrowich, Enderick Charles. *A Black Board Round My Neck.* Cape Town: Timmins, 1964.

Milton, Alan. "Teachers for Rhodesia's Tomorrow." *South African Outlook* 96 (August 1966): 129–30.

Missiological Institute. *The Role of the Church in Socio-Economic Development in Southern Africa: A Consultation Held in Umpumulo, Natal, Organized by Missiological Institute, Umpumulo in Co-operation with the Christian Academy in Southern Africa.* Durban: Lutheran Publishing House, 1972.

Mnyanda, B. J. "Native Education." *NADA* 10 (1932): 108–11.

Mokatle, Naboth. *The Autobiography of an Unknown South African.* Berkeley and Los Angeles: University of California Press, 1971.

Molema, S. M. *The Bantu Past and Present: An Ethnographical and Historical Study of the Native Races of South Africa.* Edinburgh: W. Green and Son, 1920.

Moreia, A. "The Elites of the Portuguese Tribal Provinces: Guinea, Angola, Mozambique." *International Social Science Bulletin* 8 (1956): 548–81.

Mufuka, Kenneth Nyamayaro. *Missions and Politics in Malawi.* Kingston, Ont.: Limestone Press, 1977.

Murphree, Betty Jo. "The Acculturative Effects of Schooling on African Attitudes and Values." *Zambezia* 2 (December 1970): 11–21.

Murphree, Marshall W. "A Village School and Community Development in a Rhodesian Tribal Trust Land." *Zambezia* 1 (1970): 13–23.

Murray, A. Victor. "Education under Indirect Rule." *Journal of African Society* 34 (1935): 227–68.

―――. *The School in the Bush: A Critical Study of the Theory and Practice of Native Education in Africa.* London: Longmans, Green, 1938.

National Conference on Education. *Education and our Expanding Horizons: Proceedings of the National Conference on Education, held in Durban of the University of Natal, July 9th–21st, 1960.* Durban: University of Natal Press, 1962.

Ngonyama, S. "The Education of the African Girl." *NADA* 31 (1954): 57–58.

Nyasaland. Committee of Inquiry into African Education (chairman, J. F. U. Phillips). *Report*. Zomba, 1962.

Nyasaland. Education Department. *Memorandum on Native Education and Its Effect upon Production*. Zomba: Education Department, 1927.

Olivier, Stephanus P. "Recent Adaptations of Education in Rhodesia." M.A. thesis, University of South Africa, 1943.

Orbell, S. F. W. "The Role of Environmental Factors in the Education of African Pupils." *Zambezia* 1 (1970): 41–45.

Paixao, Braga. "Discurso proferido no acte de posse de Director Geral do Ensino Colonial." *Boletim Geral Colonial* 227 (1944): 8–18.

Paiyao, Victor Manuel Braga. *Educao Politica e Politica da Educao: Tres anos en Moçambique*. Lisboa: Divisao de Publicacoes e Biblioteca Agência Geraldas Colonias, 1948.

Parker, Franklin. "African Community Development and Education in Southern Rhodesia, 1920–1935." *International Review of Missions* 51 (July 1962): 335–47.

––––––. *African Development and Education in Southern Rhodesia*. Columbus: Ohio State University Press, 1960.

––––––. "Early Church-State Relations in African Education in Rhodesia and Zambia." *World Yearbook of Education*, 1966.

––––––. "Education in the Federation of Rhodesia and Nyasaland." *Journal of Negro Education* 30 (1961): 286–93.

Pells, E. O. *300 Years of Education in South Africa*. Westport, Conn.: Greenwood Press, 1970.

Perterras, P. "Education of African Natives." *Westminister Review* 643 (December 1908).

Pistorius, P. *Gister en Vandag in de Opvoeding*. Potchefstroom: Prorege, 1966.

Plaatje, Solomon Tshekisho. *Native Life in South Africa before and since the European War and the Boer Rebellion*. London: P. S. King and Son, 1916.

Pollak, O. B., and K. Pollak. *Theses and Dissertations on Southern Africa: An International Bibliography*. Boston: G. K. Hall, 1976.

Posselt, F. "Native Education." *NADA* 16 (1939): 99–106.

Potgieter, Laetitia. *Bantu Education in the Union, 1949–1959: A Bibliography*. Cape Town: University of Cape Town, School of Librarianship, 1965.

Prozesky, M. "Teaching of Zulu in Primary Schools." *Native Teachers' Journal* (Natal) 12 (1932): 21–24.

Ranger, Terence O. "African Attempts to Control Education in East and Central Africa, 1900 to 1939." *Past and Present* 32 (1965): 57–85.

———. *The African Voices in South Rhodesia, 1898–1930.* Evanston: Northwestern University Press, 1970.

Raum, O. F. "Indirect Rule as a Political Education." *Internationale Zeitschrift für Erichung* 5 (1936): 97–107.

Rea, Frederick Beatty. "The Future of Mission Education in Southern Rhodesia." *International Review of Missions* 49 (1960): 195–200.

———. *The Missionary Factor in Southern Rhodesia.* Salisbury: Historical Association of Rhodesia and Nyasaland, 1962.

"Rhodesia: Black Power on the Campus." *Economist* 248 (August 11, 1972): 28–29.

Rhodesia, Northern. Northern Rhodesia Committee Appointed to Investigate European Education. *Report on European Education in Northern Rhodesia, May–July, 1948.* Lusaka: Government Printer, 1948.

Rhodesia, Southern. Central African Statistical Office. *Report on Educational Statistics for Southern Rhodesia.* Salisbury, 1947.

Rhodesia, Southern. *Southern Rhodesia Education Commission: Report, 1962.* Presented to the Legislative Assembly. Salisbury, 1963.

Rich, S. G. "Binet-Simon Tests on Zulus." *South African Journal of Science* 14 (1918): 477–82.

Richards, J. R. "Personality Factors and Main Subject Choice in Colleges of Education in England and Rhodesia." M.A. thesis, University of Manchester, 1972.

Rogers, C. A. and C. Franz. *Racial Themes in Southern Rhodesia: Attitudes of the White Population.* New Haven: Yale University Press, 1967.

Rosa, M. F. "Ensino rudimentar para indigenas em Angolas e na Guine Portuguesa." *Boletim Cultural da Guine Portuguesa* 6 (1951): 805–84.

Rose, Brian. *Education in Southern Africa.* Johannesburg: Collier-Macmillan, 1970.

Rowley, Henry. *The Story of the Universities' Mission to Central Africa.* London: Saunders, Otley, 1867.

Samuels, Michael Anthony. *Education in Angola, 1878–1914.* New York: Teachers College Press, 1970.

Santerre, Renard. "Problemes Africains d'education." *Revue Canadienne des Etudes Africaines* 8 (1974): 465–66.

Santos, Francisco Martius dos. *Historia do Esino em Angola.* Lisbon: Edicao dos Servicos de Educao, 1970.

Sargent, E. B. *Report on Education in Bechuanaland Protectorate.* Mimeographed. 1905.

Sasnett, Martena, and Inez Seymeyer. *Educational Systems in Africa.* Berkeley and Los Angeles: University of California Press, 1966.

Scott, H. S. "Educational Policy in the British Colonial Empire." *Yearbook of Education*, 1936.

Serapiao, Louis Benjamin. "The Preaching of Portuguese Colonization and the Protest of the White Father." *Issue: A Quarterly Journal of Africanist Opinion* 2 (Spring 1972): 34–41.

Shaw, M. "Village School in Northern Rhodesia." *International Review of Missions* 14 (1925): 523–36.

Shepherd, Robert Henry Wishart. *Literature for the South African Bantu: A Comparative Study of Negro Achievement.* Pretoria: Carnegie Corporation, Visitors' Grants Committee, 1936.

———. *Lovedale, South Africa, 1824–1955.* Lovedale, S.A.: Lovedale Press, 1971.

———. *Lovedale, South Africa: The Story of a Century, 1841–1941.* Lovedale, S.A.: Lovedale Press, 1940.

Shepperson, George, and Thomas Price. *Independent African: John Chilembwe and the Origins, Setting and Significance of the Nyasaland Native Rising of 1915.* Edinburgh: Edinburgh University Press, 1959.

Soga, J. Henderson. *Ema Xhosa: Life and Customs.* Lovedale, S.A.: Lovedale Press, 1931.

———. *The South-Eastern Bantu.* Johannesburg: University of Witwatersrand Press, 1930.

South Africa. Bureau of Census and Statistics. *Official Yearbook of the Republic and of Basutoland, Bechuanaland Protectorate and Swaziland.* Pretoria: Government Printer.

South Africa. Department of Education. Committee on Adult Education. *Adult Education in South Africa.* A Report by a Committee of Inquiry Appointed by the Minister of Education. Pretoria: Government Printer, 1946.

South Africa. Department of Higher Education. *Annual Report, 1968–1969.* Pretoria: Government Printer, 1969.

South Africa. Department of National Education. *Annual Report, 1970.* Pretoria: Government Printer, 1970.

South Africa. Department of Native Affairs. *Bantu Education: Policy for the Immediate Future.* Statement by the Hon. Dr. H. F. Verwoerd, Minister of Native Affairs, in the Senate of the Parliament of the Union of South Africa, June 7th, 1954. Pretoria: Information Service, Department of Native Affairs, 1954.

South Africa. Inter-Departmental Committee on Native Education. *Report, 1935–1936.* Pretoria: Government Printer, 1936.

South African Education Conference. *Educational Adaptations in Changing Society,* edited by E. G. Malherbe. Report of the South African Education Conference held in Cape Town and Johannesburg, July 1934. Cape Town and Johannesburg: Juta, 1937.

South African Institute of Race Relations. *Secondary Education for Africans.* Johannesburg, 1965.

South Africa SPRO-CAS Education Commission. *Report: Study Project on Christianity in Apartheid Society: Education Beyond Apartheid.* Johannesburg: SPRO-CAS Publication, 1971.

Stokes, Eric, and Richard Brown, eds. *The Zambesian Past.* Manchester: Manchester University Press, 1965.

Stoley, H. C. "The System of Education in Basutoland." *Board of Education Special Reports on Educational Subjects* 13 (1905).

Tangri, Roger K. *African Reaction and Resistance to the Early Colonial Situation in Malawi, 1891–1915.* Salisbury, 1969.

Theme: Transitional Problems in the South African Educational System, Cape Town 1961. Proceedings of the Jubilee Conference of the Faculty of Education, February 7–11th, 1961. University of Cape Town, Faculty of Education, 1961.

Trevor, T. G. "Native Education from an Employer's Point of View." *NADA* 5 (1927): 97–99.

Tunmer, Raymond. *Race and Education.* Johannesburg: Institute for the Study of Man in Africa, 1967.

———, and R. K. Muir. *Some Aspects of Education in South Africa.* Johannesburg: University of the Witwatersrand, African Studies Programme, 1968.

———, and Brian Rose, eds. *Documents on South African Education.* Johannesburg: Donker, 1975.

United Nations. *Non-Self-Governing Territories: Summaries and Analyses of Information Transmitted to the Secretary-General during 1953: A Special Study on Educational Conditions.* ST/TRI/SER.A/8/add.1. New York, 1953.

Van Rensburg, Chris, ed. *Education for South Africa's Black, Coloured and Indian Peoples.* Johannesburg, 1975.

Vatcher, William H. *White Laager: The Rise of Afrikaner Nationalism.* New York, 1965.

Verwoerd, H. F. *Bantu Education: Policy for the Immediate Future.* Pretoria: Information Service of the Department of Bantu Administration and Development, June 7, 1954.

Vincent, Joan. *African Elite: The Big Men of a Small Town.* New York: Columbia University Press, 1971.

Walshe, Peter. *The Rise of African Nationalism in South Africa: The African National Congress, 1912–1952.* Berkeley and Los Angeles: University of California Press, 1971.

Walton, James. "Factors Affecting Attendance in Basutoland Schools." *Teacher Education* 2 (November 1961): 30–36.

Welsh, G. H. *The Black Man's Schools: Some Impressions of American Education with Special Reference to the Negro in the United States, and to Desirable Improvements in the Education of the South African Bantu.* Pretoria: Carnegie Corporation, Visitors' Grants Committee, 1932.

Wilson, Monica, and Leonard Thompson. *The Oxford History of South Africa.* London: Oxford University Press, 1971.

Winter, Colin O'Brien. *Namibia.* Grand Rapids, Mich.: William B. Erdmans Publishing, 1977.

Wood, A. W. *Informal Education and Development in Africa.* The Hague: Mouton, 1974.

World Association for Adult Education. *Adult Education in British Dominions.* London: World Association for Adult Education, 1929.

Wrong, Margaret. "Education in Bantu Central and South Africa." *Journal of Negro History* 15 (Summer 1948): 370–82.

Yesufu, T. M. *Creating the African University.* New York: Oxford University Press, 1973.

Contributors

MARIO J. AZEVEDO, a Mozambican, is Associate Professor of History at Jackson State University, Mississippi. He is the author and co-author of two recently published books, *Disease and African History* (Duke University Press, 1978), and *The Returning Hunter* (Interculture Associates, 1978), a historical novel.

JACK BERMINGHAM is Lecturer in African History at the University of the West Indies in Kingston, Jamaica. His research focuses on the colonial history of Southern Africa, with special reference to Botswana.

DAVID CHANAIWA is a Zimbabwean and Professor of History at California State University, Northridge. He is the author of several books, among which are *The Zimbabwe Controversy: A Case of Colonial Historiography*, Vol. VIII (Syracuse: Eastern African Studies, 1973); *Profiles of Self-Determination: African Responses to European Colonialism in Southern Africa, 1652 to Present* (Northridge: California State University Foundation, 1976); and *The Occupation of Southern Rhodesia: A Study of Economic Imperialism* (Nairobi: East African Publishing House, 1978). He currently is finishing a book, *The African Heritage of Southern Africa*.

R. HUNT DAVIS, JR., is Associate Professor of History at the University of Florida, Gainesville. He is the author of *Bantu Education and the Education of Africans in South Africa* (Ohio University, 1972) and of numerous articles on the history of African education in South Africa. He is currently engaged in research on Fort Hare University.

CHRISTOPHER A. LEU is Professor of Political Science at California State University, Northridge. His research focuses on Third World politics, and he is working on a long-term project on the political economy of Namibia.

MANNING MARABLE is Associate Professor of History in the Africana Studies and Research Center at Cornell University. He is the author of *From the Grass Roots: Black Political and Social Essays* (Boston: South End Press, 1979) and *Blackwater: Essays in Southern and Afro-American History* (forthcoming).

277

AGRIPPAH T. MUGOMBA, a Zimbabwean, is Associate Professor of Black
    Studies and Political Science at Amherst College, Massachusetts.
    A specialist in African international relations, he is the author of
    *The Foreign Policy of Despair: Africa and the Sale of Arms to South
    Africa* (Nairobi: East African Literature Bureau, 1977). He is
    presently working on two books, *From the Rovuma to the Maputo:
    Underdevelopment and Foreign Policy in Mozambique* and *The Political
    Economy of Dependency and Underdevelopment in Southern Africa.*
MOUGO NYAGGAH, a Kenyan, is Associate Professor of History at Cali-
    fornia State University, Fullerton. A specialist on recent South
    African history, he is the author of *The Most Undemocratic Democ-
    racy: The Development of Apartheid Laws in South Africa* (forthcom-
    ing).
BRIDGLAL PACHAI, a distinguished historian and a native of South
    Africa, is Professor of History and Head of the Department of
    History at the University of Sokoto in Nigeria. For many years he
    held the Chair and Headship of the Department of History and
    Political Science at the University of Malawi and for a while served
    as the university's Acting Vice-Chancellor. His numerous publica-
    tions include *The Early History of Malawi; The International Aspects of
    the South African Indian Question 1860–1971; Livingston: Man of
    Africa; Malawi: The History of The Nation;* and *Land and Politics in
    Malawi, 1875–1975.*

Index